W9-DJP-173

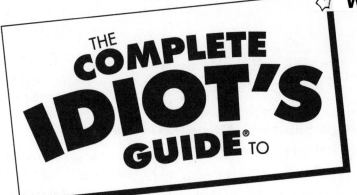

# THE COMPLETE IDIOT'S GUIDE® TO

# the Power of the Enneagram

*by Herb Pearce, M.Ed., with Karen K. Brees, Ph.D.*

## ALPHA

A member of Penguin Group (USA) Inc.

*To the memory of Andrea Szmyt, who co-taught the Enneagram with me for a number of years. We had many journeys together exploring the Enneagram and its value in the world.*

## ALPHA BOOKS

Published by the Penguin Group

Penguin Group (USA) Inc., 375 Hudson Street, New York, New York 10014, USA

Penguin Group (Canada), 90 Eglinton Avenue East, Suite 700, Toronto, Ontario M4P 2Y3, Canada (a division of Pearson Penguin Canada Inc.)

Penguin Books Ltd., 80 Strand, London WC2R 0RL, England

Penguin Ireland, 25 St. Stephen's Green, Dublin 2, Ireland (a division of Penguin Books Ltd.)

Penguin Group (Australia), 250 Camberwell Road, Camberwell, Victoria 3124, Australia (a division of Pearson Australia Group Pty. Ltd.)

Penguin Books India Pvt. Ltd., 11 Community Centre, Panchsheel Park, New Delhi—110 017, India

Penguin Group (NZ), 67 Apollo Drive, Rosedale, North Shore, Auckland 1311, New Zealand (a division of Pearson New Zealand Ltd.)

Penguin Books (South Africa) (Pty.) Ltd., 24 Sturdee Avenue, Rosebank, Johannesburg 2196, South Africa

Penguin Books Ltd., Registered Offices: 80 Strand, London WC2R 0RL, England

## Copyright © 2007 by Herb Pearce

All rights reserved. No part of this book shall be reproduced, stored in a retrieval system, or transmitted by any means, electronic, mechanical, photocopying, recording, or otherwise, without written permission from the publisher. No patent liability is assumed with respect to the use of the information contained herein. Although every precaution has been taken in the preparation of this book, the publisher and authors assume no responsibility for errors or omissions. Neither is any liability assumed for damages resulting from the use of information contained herein. For information, address Alpha Books, 800 East 96th Street, Indianapolis, IN 46240.

THE COMPLETE IDIOT'S GUIDE TO and Design are registered trademarks of Penguin Group (USA) Inc.

International Standard Book Number: 978-1-59257-694-4
Library of Congress Catalog Card Number: 2007928985

12  11  10    8  7  6  5  4  3  2

Interpretation of the printing code: The rightmost number of the first series of numbers is the year of the book's printing; the rightmost number of the second series of numbers is the number of the book's printing. For example, a printing code of 07-1 shows that the first printing occurred in 2007.

*Printed in the United States of America*

**Note:** This publication contains the opinions and ideas of its authors. It is intended to provide helpful and informative material on the subject matter covered. It is sold with the understanding that the authors and publisher are not engaged in rendering professional services in the book. If the reader requires personal assistance or advice, a competent professional should be consulted.

The authors and publisher specifically disclaim any responsibility for any liability, loss, or risk, personal or otherwise, which is incurred as a consequence, directly or indirectly, of the use and application of any of the contents of this book.

Most Alpha books are available at special quantity discounts for bulk purchases for sales promotions, premiums, fund-raising, or educational use. Special books, or book excerpts, can also be created to fit specific needs.

For details, write: Special Markets, Alpha Books, 375 Hudson Street, New York, NY 10014.

**Publisher:** *Marie Butler-Knight*
**Editorial Director:** *Mike Sanders*
**Managing Editor:** *Billy Fields*
**Acquisitions Editor:** *Paul Dinas*
**Development Editor:** *Lynn Northrup*
**Senior Production Editor:** *Janette Lynn*
**Copy Editor:** *Michael Dietsch*

**Cartoonist:** *Shannon Wheeler*
**Cover Designer:** *Kurt Owens*
**Book Designer:** *Trina Wurst*
**Indexer:** *Julie Bess*
**Layout:** *Brian Massey*
**Proofreader:** *Aaron Black, Mary Hunt*

# Contents at a Glance

# Contents

## 5  Type 3: The Success Striver/Winner     61

# Introduction

People are fascinated by personality differences and personality typing systems. Why are you and I so different? What makes you tick? Who am I? Why is it so hard to change? Why am I attracted to a certain personality type, even when it's such a challenge?

The Enneagram, a system that explains nine personality types, is such an accurate predictor of personality, motivation, and behaviors that people who discover it often feel they are having a psychic reading. They'll ask, "How can you know me so well? How can you figure me out and describe me so accurately? Why do you accept me, even with all my baggage?" The answer is the Enneagram. Understanding and relating are so much easier when you understand someone's motivations.

The Enneagram explains personality in a fun and understandable way. It also challenges you, as it hits on your strengths *and* weaknesses. It explains why you are attracted to certain people and experiences. It also explains why you hide parts of yourself and avoid certain other experiences. In this book, you'll have an opportunity to explore yourself in depth.

As we highlight the unique qualities and psychological underpinnings of each of the Enneagram's nine personality types, you'll also discover your own! You'll learn strategies for relating well to each personality style and also what actions to take to grow within and beyond your own type.

You'll explore how the types show up in everyday life, at work, and in all your relationships. You'll see how to heal past relationships and learn many new avenues for interacting with each type—whether friends, relatives, lovers, partners, or bosses. Welcome to the power of the Enneagram! Bon voyage!

## How to Use This Book

This book is a beginner's course in understanding the Enneagram. As you read, you'll gain an understanding of the nine unique personality styles that form the basis of the Enneagram system and learn how to use this knowledge to greatly enhance your life.

**Part 1, "The Enneagram: Its History and Benefits,"** introduces the system, defines basic Enneagram language, references its history, and explains, through real-life examples, the practical benefits of the Enneagram for your personal and professional life.

**Part 2, "The Enneagram Types,"** goes into depth about each type's characteristics and introduces subtypes—positive traits, limiting traits, type traits in childhood and parenting, in growth and relationships, and in decision-making and leadership.

**Part 3, "What's Your Enneagram Type and Others' Types?"** explains the process of typing and provides accurate and respectful ways to type yourself and others. You'll learn how family and culture have influenced your type.

**Part 4, "How to Apply the Enneagram,"** focuses on the practical use of the Enneagram in your life, regarding personal growth, romance and relationships, friends and family, and work and career.

## Extras

Throughout each chapter, you'll find tidbits of information that will help your understanding of the Enneagram.

**Warning!**

You'll want to check out these cautions, concerns, and corrections regarding the types.

**Lifelines**

Here you'll find important tips and advice to enhance your understanding of the Enneagram.

**def•i•ni•tion**

These are definitions and explanations of Enneagram or related language.

**Insights**

Check these out for information, personal stories, and real-life quotes from each type.

## Acknowledgments

I want to acknowledge my personal editor and co-writer, Karen Brees, who spruced up my writing in amazing ways. As I read her rewrites, her creative use of language constantly delighted me. We had a blast writing this book together and getting to know each other through daily e-mails.

I want to thank Paul Dinas, acquisitions editor, who answered innumerable questions regarding this project; and also Lynn Northrup, development editor, who did likewise. I wouldn't have written this book without my literary agent, Andrea Hurst, who asked if I were interested. I said *yes*, without a moment's hesitation. Thank you.

I am very grateful to Melanie Joy, a dear friend who contributed many hours of support, encouragement, brainstorming, ideas, feedback, and discussion about the types. I want to thank Joy Hartwell for her insights; John O'Leary, my Enneagram discussion partner and occasional co-teacher; Walter Ness, Annette Brubaker, Theo and Katja Swartz, Karin Stephan, Ken Jenkins, Cory McCarthy, Rick Charnes, Sheryl Lawrence, Lee Anne Klemyk, Erik Williams, Maureen McConnell, Evan Gorman, Evan Mulvaney, Loretta Betts, Betty and Maryjane Corgnati, Deb Harrison, Jane Laroque, Arnie Rosen, Matt Pallaver, and Donna Cognac for their ideas and interviews; and the many other students and friends I interviewed, who gave me ideas and well wishes.

Thanks to the countless clients, Enneagram students, and workshop attendees, over the last 16 plus years, who contributed greatly to my Enneagram knowledge, enjoyment, and growth. I've loved every second and wouldn't have been able to write this book, without those experiences that enriched my life and my practice.

Helen Palmer and David Daniels, with whom I trained to become an Enneagram teacher, deserve special recognition. Their teacher training and subsequent workshops, along with Helen's books, have provided guidance for me throughout the years.

Along those same lines, Don Richard Riso and Russ Hudson's training, workshops, and books have been extremely beneficial for both my personal and Enneagram growth. Riso, Hudson, Palmer, and Daniels have contributed immeasurably to developing psychological understanding of the types.

Thanks also to Ruth Duffy and Virginia Sampson, both spiritual directors and my first Enneagram teachers at Campion Renewal Center in Weston, Massachusetts; and Barbara Hastings, a student of Helen Palmer and one of my first Enneagram teachers.

I'm indebted to all those throughout history who developed typing systems, particularly those related to the Enneagram. Among them, George Gurdgieff, Oscar Ichazo, and Claudio Naranjo, who developed much of the original ideas and early writing on the Enneagram.

And lastly, I want to thank my mother, Daisy Pearce, who has so deeply contributed to my life. Both Type 9s, we have had a fairly easy road together. She has been one of my Enneagram students! I also thank my father, David Pearce, my brother, Stephen Pearce, and my sister, Pamela Pearce.

## Trademarks

All terms mentioned in this book that are known to be or are suspected of being trademarks or service marks have been appropriately capitalized. Alpha Books and Penguin Group (USA) Inc. cannot attest to the accuracy of this information. Use of a term in this book should not be regarded as affecting the validity of any trademark or service mark.

# Part 1

# The Enneagram: Its History and Benefits

Looking for answers to life's basic questions? Who am I? How can I relate to others on life's journey? An ancient body of knowledge, the Enneagram has been rediscovered, growing rapidly in popularity since the 1970s. Both guide and teacher, the Enneagram describes nine personality styles, each of which experiences life from a type filter that both enhances and limits life choices. In these chapters you'll learn how the Enneagram can benefit you, a bit of its history, and see why more and more people are using this system for personal growth, relationship enhancement, and career enrichment.

# Introducing the Enneagram

## In This Chapter

- ◆ What the Enneagram is—and what it's not
- ◆ Your first look at the nine personality types
- ◆ Breaking the types into subcategories
- ◆ From long ago to modern day—a brief history
- ◆ Harnessing the power of the Enneagram

What is the Enneagram? Excellent question! The Enneagram seeks to understand why people do what they do and why people are the way they are. The Enneagram teaches that there are nine different personality styles in the world. Every single person on the planet is one of these nine personality types. Discovering your own type and learning about your personality strengths and tendencies is a journey of discovery. Does that mean everyone who is the same type will be the same? Not at all! And that's the intriguing part. The Enneagram doesn't put you in a box. Rather, it helps you understand your core type and all the other types' perspectives. It gets you *outside* the box, so you begin to appreciate your uniqueness and the uniqueness of others.

We're here to reveal the secrets of the Enneagram, so that you will have the advantage in areas such as charting your career path, pursuing your heart's desire in romance, dealing with difficult people, and learning to develop your talents and personal qualities on your life journey. You'll learn exactly what the Enneagram is, what it isn't, and how to use its power to enhance your life.

# The Enneagram Explained

It's always easiest to break something down into its parts when we're learning, and the *Enneagram* is no exception. It's a body of knowledge, it's a tool, and it's a road map:

- ◆ The Enneagram primarily relates to a body of knowledge, stretching back to ancient times. It seeks to understand the human psyche. It looks for answers to common questions: What motivates us? What pushes our buttons? Of course those are modern terms, but the Enneagram fits our modern life very well.

- ◆ The Enneagram is a tool. Once we understand how to use it, the Enneagram will help us to analyze personalities, situations, and dilemmas. With that information, we can choose the appropriate course of action. Forewarned is forearmed!

- ◆ The Enneagram is a system that can greatly assist in spiritual growth. If you want to reduce fear and anxiety, see life with greater clarity, and have some fun learning and letting go of your ego, the Enneagram provides you with a road map for that evolution.

## def•i•ni•tion

The name **Enneagram** derives from the Greek root *ennea*, meaning 9; and *grammos*, meaning drawing, type, or figure. The Enneagram is a theory of personality types, describing nine core types, each of which has a filter or lens that deeply flavors one perspective over the others. The lens is both an amazing strength and an amazing limitation.

# What It Isn't

The Enneagram isn't a full description of every aspect of personality. Race, culture, subcultures, gender, birth order, and family history all play major roles in personality formation which the Enneagram doesn't necessarily address. The Enneagram only considers the *lens* from which your personality expresses itself, on a fairly consistent basis. It doesn't claim you are only and always just one type, though it does state you are *pulled* by one type that tends to define you. At different times in your life, during times of stress, as well as times when life is going smoothly, you will move among all nine types, taking on characteristics of each. In upcoming chapters you'll learn how this works and how to use these characteristics to benefit you.

# How It Works

Have you ever looked at a couple and thought, *He's not her type.* Where does that idea come from? Or you'll be watching a movie or a television show and realize that a certain actor or actress is typecast?

At some level, we realize there are specific types of people. The Enneagram teaches that there are nine types of people and numbers those types from 1 to 9. Each one of us is one of those types, and the type we are is called our core type. For example, your core type may be 4 and your best friend's may be 8. (In a little while, you'll find out exactly what that means.)

Here's an analogy to simplify the explanation. Just as the musical octave's eight notes can create complex symphonies, each of us has some qualities of all nine types within us. This creates richness and diversity. It can also create problems! If our symphony has too many wrong notes, it's just noise. If our type has too many negative qualities working overtime, we get depressed and frustrated, and we may have difficulty in our work and personal lives. The Enneagram plots out those qualities, shows us where we fall short, shows us where we're doing well, and helps us get on an even keel. So far, so good? Good!

## An Overview of the Nine Types

Here's an introduction to the nine types of the Enneagram. Each type has its own chapter in Part 2:

**Type 1: The Perfectionist/Improver.** Type 1 has an ideal view of how life should be and wants reality to conform to that view. 1s examine everything, including themselves, with an eye toward correction and perfection.

**Type 2: The Giver/Cheerleader.** Type 2 wants to help people, as a way to be loved and accepted. 2s need people to need them. A positive personality, the 2 loves to give, but can lay on the guilt if unappreciated.

**Type 3: The Success Striver/Winner.** Type 3 is the U.S. cultural ideal and focuses on goals, success, accomplishments, winning, and producing. Image is everything, and 3s generally target areas for goal-setting, where they can succeed.

**Type 4: The Romantic/Depth Seeker.** Type 4 is the nonconformist, working to cultivate individuality or specialness in order to be noticed and admired. The 4 is drawn to beauty, individual self-exploration, and a search for meaning.

**Type 5: The Observer/Knowledge Seeker.** Type 5 tends to be private and engaged in thinking, observing, and making sense out of life, particularly in knowledge-gathering, theory making, and integrating different aspects of knowledge and learning.

**Type 6: The Guardian/Questioner.** Type 6 tends to question everything, particularly issues of safety and security. 6s worry, analyze in depth, and try to solve concerns in advance. They feel more secure in the truth, no matter how negative, than with positive images.

**Type 7: The Optimist/Fun Lover.** Type 7 sees the world in the best possible light. 7s like positive thinking, fun, adventure, and newness. They prefer risk to repetition and like to be around people that are happy, ready for change, and can move on the spur of the moment.

**Type 8: The Director/Powerhouse.** Type 8 likes to be in charge. 8s want control of their own lives and often others' lives, too. 8s act quickly and can't stand ambivalence. They prefer action, directness, and strength.

**Type 9: The Harmony Seeker/Accommodator.** Type 9 prefers to avoid conflict. 9 tends not to initiate but "goes with the flow." 9s appear easygoing, and they like comfort, constancy, and little change—unless they initiate it in stages.

> **Warning!**
>
> Resist the temptation to tell people you know what their core type is. You could very easily be wrong! It takes time to learn the Enneagram.

Is it nature or nurture? Parents often remark that their children have unique traits from birth, particularly in comparison to their siblings. Although this is true, our upbringing and family patterns also affect who we become. Some people think their type is spiritually generated—a prechosen path of strengths and obstacles to learn from in this lifetime. Whatever the case, nature and nurture combine to work their miracles and it's up to you to choose a side in this ongoing argument. Most Enneagram teachers agree that nature (physical and emotionally preset genes and disposition) plays a bigger role than nurture (environment and upbringing).

Now that you've been introduced to the nine types, you might have already found either yourself or those you know in these broad categories. Each type has strengths, tendencies, and areas of needed growth. However, if that's all there were to the

Enneagram, it would be very basic and not all that accurate. Fortunately, that's just the beginning—sort of the overture, to continue our symphony analogy. There are other parts to the types. These parts are called wings, Instinctual subtypes, centers, Growth type, and Stress type. Taken all together, they paint a portrait of you that is uniquely you.

# Wings

Each core type has two wings. Wings flavor the way you exist in your core type, sort of the way salt and pepper enhance your food. You'll find your wings on either side of your type number. For example, wings for a 7 are 6 and 8. Wings for a 1 are 9 and 2. Where does the flavor come from? It comes from the qualities of the types next to you. You, in essence, *borrow* some characteristics of that neighbor type. One of your wings is generally stronger than the other. It's called your strong wing and its characteristics show up in day-to-day life. You'll discover more about wings in the type chapters in Part 2.

# Instinctual Subtypes

Each type has three subtypes, called Instinctual subtypes. These add complexity and variety and relate to three basic survival instincts, all of which are essential in your development. One of these subtypes, however, is more of an *obsessional* focus and *self-esteem* concern throughout your life. It operates in the arena where you have your most life challenges and have the most to learn and grow. A subtype area that's always been easy for you is *not* your subtype. You'll find their descriptions in Part 2, but for now, here's a subtype summary:

♦ **Self-Preservation subtypes** focus more on issues and concerns regarding basic, personal survival. These issues are related to security, protection, food, the home, comfort, money, planning for the future, and health.

♦ **Social subtypes** relate to the herd instinct and focus more on issues of social rank, position, prestige, social recognition, causes, group or community inclusion or exclusion, and group or social acknowledgement or appreciation.

♦ **Sexual subtypes** focus on issues relating to the mating instinct and are obsessed and often stressed about sex, romance, relationships, love, rejection, jealousy, and commitment.

Your subtype tends to be a lifelong area of concern or stress. This subtype focus may shift a bit, due to current life circumstances. If you are moving, you'll be focused on self-preservation issues; if pursuing a relationship, you'll be focused on the Sexual subtype; and if you're worried about your job or whether you will be accepted in a certain group, you'll focus on the social arena. Once those areas are satisfied, you'll move back to your primary subtype concern.

## Centers

Our musical analogy will help here. Visualize yourself as the conductor of the symphony orchestra. The orchestra before you is grouped into sections: woodwinds, strings, percussion, and brass. Within each section are similar types of instruments. In much the same way, the Enneagram divides the nine types into three sections called centers or triads. Each center perceives reality, first and foremost, through a similar focus of attention that is different from the other two centers. These three centers are Body (or Gut), Image (or Heart), and Head. Here's a brief summary of how these centers work:

- **The Body types (or Gut types)** are 1, 8, and 9. Body types tend to be more basic, with no frills—things are what they are. Body types perceive life from body instinct. They prefer a direct form of expression and love honesty.

- **The Image types (sometimes called Heart types)** are 2, 3, and 4. Image types perceive the world from an image they create and project. They want to be seen from that perspective and be rewarded for what they can produce from that image projection.

- **The Head types** are 5, 6, and 7. Head types perceive life from the mind or mental representation and like to plan, think, and understand before they move. *Cogito ergo sum.* I think; therefore, I am.

> ### Insights
>
> Here's a simple exercise to figure out what your natural center might be. View ordinary objects in a room. Head types tend to view objects visually, descriptively, and analytically. Image types view objects from how the object affects them personally and emotionally. Body types tend to merge with the object, experiencing direct or visceral sense from it. Try all viewpoints with the same object!

You'll find out more about Body, Image, and Head types in Part 2.

## Growth Type

You've already learned that the Enneagram is a tool for personal growth, so it's only logical that it provides you with a Growth type! Your Growth type is one of the nine types, other than your core type. When you seek out the best features of that type and try to emulate them, that makes for growth! When you're consciously aiming for personal improvement, and when your life is going along smoothly, you'll be learning from your Growth type.

## Stress Type

What would life be without stress? Hard to know, because it seems to be programmed into the solar system. The Enneagram teaches that during these stressful times, you first spiral down within your own type, acting out your type's absolute worst traits. If things get even worse, you then take on the worst traits of your Stress type, which is another of the nine types, apart from your own.

**Lifelines** _____

Sometimes people try to hide their type, even from themselves, particularly if they've been hurt or rejected for their type perspective. It's important to remember that each type is as valid as another. Affirm your type!

It's actually a good idea to develop the best qualities of both your Stress type and your Growth type. Your Stress type teaches you to recognize when things are getting bad in your life (you'd better get to growing), and your Growth type is both a reflection of how well you are doing and a model for those positive traits to develop to maintain your well-being.

You'll find a complete description of each type's Growth and Stress types in Part 2.

## Gender

Generally, the types are somewhat evenly distributed, although there do seem to be more female 2s and 4s and more male 5s. On average, 1s, 3s, 7s, and 8s tend to be more self-directed and assertive and often associated with the masculine; 2s, 4s, and 9s tend to be more feminine and relationship-oriented. 5s tend to have a masculine orientation, but regarding focus and detachment they are not always assertive, and 6s vary. Of course, there are exceptions. Because the Enneagram doesn't pigeon-hole you, you'll find infinite variety.

## Introvert-Extrovert

It's generally easier to type an extrovert than an introvert. While every type can contain introverted or extroverted versions, Type 5 seems to be the only type with introverts as the vast majority of its members. Introverts, in general, are more self-reflective and don't reveal themselves immediately. Extroverts are more expressive and show who they are more readily and are easier to type because of this. 1s and 6s have a fairly even mix of introverts and extroverts. 4s, 5s, and 9s tend to have more introverts. There are generally more extroverted 2s, 3s, 7s, and 8s. There are many exceptions to this tendency, so always be open to an introverted or extroverted version of each type.

Core types, wings, Instinctual subtypes, centers, Growth type, and Stress type—these are the elements you'll be concerned with as you begin your journey into the power of the Enneagram. Now that you know the main parts, let's take a brief look at where this came from. Here's Enneagram History 101—the short version!

# History of the Enneagram

*In the beginning* … Actually, we're not sure where the beginning is. The origins and early history of the 9-type symbol are steeped in mystery. We find elements of it in the Jewish Kabbalah, Christianity, *Sufism*, Buddhism, and Taoism. Also, the Babylonians and the Egyptians seem to have had a fascination with the 9-type symbol or nine stages of spiritual development.

## def•i•ni•tion

Sufism is system of mysticism within Islam.

Some believe that Philo, a Jewish, neo-Platonist philosopher, introduced this 9-type tradition into Judaism, where it appears as the Kabbalah and the spiritual growth system called The Tree of Life. The Kabbalah references nine stages of development, with a tenth one that unifies the nine.

The symbol of the Enneagram is an ancient cosmic symbol, with nine lines that include a triangle, creating a unique star pattern inscribed within a circle.

The Greeks got really involved, with Pythagoras, Plato, Plotinus, and Homer all having a hand in some aspect of the Enneagram symbol. Pythagoras used the symbol, as he considered the sacred meaning of numbers and speculated about personality types. Plato spoke of nine divine forms and something called *mystical mathematics*. Plotinus wrote a text called *The Enneads*, and Homer's *Odyssey* and *Iliad* have been linked to the Enneagram's nine types or nine spiritual journeys.

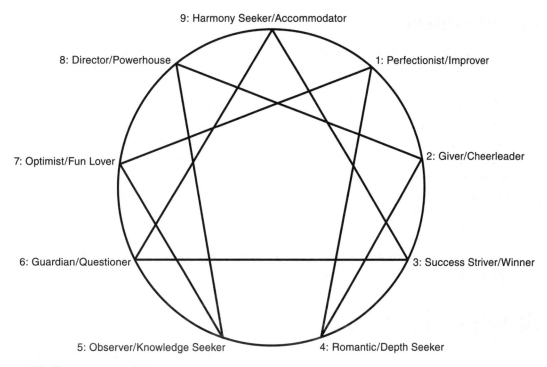

9: Harmony Seeker/Accommodator

8: Director/Powerhouse

1: Perfectionist/Improver

7: Optimist/Fun Lover

2: Giver/Cheerleader

6: Guardian/Questioner

3: Success Striver/Winner

5: Observer/Knowledge Seeker

4: Romantic/Depth Seeker

*The Enneagram symbol.*

Variations of the Enneagram symbol also appear in Islamic Sufi traditions, perhaps introduced by the Arabian philosopher, al-Ghazzali. Around the fourteenth century, an order of Sufism is believed to have preserved and passed on the Enneagram symbol. This order is variously known as the *Brotherhood of the Bees* (because they collected and stored knowledge) and the *Symbolists* (because they taught through symbols).

We can speculate endlessly about ancient origins of the Enneagram, but one thing is clear: many spiritual and religious systems and theories taught about differences, how to move beyond ego, and how to lessen suffering. Let's fast forward to modern times, because that's when we live! A few names are important here:

◆ George Gurdjieff (1879–1949) used the nine spiritual qualities associated with the Enneagram to explain the cosmic laws of the universe. A teacher, he studied mystery schools of wisdom and traveled extensively.

◆ Oscar Ichazo (1931– ) a philosopher, psychologist, and teacher, is considered by many to be the father of the modern Enneagram. He is the one who created and developed the modern descriptions of the nine Enneagram types.

◆ Dr. Claudio Naranjo (1932– ) Chilean-born anthropologist and psychiatrist, studied with Oscar Ichazo. Through his many interviews with each type, he added to the psychological understanding of the types.

Each man advanced the cause of the Enneagram, contributing new dimensions of thinking and new levels of complexity.

Since the 1970s, the Enneagram has been growing steadily in popularity. There are many reasons for this, but probably the complexity of modern life, with its fast pace and increasingly impersonal interactions in business and in everyday life, are responsible. We need the human connection and we need to relate to others from a position of awareness and strength. The Enneagram provides both the means for making those connections as well as that strength.

Today, some of the most well-known Enneagram teachers and writers of the Enneagram are Helen Palmer, David Daniels, Don Richard Riso, and Russ Hudson. Enneagram teachers and groups are located all over the world. Millions of people are becoming aware of the Enneagram, and their numbers continue to rise! There is an International Enneagram Association and an annual conference.

# The Power of the Enneagram

The Enneagram provides a major shortcut to understanding the self, offering tools and action steps. Each type has a growth path very unique to the type. If you take advice from others of different types (quite likely), and do what others tell you to do, you might be going against the grain of what *you* need. Of course, listen to your intuition around growth, but you will find that the Enneagram accurately predicts your life journey, issues, and resolutions and brings you clarity and the confidence to act in ways best suited for you.

## Personal Understanding and Growth

The Enneagram is one of the clearest descriptions of how people perceive their reality and organize their thoughts and actions around those perceptions. The Enneagram will help you understand yourself—what runs you and what limits you. You'll see why you do what you do and how you expect others to respond to you in *your* type world, not the type world in which they live. Don't take it personally! Growth only comes after you've faced the truth of who you are. Prepare for humility—yep, another object lesson! The Enneagram's type descriptions are clear and objective, so you'll see that others of the same type have very similar motivations and actions.

## Relationship Dynamics

You will discover the world's richest gold mine in the Enneagram. An Enneagram workshop or two can help you gain insight into your relationships (see Chapter 2 for more on workshops). You can actually understand what's happening and why. Once the nature of your differences become clear, you'll watch the tension disappear! (Sounds sort of like a commercial jingle, doesn't it?) The reality is, though, that everyone becomes less of an enigma. You'll understand your partner and have the bonus of having your partner understand you. (Warning: you might become an instant Enneagram addict!)

Everyone you know will make more sense to you. You'll feel secure in knowing them and what is important to them. They will love you for it! You might not like the way people may act, but you can eliminate wondering why they are the way they are. They'll wonder how you suddenly became so smart!

| Insights |
| --- |
| Ask other types what they struggle with—what's difficult. When you develop understanding and compassion for each type's inner and outer struggles, you'll have realistic expectations and better relationships. |

Using the Enneagram will greatly improve your own sense of compassion for people, knowing the different types and their personal struggles. You won't compare another type to yourself so readily but rather you'll compare them to the challenges within their type. With understanding comes empathy. Your confidence will soar, because you'll know what to say (and not say) and what to do (and not do). You'll know how to educate each person about your type, what your sensitivities and challenges are, what you can handle, and what you can't. You can become a coach, helping those you care about enjoy shared and different type strengths.

You'll learn why and how past relationships played out the way they did. So many conflicts in relationships are directly related to type differences and misinterpretations, as well as to maturity differences within each type. You'll look at your past history with new insight. You won't repeat as many mistakes, and you'll get better at choosing to relate to people whose types are compatible with yours.

| Insights |
| --- |
| People often say that one or two sessions of couples work with a therapist, well-versed in the Enneagram, is worth months of work with another therapist, working solely with communication skills. The Enneagram gets right to the point, targeting differences and providing couples with immediate skills targeted just for them. |

## Career Growth

It's so important to have work that you love and that also fits with your type strengths and challenges. The Enneagram helps inform what work paths or careers might be more satisfying than others, in addition to improving relationship dynamics directly related to work issues. Working against your type or dealing with type prejudices can be exhausting.

It's important to be in work settings that value your type and your form of productivity and creativity. It's equally important to be understood for the challenges of your type, so that co-workers and management don't have unreasonable expectations. You can educate others in this capacity. Knowledge of your co-workers' and supervisors' types can also help you understand their perspectives, expectations, actions, and type language. You'll be able to modulate your own language and work actions to balance your type with others' type expectations and goals.

Now that you've got the basics of the basics under your belt, you're ready to see the role the Enneagram can play in your life!

## The Least You Need to Know

- The Enneagram describes nine unique types or ways of seeing life.
- Wings and Instinctual subtypes flavor each core type, adding depth and complexity.
- Your Stress type and Growth type influence the way you handle life's challenges.
- The Enneagram has a rich history, reflecting peoples' timeless search to understand the fascinating personality differences that make us who we are.
- The Enneagram has benefits for relationships, personal growth, and career success.

# Using the Enneagram Today

## In This Chapter

- ◆ You and the Enneagram
- ◆ Tips on how to approach Enneagram learning
- ◆ The Enneagram in counseling, coaching, training, and business
- ◆ Using the Enneagram for growth

A great tool for personal growth in everyday life, the Enneagram is also used in the business world for team development and motivating employees toward career growth via development of personal strengths. In schools, it's being taught to teachers to aid them in understanding their students and to students for self-understanding, as well as for relating to peers. More and more psychotherapists and social workers use the Enneagram in counseling, to help them better understand their clients. We'll take a look at each of these areas.

## Using the Enneagram in Your Everyday Life

The Enneagram's best use is for everyday life purposes. As you've already seen, it's a practical tool to understand yourself and others and expand your options for personal growth in both work and relationships. It's also a great aid for developing strengths outside your type. As you learn more about the Enneagram and start using it on a daily basis, keep seeing and enjoying the world of differences.

With nine different perspectives on life, which you'll read about in detail in Part 2, the Enneagram types enrich our understanding and broaden our horizons. Notice how true to type people are, and have some fun people-watching. Enjoy what's good in each type and don't let the *not so good* upset you. Have compassion for others. People, on average, are just being who they are and tend to treat everyone the same way. Don't take things too personally. The more you know about the different types, the more you can predict behavior in others.

## Type Strengths Can Help You Grow!

Ask questions of the types. Learn from them. Educate others about your type. Never assume others really understand you. Never even assume you understand yourself. Examine your type's values and decide whether you want to keep them! The types are options, on one level, and yet a strong magnet to keep repeating what you are familiar with, on another. The Enneagram gives you more options to be in charge of your life and, at the least, make sense of it! You can practice using the strengths of each type. Choose a type to develop, outside your own type, and begin imitating positive behaviors of that type. For example …

- To develop 8, start being more assertive, direct, and clear. Don't think too much. Just act and trust your gut. Get an 8 friend or coach to help you.

- To develop 9, practice relaxing more, focus on peace and harmony, take breaks, and pursue hobbies and interests, as well as work.

Practice being that type every day, and don't expect instant results. *Fake it till you make it.* Practice makes perfect. Once you've mastered one positive trait, keep it! And then start developing another one. You'll never run out!

## Working at Positive Changes

Type growth and change is challenging and takes time. We all repeat some of the same dysfunctional patterns. Work at some positive type change daily:

- If you are a 2, ask for help!

- If you are a 4, attempt to *not* make a crisis out of your current issue. Try on new perspectives and behaviors.

◆ If you are a 3, with a driven nature, take breaks between projects. Go on a short vacation (you can plan your next project).

◆ If you are a 9, go into action when you are anxious. It feels counter-instinctive, but it's the right move.

Don't hate your type when you are frustrated with its limits. Be aware of your strengths and surround yourself with good examples of each type, particularly your own. Keep learning about type differences through reading, reflection, workshops, and websites (see Appendix E), and asking type questions of your friends and others with whom you come in contact (see Appendix C). The world is more beautiful when you really understand, enjoy, and respect its differences.

**Lifelines** _____

Think of how your own type and others' types have affected you. See this objectively, without major judgments, but if some feelings come up, let them. It can be powerful to see that your perspective has both limited and enhanced your life. In a strange way, it's helpful to see that your life has been somewhat predictable. You haven't always been in charge of it—your type has!

# Case Studies Shed Light

Here are two case studies involving two very different couples. The Enneagram helped them solve problems and learn to enjoy each other's differences.

## Perfectionist Meets Optimist–Objective: Harmony

A Type 1 woman is married to a Type 7 man. 1s and 7s are great together, when they learn from and support each other's differences. Getting there, however, can be difficult.

She complains that her husband is not serious enough, laughs at everything, doesn't worry about money, doesn't have a steady career. His ventures in the world of work, starting a company and a stint as a salesman, haven't panned out. She is self-employed as a nutritionist. They're not getting rich too quickly.

He decides it's time to grow! He takes temporary employment in construction. Learning on the job, he builds his skill base, fixing houses—painting, wallpapering, building, wiring, plumbing—and eventually builds a full-time business, which becomes a success. He enjoys it, as well. Important for a 7! Husband and wife begin working together—buying houses to fix and then sell. They become real estate agents and develop a profitable business.

Even though he's always in good spirits (doesn't sound too bad!), he still isn't overly serious and doesn't talk about weighty subjects, but he's reliable, cheerful, and supportive. He likes his wife's more serious and grounded nature. They share outdoor activities and she lightens up, exercises more, laughs more, and accepts her husband the way he is—which is perfect for her, really. 1s go to 7 to grow, just as 7s go to 1 to become focused.

## How Do I Love Thee?

One Type 9 man learns the Enneagram to understand his Type 4 girlfriend, whose approach to life is radically different from his. She thrives on intensity and strong expression of feeling—full tilt—whether of joy or abandonment. She wants personal attention, praise, and depth of expression. He's calmer, even-keeled, and enjoys simple pleasures.

They find a way to bridge the gap. She works at being calmer, not overdramatizing, or blaming him for her pain. He likes his newfound, more passionate self. He becomes more dramatic (he has done some community theater) and acts out his undying love (even if it's a bit staged). He plucks two of her favorite flowers from an abandoned garden! She loves the specialness of it and the unique presentation (he's on his knees, when he gives her the flowers). Learn your opposite. There's much to gain personally and relationally.

# Help Me, Counselor!

The Enneagram is a remarkable tool for psychotherapists, social workers, healers, and teachers of any type. As a matter of fact, it's useful in any of the helping professions. It gets right to the point and speeds up counseling, often creating minor or major miracles of change. Everything you say with Enneagram language can be backed up and verified by the client—making the Enneagram practical, verifiable, and instantly useful.

Knowing your type and your clients' types will allow you to be more open to your own preferences and type limitations. It will also filter the natural tendency to make the client the same type as you, the therapist. You'll know the client's type growth cycle, understand the particular struggles of that type, and not push too far past a type's current limitations.

Your accurate use of language and empathy will help the client feel comfortable, trusting, and supported—necessary prerequisites for making positive growth. You'll understand type risks and spot backsliding from a type perspective. You'll be more aware of clients' differences and better prepared to address them appropriately. The more skilled you are with the Enneagram, the more you can type clients in an interactive process, talk about type strengths and defenses, and reflect on relational dynamics.

Because the Enneagram is an objective way of seeing reality, clients can learn about their automatic reactions and avoidances, start to notice those reactions, and learn more functional ways of being and behaving.

In other fields involving healing, psychic work, or bodywork, you'll feel more confident in providing the services your clients really need, they'll be more satisfied with these services, and your skill level will have less trial and error and more dead-on accuracy. The only bad news—you might have to attract more clients, because you'll work more quickly and more efficiently. Of course, satisfied clients will tell their friends!

> **Insights**
>
> There are a number of Enneagram training programs that certify Enneagram teachers and trainers. Enneagram workshops (discussed later in this chapter) address understanding the types, growth for each type, how to relate to each type, type and romance, and tips on typing.

## The Motley Crew: Integrating Differences

An Enneagram therapist counseled an entire family—a Type 6 wife; Type 5 husband; Type 9 son, age 16; and Type 7 daughter, age 12. The wife complained about lack of attention from her husband. (This is a constant complaint about Type 5 men, as they tend to be private, liking time alone and engaging in more intellectual topics than in emotional or relational ones.) As a 6, she challenges and questions him. She likes clear communication and agreement on problems and potential dangers involving child rearing and financial matters, but he doesn't talk about much, unless it's a serious, current issue. She wants advance planning and also to convince him to see what she sees.

He's objective, isn't riled easily, and also has a touch of 7. When home from his computer-oriented job, he wants to be on the computer at home, ride his motorcycle, or have light conversation, if any at all. She interprets his lack of attention toward her, and seeming unconcern about safety, as a sign of problems between them. She further exacerbates the situation by more questions, challenges, and upsets, and he responds with more withdrawal; then she does the same. The 9 son mediates family differences and the 7 daughter wants to have fun, reacts negatively to mom's control and concerns, and allies more with dad.

Through education and counseling, the wife learns to understand her husband's nature and works at accepting his tendencies toward more quiet, interesting, intellectual discussions and humor. He understands she tends to be problem-oriented and wants his input. He learns to talk more, check in with her, make more physical contact, and understand her nature. They need closeness in differing ways.

Not all the problems are solved, but coaching the mom to relax more, notice possible misinterpretations, find ways to bond through fun and more objective understanding, and lower the judgments and interpretations, rather than having strong reactions, helps the whole family situation.

> **Warning!**
>
> Whether families pull together or pull apart is in their make-up. The more tolerance for differences and learning, the more families stay together. The more pressure for conformity, the more they tend to pull apart or explode!

## The Optimist and the Director: Action on the Set!

A 7 woman and an 8 man, a couple, seek counseling. The 8 favors a direct method of speaking and is focused on loyalty, honest talk, and understanding his partner's motivations. "Give me the dark side, and I can handle it," says the 8. For the 7, however, talking about fear, anger, and sadness is frightening. She makes a major breakthrough in confronting her boyfriend by talking about her upset with him over forgetting to bring the pet food to her house. For him, this is easy to hear. For her, well, it's taken weeks, thinking about sharing this, and she's greatly relieved to say, "I'm angry!" The therapist highlights the breakthrough, for the 8 would have missed the importance of her communication, as well as her need to be assertive—exactly what an 8 likes!

## The Giver and the Observer: Open Up, Share More

A 2-5 couple has couple counseling. The 2 female wants more personal attention and wants the 5 man to share more of himself and what he is thinking. He wants her to be less emotionally reactive and spell out exactly what she wants, rather than hint at it.

He tends to make independent decisions, without consulting or collaborating with her. This irritates her. She is trying to be more independent in her work (growth for

2 is to be more independent) and less dependent on him. She's also trying to break away from overgiving, which is difficult for her.

The therapist coaches him to share more, even if mundane information is all he's mulling over. Also, he's coached to be more emotionally expressive and more romantic. He needs to acknowledge his dependence on her, to a greater degree.

## The Harmony Seeker Learns Assertiveness

A 9 woman is struggling with the death of friends, an ill husband, and a daughter with anorexia—plenty to manage. She needs support. Outwardly, she needs to be assertive, while inwardly feeling entitled to her own desires and goals. She wants to relate to others and negotiate with a clear picture of who she is and what she wants.

The Enneagram therapist shows empathy for the difficulty of the woman's situation. This is affirming for the 9. Daily practice of self-nurturing techniques and learning to say *yes* to herself and *no* to others, when this is necessary, reinforces the 9's right to self-clarity. She is counseled to negotiate her needs, rather than giving in.

## It's Lonely at the Perfectionist Top of the World

A Type 1 man deals with issues of self-judgment and also with issues with his girl-friend. The Enneagram therapist educates him about the tendencies of Type 1 to self-judge and feel imperfect and angry. He is coached on how to notice mind tendencies throughout the day, soften judgments, normalize disappointments, and be patient. Learning alternative ways to think and the use of affirmations is helpful.

The 1 man learns that it's common to sometimes feel ambivalence about a romantic partner. This relieves some guilt. He learns to refocus on what's positive. He also learns that it's perfectly fine to have some needs met with other friends. His negative thoughts decrease as he learns options to balance his thinking between the positive and the less-than-perfect experiences.

## When I'm Good, I'm Very, Very Good; When I'm Bad ...

All the types are good at their type strengths but need to develop strength from their weaknesses. In individual counseling, here's a summary of what the types seek:

◆ 1s seek to be less self-critical and more accepting of ambivalence and gray areas, both within self and from others.

- 2s seek to nurture themselves and back away from too much focus on others.

- 3s seek to explore the inner self and accept that occasional failures are a normal part of life.

- 4s seek to leave the extremes and tend more to neutrality.

- 5s seek to feel more and learn how to connect to others more deeply.

- 6s seek to feel less anxiety.

- 7s seek to listen to others' pain, as well as to their own.

- 8s seek to learn to control their need to control.

- 9s seek to be more assertive and learn how to express anger.

# Coaching the Coach to Coach

Coaching is an offshoot of counseling. Counseling often relates to more in-depth understanding of motivations, deep-seated issues, and dysfunction. Coaching is more related to necessary action steps to produce results in the client's life, without considering defenses and past history. Generally coaching is done over the phone, with only the first session in person.

**Lifelines**

Good coaches or therapists also understand and develop the type qualities of their clients to enhance their own growth, as well as to deepen empathy. You are more successful when you really can understand the world from others' perspectives.

When you know both your type and your clients' types, you have a much better shot at knowing how to individually coach them. They'll feel understood, and you'll be on the mark about knowing what action steps are more in alignment with your clients' types. You won't expect or try to make your clients move beyond their capacity or re-create themselves in *your* type.

It's not unusual for your clients to unconsciously pick the same type coach for comfort and familiarity or a more *opposite* type, sensing that your skills and strengths are exactly what they need. Conversations about goals, approach, and your personality differences as coach-client are all-important to best utilize the time and money spent for coaching.

Separate from client success, the coach also needs to feel successful, satisfied, confident, and clear about what is happening, with regard to personality dynamics. Good coaching programs include the Enneagram or other personality-based training to understand how personality differences interface with coaching, communication, goals, and success. Consider the following coaching tips for the nine types:

♦ 1s need coaching to lighten up, let go of the small stuff, and see that all perspectives have value.

♦ 2s need coaching to make sure they are identifying personal needs, getting the returns they are looking for, and learning how to not overgive.

♦ 3s already tend to be success-driven but might want to increase that success with some fine-tuning from an expert in their field. They also might need help with personal goals and improving relationship dynamics. Talk about action steps, bottom lines, and how to quickly deal with obstacles is already comfortable language for a 3.

♦ 4s need coaching to help them learn to assume responsibility for the consequences of their actions, rely on themselves more for personal validation, and accept constructive criticism without feeling personally devalued.

♦ 5s need coaching to express more, show passion, and accept subjective reality.

♦ 6s need support to see best-case scenarios, work with anxiety reduction, and feel secure in the present moment.

♦ 7s need a positive coach but also one who can support commitment, depth, and completing goals.

♦ 8s need to experience that it's normal to feel insecure and be less bold but still self-connected. 8s need to be coached with directness but also with sensitivity to hidden needs.

♦ 9s look for support in dealing with conflicts and not retreating from them. They need to know that, at times, others will be upset or disagree with them, and that this is normal—not a reason to withdraw. Being self-centered, assertive, expressing anger, and clarifying goals, are important for 9s.

# More Bang for the Buck

Business is always about the bottom line. When employees find themselves in positions they don't want, they're likely to be uninterested and inefficient, with the result that time, money, and other resources are wasted. Team up your employees with

**Warning!**

Make no assumptions that any one type is right for a particular job. Typically, a type is good at that type's strengths, but sometimes people are more motivated to try on something that's more of a challenge in order to develop new skills.

a role or job that excites them, one at which they already excel or one they're motivated to learn. The Enneagram provides information that helps with the right placement, one that's decided between management and the prospective employee.

As a tool, the Enneagram can help people utilize the best strengths of their type, enhance communication, work together as a team, and provide useful information to increase production and sales.

## Let's Hear It for Team Spirit!

Once you know everyone's type and subtypes, you know the make-up of the team. One type may be overrepresented, or one type may dominate, at the expense of another. As team training leader, you can give a quick evaluation of type and team strengths, noting how the group's type makeup might affect productivity. You can focus on how to utilize the strengths of each team member. For example, if Image types 2, 3, and 4—types who tend to focus more on presentation and style—are missing, adding one of these types will provide the team with strategies to promote group image, advertising, and certain aspects of sales and enhance your chances of success.

## Bury Your Prejudices

Teams and groups often benefit from having a range of types. This mix allows all issues to be fully explored and developed. Type prejudice (judgment or punishment against certain types) can deeply affect outcomes. It can create fears, holding back, more judgments, withdrawal, stalling, and it can ultimately result in serious loss of time and energy. The Enneagram can be an objective tool in groups or organizations to comment on type values, including prejudgments, inclusions, or exclusions. Once type is understood, there is more patience and more support for efficiency, clarity of language, and verbalization of concerns. Speed and outcome are always positively affected with knowledge, acceptance, positive support, and fun. It's win/win all the way around.

## We're All Leaders Here, but We're Leading Nowhere Fast

One executive team discovered that everyone on the team, with the exception of one member, was a leadership-action Type 3 or 8. The lone different member was a more analytical 6. The Questioner 6 was trying to be more like other team members but felt misunderstood and left out of group decisions. The 6's tendency was to over-analyze, which slowed down action steps for others.

The leadership types were coached to learn what to expect from the 6 and utilize the 6's strengths, instead of their previous tendency to act quickly, considering only their own ideas. Once the 6 realized his role as a strategic planner and analyzer was wanted and could be utilized more clearly, he felt more valued. Go team!

## You Can Take This to the Bank

An 8 team leader in a bank ran roughshod over everyone, and everyone was afraid of him. To top it off, the VP was also an 8. Some 8s are inspirational and more egalitarian, but these 8s were "my way or the highway" types. During team training, the Enneagram leader and employees egged on the president and the VP, during two different role plays, to act out alternative ways of handling complaints. With the tension cleared, the leader offered options and responses that engaged everyone. A little humor helped, along with specific coaching tips on how to directly approach an 8 and also, for the 8s, on how to soften their perceived harshness. There was a little less quaking in the boots!

# The Enneagram as a Training Tool

Numerous training programs use the Enneagram as a tool for creating understanding or for personal enhancement. Enneagram trainings and presentations are held during annual retreats, teambuilding experiences, club meetings, conferences, or award dinners. The venues are numerous and varied. Many social service agencies use the Enneagram in training staff to work with clients, to understand how and why personality conflicts arise, and what to do to resolve conflicts and work together more effectively. The benefits extend beyond the workplace to the family setting.

## Head Start Program Works for Adults, Too

A Head Start program uses the Enneagram at trainings to help staff understand child/parent differences and work together more effectively. Everyone gets typed and participates in fun exercises to help in understanding each type.

Social service agencies often contain many 9s, who like to create harmony and understanding. However, conflicts arise and underlying tensions can build, particularly with the more assertive types. 9s and 2s receive coaching to be more direct, 4s get support to conform more—while still retaining their individuality—and 7s keep the antics going. No one can keep the mood light the way 7s can. Every type is validated and Enneagram ribbing continues for months!

| Insights |
| --- |
| Feedback from team training generally includes comments such as, "Wow, this is fun!," "This explains their behavior," "Now I understand why they are doing what they do," "I know how to talk to each person," "We've been joking with each other more," and "We talk about it—the Enneagram—all the time." |

Good training speeds up the process of learning to understand personality. It can also prevent conflicts that otherwise might take many years to work out. Conflicts are often avoidable, once people gain insight into how to relate to others from *their* world view. Most people tend to think their own view is the right or normal one. Some people, however, do the opposite and diminish their own perspectives by putting others' perspectives up on that proverbial pedestal. Enneagram workshops that address understanding the types, growth for each type, relating to each type, type and romance, tips on typing, and other topics help people quickly understand how this important tool fits into their daily lives.

## Finding an Enneagram Trainer or Workshop

Where is the Enneagram taught? A better question might be, "Where *isn't* the Enneagram taught?" In every instance, the experience has been positive, informative, and entertaining! It's been taught in …

- Real estate firms.
- Banks.
- Computer tech firms.
- Manufacturing companies.
- Pharmaceutical companies.
- Consulting firms.
- Social service agencies.
- Religious denominational headquarters and churches.
- Conferences.
- Educational settings.

# E Is for Enneagram

In educational settings the Enneagram has practical application for personal growth and relational dynamics. The Enneagram is taught in a variety of educational arenas, including yoga centers, bookstores, churches, secondary schools, and colleges. In colleges, it's frequently found in courses focusing on personality and counseling.

Children as young as 8 take basic Enneagram workshops and easily pick up the concepts and personality descriptions. Upon hearing the types described or acted out, children have drawn their own diagrams, using vegetables or fruits or names of friends who, in their perceptions, fit the types. Also, students can learn *how* they learn and how to relate to other students, as well as to their teachers.

The Enneagram can be used with students in secondary schools to teach …

- 1s to relax the perfection drive and not try so hard.

- 2s to ask for help and also ask if others want help.

- 3s to pursue their true desires, even if this means the 3 doesn't come out on top.

- 4s to handle their feelings and realize hurts are often unintentional.

- 5s social skills and emotional education.

- 6s to calm themselves and focus on the positive.

- 7s to experience all their feelings more deeply, not just the exciting ones.

- 8s appropriate ways to join in, because their directness and need to control are sometimes seen as bullying.

- 9s to be self-directed.

Likewise, teachers need to see how their type strengths and limitations affect their students and look at alternative teaching methodologies that include all the types' perspectives. Each type has some areas that need work:

- 1s can be too rigid and not flexible enough to work outside their comfort zone.

- 2s can be too pleasing and over involved.

- 3s can push students too much toward success.

- 4s can take events and actions too personally.

- 5s can be overly dry on knowledge and not connect with their students.

> **Insights**
>
> Nothing has ever given me the insight the Enneagram has given me. This stuff actually works. People make sense. I understand myself. I feel more confident.
> —Paul, 42

- 6s can focus too much on preparedness—what-ifs.

- 7s, focused on fun, may miss what's serious.

- 8s may be overly directive and authoritarian—sometimes frighteningly so.

- 9s may not be definite and specific.

So, let's get started! It's time to learn more about the types, your own type, and ways to make your life fabulous!

## The Least You Need to Know

- The Enneagram provides valuable tools to help you understand your psychological makeup, feel confident in your interactions with others, and live your daily life with more clarity.

- Counselors and coaches can learn how types influence behaviors and can develop active strategies to support client growth and change.

- Business leaders can use the Enneagram for leadership development and staff trainings to increase sales and profit.

- For team development, the Enneagram can explain the type perspective of everyone on the team, reduce conflict, and promote efficiency.

- In education, the Enneagram can help explain how students learn and provide teachers with information to best provide instruction.

# Part 2

# The Enneagram Types

In these chapters you'll get a detailed look at each of the Enneagram's nine types, along with the subtypes and wings that further subdivide each type. Which type describes your driving force and that of the important people in your life? Remember, type is more about what motivates you than about exact behaviors. Understand the type as a whole, rather than trying to see how you or others fit exactly with each part of the type description. If you have changed a great deal during your life, the type you have grown into might not be your original type, but most likely your Growth type. You'll see how all the pieces fit neatly together in these chapters.

# Type 1: The Perfectionist/ Improver

## In This Chapter

- ◆ Living by the rules
- ◆ I'm here to fix me, you, and the rest of the world
- ◆ Oh! The pressure to be good is killing me
- ◆ Let's see, there's guilt, and resentment, and …
- ◆ Doing it right—no time to play and relax

Perfectionist/Improvers strive to make everything right, have high ideals, and expect the same traits in others. 1s have a hard time with ambivalence and the gray areas of life. It's always an either/or proposition for the 1: black or white, good or evil, right or wrong. That someone could be good and bad at the same time is difficult for the 1 to accept.

## Understanding the Type

1s believe there is only one way—the right way! Their ideal vision of how life *must* be lived drives them along on the path toward perfection. We all aim for ideals to some degree, but 1s go overboard in a sink or swim effort to do *everything* right. When the results of their best efforts fall short of perfection, guilt and upset haunt them.

*Perfectionist* 1s focus attention on what's *not* working more than what *is*. They tend to measure everything against how well they're doing to meet often unattainable goals. There's an anxious awareness of making a mistake, of being judged, of failing to meet the mark. They can't accept that humans are fallible, especially themselves, and they also don't accept that truth and rightness may come in more than one version.

*Improver* 1s make what is better. They don't buy into image or surface values. Concerned with ethics, they want to know whether others have hidden selfish motivations cloaked in an image of goodness. They look at what's real and how it can be improved. 1s are often in the forefront of reform, whether religious or political. 1s tend to be one of the dominant types in religion, believing in universal values and in good overcoming evil.

# Positive Traits of the Type

As a 1, you're generally conscientious, reliable, accountable, thorough, moral, and willing to sacrifice your own desires for the greater good. Self-motivated, you do what you can that, in your eyes, is good. You fight the good fight, become Don Quixote with a dollop of realism, and work hard to put your values into action. You believe that *everything* worth doing is worth doing well. In a nutshell, positive traits of 1 include …

- ◆ Honesty
- ◆ Accountability
- ◆ Fairness
- ◆ Social and moral ethics
- ◆ Reliability, commitment
- ◆ Practicality

| Insights |
| --- |
| Famous 1s include John Bradshaw, Henry David Thoreau, Al Gore, John Lennon, Jimmy Carter, Tom Brokaw, Peter Jennings, Colin Powell, Judith "Miss Manners" Martin, Queen Elizabeth II, Margaret Thatcher, Martha Stewart, and Hillary Clinton. |

Whether it's recycling, reorganizing, managing, politicizing, or making a perfect product, if you're a 1, whatever you do, you do it well. You are the quality-improvement managers of the workplace. You want to make the world a better place and right the wrongs of the universe.

1s create quality. Given a preference, your creations would have meaning and integrity

**Warning!**

Don't let unnecessary worry get the best of you. Valedictorian of her high school class, Jenny had always made straight As. She worried throughout college about making a B. She was a 1!

for everyone. 1s think of the whole, what's best for everyone. Following the Puritan ethic of hard work, selflessness, and sacrifice for the greater good, the 1 philosophy laid the foundation of the United States. The seventeenth and eighteenth centuries were rather 1*ish*—integrity, honor, the highest aesthetics, sacrifice, duty, beautiful penmanship, and high-quality craftsmanship.

If you're a 1, you are an improvement junkie, constantly focused on self-betterment. Your bookshelves may be crammed with a good selection of *How To (Improve Yourself) in 30 Days*. You're always focused on the future and how it could be better, if you work hard, practice diligently, and hold the right values. Self-motivated, you're a self-starter.

You have an aesthetic sensitivity and may pursue artistic endeavors. Perhaps you teach yoga in the most beautiful and complete way possible in an attractive environment, or you're an interior decorator, or you design solid buildings with careful attention to line and form. You appreciate how objects ideally relate to each other. You love order and balance and connectedness. You delight in the order of the universe and its myriad forms. You are quite possibly the world's best suitcase packer!

You tend to be serious but do best when you allow yourself to use your sense of humor. When developed, you can play and live life to the fullest, letting go of the idea that you have to earn whatever you enjoy. The cherries are ripe for the picking! You throw the best parties with plenty of food and lavish decorations, paint, write children's books, play exquisite music, and sing.

That you are competent and complete your projects on time is a given. You do what you say. You strive for the highest ideals. You can be relied on because you are unselfish and will do what's right and aren't afraid of hard work. You are honest, forthright, and a model for others of what is fair and just. Higher qualities of 1s include integrity, unselfishness, and adherence to high ideals.

# Embracing Your Spiritual Side

1s tend to either be religious or have a spiritual bent. You may believe in a divine structure at work in the universe. You tend to believe in universal truths and have a hard time with randomness or bad things happening to good people. You are comfortable in religious systems with clear rules and guidelines for living a spotless life, along with lessons or punishments for when you falter.

## Lifelines

Social reformer 1s include Ralph Nader, Harriet Tubman, Frederick Douglass, and Mohandas Gandhi. Religious reformer 1s include Mary Baker Eddy, Mother Ann Lee, St. Paul, and Pope John Paul II.

1s often are founders of spiritual communities or religious groups that strive for higher ideals. There are no shortcuts. You live what you espouse, believing you are only as good as your actions. You like to model what is good, work hard, and be accountable. You expect the same of others. You like simplicity and believe when things are lived well they run like a divine clock. The Shaker communities of New England and the Midwest fit this model perfectly.

# The Dark Side

We know that 1s are driven to be good and respectable, always working to deny *bad* needs, drives, and instincts, along with suppressing needs for pleasure, selfishness, comfort, or expressions of anger. At some point, however, this darker side may emerge and can manifest in many forms. You try so hard to not be dark that you bring it out.

On vacation, for instance, 1s might act out hidden sexual desires, lash out at others, or take to addictions—such as excessive drinking—as a way to quell the stress of the perfectionist drive. Because you don't like your dark side to come out, you will punish yourself for such actions or thoughts, promising better behavior in the future. You can struggle with your good and bad sides for a long time, until you can accept self-centered needs, human mistakes, and the frailties of life as normal.

Worst traits of the type include these foibles:

◆ Being overly critical

◆ Being blind to or hiding the dark side

◆ Feeling resentful

- ◆ Faulting, being stingy with praise

- ◆ Acting goody-goody

- ◆ Seeing the world only in black and white

1s can struggle with eating disorders, workaholism, and procrastination—all ways to manage stress and inner demands. Some 1s also can struggle with aspects of OCD (obsessive compulsive disorder), releasing anxiety in obsessive behaviors such as washing hands, checking doorknobs, straightening, and cleaning. 1s have a special stress of having to be good, while holding it together.

 **Lifelines** _____

A Type 1 follow-the-rules naval officer aboard an aircraft carrier secretly timed and wrote up sailors who took showers that lasted beyond the 30-second rule. His nitpickiness was hated and, upon docking in the United States from an overseas cruise, his car was crushed by a ton of bricks from the flight deck. The moral of the story? Have some flex with rules!

1s do a great job but sometimes can't seem to start the job. You fret about perfection and judgment and don't want to tackle the uphill effort. You might put off action and goals until you're ready for perfecting the task or have enough research or experience to make sure it will be well done. Just start, learn from mistakes, have realistic limits, and don't worry about the little spot no one will ever notice anyway!

Your strong inner critic motivates, guides, finds fault, and punishes through shame or fear when your efforts don't measure up to strong standards. Because the attention goes to what's not working rather than what is, it's impossible to feel very secure. The effort to get there increases tension, inner judgment, anxiety, and concern about being judged by others. Only perfection, achieved or imagined, relieves the tension of such a drive.

The reward is living up to your standards and reprieve from punishment, *if* you do things right. But being 1 percent off can create as much mental anguish as being 50 percent off. It's hard to know what is normal, because the inner expectations are so high. A 99 percent on a test just isn't enough.

1s suffer needlessly! You project that others are as critical as your inner critic, so you work hard to avoid other's criticism, not realizing people often don't need perfection or the stress that goes along with it and are more accepting than you imagine.

# Stress Type

The Stress type of 1 is 4, the Romantic/Depth Seeker. The stress of holding everything in brings out 4 emotions of self-pity, insecurity, sadness, anger, and need for comfort. 1s don't realize that no one holds it together as an adult. The childhood needs for caring, acceptance, and the allowance of hurt and pain of life are natural to feel and experience.

If you're a 1 and under stress, you need to notice your hopeless feelings, emotional demands, and reactivity as a reflection of an impossible drive for perfection. Accept what you feel as okay, allow things to flow at their own pace and rhythm, and forgive yourself and others for being human. You'd do well to go to the positive side of 4 and accept feelings as normal and a reflection of unmet needs.

# Decision-Making

1s are, or want to be, decisive and correct, so you either procrastinate, for fear of being wrong, or go for strong definition and clear action. Your decisions are backed by research, careful thought, and a desire to please your superego. You stand behind what you think, until another voice pipes in that may cause you to reevaluate.

1s could do well to make experimental decisions, evaluate, and then make a final decision. It would cut the procrastination and force you to deal with the complexity of human nature beyond right-wrong options. As you mature, you deal with complexity more easily. You still form opinions but with more compassion, tolerance for difference, and an understanding of people's motivations. People expect you to be human and aren't evaluating you critically as much as you think. Some are, but they're probably 1s, too!

# Picking the 1s Out of the Crowd

As a 1, you are passionately committed to what you believe in and are reactive if people have opposite beliefs. You tend to be focused and sometimes have a rigid or unrelaxed quality. You can be harsh or critical without being aware of it, as you become anxious when you perceive things are *wrong*. Generally you have clear values and tend to act according to them.

## Nonverbal Cues

When looking to identify 1s, be aware of sharp, defined hand gestures; finger-pointing; polite, appropriate, and correct behavior; and conservative dress. 1s also tend to …

♦ Tighten their jaws.

♦ Sit straight and have correct posture in whatever they're doing.

♦ Do what they say.

♦ Maintain a clean and orderly work environment (home may sometimes be a bit messy).

♦ Show disapproval by withdrawing or withholding rewards.

## Verbal Cues

With a critical, teacherly tone and manner, 1s talk about *right ways* and how things *should be*. Your words are emphatic, definite, and their delivery is self-assured. You have thought it all through, and work to convince others that your opinions are the correct ones. You also tend to point out others' *incorrectness* in the process! You quote from ethical standards. You often try to control your anger but it seeps through. More developed 1s soften their words and listen well, supporting others in doing what is right for them.

## Maturity Within Type

Developed 1s are ethical but also sensible, having learned that perfection is a rigid, cold companion. Open to feedback, you understand that human nature is fallible. You find the path that is right but also fun and accept complexity, change, and some mistakes. Living life with great integrity and commitment, you sacrifice for the betterment of everyone, yet still take care of yourself.

Most 1s go back and forth between the stress of living ideals and loosening up the strictures of a crime-and-punishment approach to life. Still struggling with life from a good-versus-bad perspective, you have difficulty with the gray areas. At the same time, you're open to some feedback and have a strong desire to learn and improve. However, those obsessive tendencies can mark you as unapproachable and removed.

**Warning!**

Accept your dark side. Acceptance decreases the odds of acting it out! Look at the differences between Type 1 televangelist Jimmy Swaggart, who preached right and wrong but acted out his dark thoughts, and Type 1 Jimmy Carter, who accepted lustful thoughts as normal, though not to be acted on.

If only you could tell them how things *should* be done! Undeveloped 1s care only for people who are on the *right* side and so miss out on life's beautiful complexities and make everyone miserable! Your outlook on life and judgments of others are overly controlled. You scold and preach and blame yourself and others for being *bad* and drive people away with cold withdrawal or out of control anger or sarcasm. Depression and addictions rev up and rigid boundaries get even tighter. Other folks run away or manage with the help of good therapists. "Right or wrong it's gotta be, and there ain't nothin' in-between."

# Type 1 Childhood

1s are the good kids trying to imitate the values adults have taught them. They write with their best penmanship, help others, take careful notes, and study hard. They try to stay clean, practice their instruments, and go to church. They work hard to obey their parents. They are the model students and make good grades. For 1s, child*hood* is child*good*!

**Insights**

I tried to do well in school and to be correct. I rebelled to some degree, acting out against rules my parents expected. I could be stubborn and not do what I was supposed to. I was outspoken. —Sue, 40

1 children often struggle inside, with badness, bad thoughts, and managing their anger. They can feel bad for feeling angry, not making a good grade, or not meeting parental expectations. They may miss a healthy side of play and the good aspects of a lighter approach to life. When the pressure is too much, they sometimes act out bad boy/bad girl traits. Generally, this is followed by guilt and the cycle repeats. It's wrong to be so good!

# Type 1 Parents

Type 1 parents are ordained from birth to teach their children the *right* way. Be careful; you're dealing with a child who needs to be a bit selfish and someone who's not thinking about *Robert's Rules of Order* or the correct way to be a kid. Give them some breathing room while you guide them. A little disorder, growth curves, and fun times are totally in order.

Praise your kids for a clean room and straight As, if that happens, but realize that may not happen, unless you have bred another 1! Create a fun, lighter household. You'll love it and your kids can laugh with you when you are getting too uptight or controlling. Apologize if you go overboard. Share fun activities together. You're all learning about life, together.

# What the 1 Thinks About

1s think a lot about what's wrong and how to correct it. You derive excitement from making improvements and experience frustration when you can't. You dwell on mistakes and regret they occurred. You think about how to not repeat them in the future. Punishing, self-anger, or blaming thoughts can occur. You think about ideal realities and what a job well-done looks like. Other things 1s think about include …

- ◆ I wish I could clean that corner—it's driving me crazy.
- ◆ Why are they late? Don't they respect me?
- ◆ I won't start this, unless I can do it well.
- ◆ I've got to do the right thing, no matter what.
- ◆ Why don't they finish the job? Make it perfect?

What 1 adults *wish* they could say:

- ◆ It doesn't matter if it's not totally clean. I need to rest.
- ◆ I'll bring a book to read if they're late. That's just the way they are.
- ◆ I'll just start it and see where it goes.
- ◆ Oops! I made a mistake. Everyone does.
- ◆ It's not perfect but it's good enough.

# Relationships

If you're a 1, you tend to use willpower and effort to change anything, something, everything! This works in its own way for self-generated tasks but is often met with resistance by others who don't want change. This causes more fighting and more resistance. If you're experiencing this, learn to go with the flow more often, develop a warmer approach, and be more attuned, with a deeper part of yourself as the guide— the part of you that has a softer, less harsh approach to life.

In relationships, you expect others to be responsible and show up on time. You project that others are rejecting your flaws and imperfections, when it's quite the opposite. Through your moral teaching and righteous demands, expectations, and rules, you are actually the one rejecting others.

1s have high standards, seeking a near-perfect mate with the right values. This is certainly tough for anyone to live up to. You might criticize standards of cleanliness, the best way to chop vegetables, and which, if any, TV shows are best to watch. At the same time, you will stand by your partner, if this person is doing what is right, working hard, and is generally committed to making a relationship work.

> **Insights**
>
> I am very afraid to divulge my selfishness. I hold myself to standards of grace and nobility. It's the only way to be. That locks me in. It inhibits and isolates me. How to break through this pristine position without being self-destructive?
> —Monica, 55

1s will often own up to their mistakes, if someone is generous with forgiveness. If *someone* admits mistakes, *you* are generous with forgiveness. If they don't, your memory is long and arduous. 1s may look to others as models for more flexibility and humanness, and you long for the day when you can just enjoy life, mistakes and all. 1s can envy people who seem to relish life without effort.

# Tough Lessons

1s are susceptible to guilt. You imagine others will judge and shame you to the same degree you judge yourself, when in fact they probably aren't judging or even aware of what you are going through. High standards, good/bad thinking, and perfection are a setup for stress, constant evaluation, and anxiety. Loving support, acceptance, and trust in best outcomes are often forgotten.

You can see anger as a *bad* emotion and, because you're supposed to be *good*, you struggle. Anger often comes out as blaming, scolding, teaching, finger-pointing, irritation, resentment, and frustration. Call anger for what it is, accept it, and see what the anger is telling you about what you really need. You can live in *should have, could have, would have*, and obsess about what was missed. Take ownership of what is true and be easier on yourself and others.

You may feel irritated and resentful that others aren't sharing the load. You don't realize that sometimes the load you take on is self-inflicted! Realistically access what you want to take responsibility for and do more of what you want, rather than what you *should*.

You like order and cleanliness and almost always have that at work. At home, however, you may relax your high standards or even be messy at times—you're rebelling against the relentless pressure. You have to let it out somewhere! A touch of anger against your inner critic can be healthy. And a little messiness is fine and sometimes recommended. Learn to see anger as normal and be more okay about wants, pleasure, and the complexity of life. Anger is good when it helps you get in touch with needs, boundaries, and what you desire.

Take some time off from your steady work diet to enjoy life. Savor your successes and live in the moment, rather than moving on to the next item that needs improvement. Best to settle your mind and not over-listen to brain talk about what needs to be done next and what could be better. You've done enough! Rest! Recreate!

> **Warning!**
> Studies have shown that worry and perfectionist demands increase stress on the body. High blood pressure, muscle tension, and tight breathing result. Relax and live better and longer!

# Growth Type

The Growth type of 1 is 7, the Optimist/Fun Lover. Like the 7, play, have fun, laugh, don't take life so seriously, have a good time, ride a little more on the surface of life, and enjoy what it has to offer—amusement parks, endless worlds to explore, good times with friends, and trying out new possibilities. Who cares if it's perfect, not totally right, or examined too deeply? Your perfectionist drive is internal, and others aren't demanding what you think they are. It's okay to enjoy life on Earth and not wait until heaven to indulge in the pleasure! Nobody likes a martyr!

Growth for 1s includes some 7 qualities, among others. Because 1s like to improve, the list will be long!

- ◆ Have more fun.
- ◆ Accept human fallibility.
- ◆ Accept mistakes as part of learning.

- ◆ Relax.

- ◆ Get more massages.

- ◆ Go to the beach.

- ◆ Forgive people, yourself included.

- ◆ Soften the judgments.

- ◆ Ask before teaching.

- ◆ Seek more comfort and ease.

- ◆ Realize that life is perfect as it is.

- ◆ Accept the complex nature of existence.

- ◆ Focus on the positive.

# Creativity and Development

Because 1s generally aim toward a perfect job and are often aesthetically inclined, anything made or managed by a 1 is not only made well, but often has aesthetic appeal. Older homes, with their painstaking craftsmanship, have more solidity and beauty than many of today's hastily made houses. 1s appreciate and create from the best of both tradition and innovation, but the product has to be good.

**Lifelines**

The Shakers were a spiritual community led by Type 1 folks. Their furniture, baskets, food, and clothes were designed for practicality, had eye appeal, and approached perfection.

Let your art carry some imperfections as part of the perfection. Mistakes are part of the beauty. In the Navajo tradition, all weavers included a purposeful flaw in the cloth, so as not to incur Spider Woman's wrath! Imperfections are part of life. Don't procrastinate or throw away started art because your inner critic can't accept some flaws.

# Work and Career

1s are a perfect fit in jobs that require precision. Quality managers, ministers, editors, judges, picture framers, financial officers, and bank personnel fill the ranks. 1s tend to follow rules and regulations but you'll try to change them, if you perceive the rules as unethical, outdated, or unfair. If you're a 1, you won't expect others to do what you don't model. You struggle with your tolerance toward those who don't fit the model. Your career growth lies in acceptance of differences and of alternative ways to meet the goal.

Careers that also fit 1s are schoolteachers, accountants, food and nutritional coaches, town managers, and architects. It helps to stay open to options, even to change small parts of something that could work better or include other's wants, even if imperfect. Give workable relationships, speed of production, and enjoyment the same importance as perfection.

# Leadership

1s are natural leaders who love to take charge! Your drive for perfection creates a need to control both the situation and other people to get the job done right. Be careful of your tendency to micromanage, as this can backfire. While you're checking to be sure everyone is on task, remember to include others' differences, options, and fresh perspectives. There are many right ways to accomplish a task. This is a struggle, as you *really, really* want to take over and teach others the *right* way. If you consistently steamroll over everyone, anger and retaliatory actions may litter your path and short-circuit your engine!

Your contributions extend beyond your excellent quality-control management talents. As a 1, you can model integrity, ethics, self-sacrifice, a can-do attitude, and encourage people's best qualities to come forth. When you are in good form and balance your perfectionist drive, you are the cream of the crop!

At the same time, don't be blind to your dark side. If you aim for being too good, you may react with your selfish side. Seek the middle ground. Listen to feedback and communicate. Be open to learning, instead of always teaching. Remember—all things in moderation—including perfection!

# Digging Deeper into the Type

There are different kinds of 1s, based on wings and subtypes. 1s with a 2 wing have more of a helper side, while the 1 with a 9 wing is more detached and philosophical. Self-Preservation subtype 1s are serious about keeping their home environment, money, and future plans in order. Social subtype 1s want to seriously change the world, and Sexual subtype 1s want to merge with their ideal partner.

# Wings

As with all types, the 1 has specific wings that influence behavior. These are the 1 with 2 wing (1/2) and the 1 with the 9 wing (1/9):

◆ **1/2: Moralist/Helper.** If this is your strong wing, you'll generally extrovert your moral values in a public or one-to-one forum. You speak the word, whether others want to hear or not! On one hand, you want to please, like the 2, but you also help others do what's right. People may refer to you as a do-gooder. With the 2 wing, you have some concern for your image. Downside? Make sure others want to hear your message.

◆ **1/9: The Moralist/Philosopher.** More introverted than the 1/2 , you're more of a philosopher and more likely to write than preach your values. More peace-driven, there's no image-orientation here. You model by example, though you can talk more than act. Examples of 1/9s include Gandhi and Thoreau. Gandhi didn't preach his beliefs as much as live them. Downside? Make sure you are out in the world. Lead by example, like Gandhi.

# Instinctual Subtypes

There are three Instinctual subtypes for the 1:

◆ **Self-Preservation subtype: Responsibility and Security.** If this is your subtype, you like to have everything planned out, the house in order and clean, retirement funds saved, health foods ready, and exercise plans posted. Your nemeses haunt you, though. There are germs you can't control, the stock market drops, and there's that pesky craving for chocolate! Downside? Too much hard work, anxiety, and concern about getting every nook and cranny polished will wear you out. Stop worrying about your future. So much is really beyond your control, anyway. Chill out!

◆ **Social subtype: The Crusader/Improver.** The Crusader is the prophet and the improver who starts and helps the right causes—recycling, Planned Parenthood, Right to Life, or saving a historical site. You can speak up in groups and don't need approval, when you know you're on the right side. You are the Voice of God and forward the correct agenda. Downside? You're always on a mission. Your focus on the goal causes you to forget how to relate to people in their world. Make sure your presentation has a positive focus.

◆ **Sexual subtype: Looking for the Perfect Partner.** This subtype is looking for love and romance with the ideal mate—someone who has the same values, lives with honesty and integrity, and whose heart is directed only at the 1. Loyalty is essential and expectations are high. The mate can be compensation for your own lack of perfection. Jealousy is possible. Downside? Who wants to be perfect for someone else or be judged by someone else's ideals?

## The Least You Need to Know

◆ 1s keep society moving in an improving and positive direction, and they pay a price for this.

◆ When 1s add doing what's right to a passion for having fun, pleasure, and joy in life, they shine!

◆ 1s try hard to be good, when goodness may not be what's needed at the time.

◆ 1s' commitment to honesty and integrity works well, when tempered by sensitivity, compassion, and acceptance of moral complexity.

◆ 1s are trying to be good and need help to be *bad*—to play first, without having to earn the right.

# 4

# Type 2: The Giver/Cheerleader

## In This Chapter

◆ Pleasing yourself while pleasing others

◆ Where are my needs?

◆ Sunny on the outside—where are the clouds?

◆ Relating without helping

◆ Learning to receive

Giver/Cheerleaders focus on what you want but also on what they want you to be for them. 2s deliver but want credit for it. With your needs highlighted, 2s try to hide their own, and their constant smiles may hide their internal frustration. They aim to please and are disappointed if they can't. Who could refuse such giving?

## Understanding the Type

Let me help you! Think of me as the *mother archetype*. I'm really good at helping, and I know what you need. Of course, I am also the punisher who can withhold what you need. Bottom line? I need you to be dependent on me to provide for you, so you will love me. Be dependent on me, yet don't def•i•ni•tion _____

An **archetype** is the prototype, the original model or pattern from which all other things of the same type are made. **Mother archetypes** encompass all the virtues and vices of motherhood.

consume me. If this describes your approach to life, welcome to your type. You are a 2!

If you're a 2, you want others to be dependent on you but want your own independence, as well. However, you fear others will reject you if you're too independent. If others are taking advantage of your good nature, wanting too much and being ungrateful for your giving or overgiving, you may suddenly reach a limit. It comes as a shock to realize you have needs, too. Suddenly you can't stand the neediness and demands and may react by doling out the punishments or angrily setting limits.

It's a strange dance, isn't it? You struggle to balance the back and forth between dependence and independence. You can't stand having to need people. It seems like a weakness. Rather, you want people to need *you*. And if they praise you, well, then the sky is the limit. The dance continues.

2s are more likely to be women, though there are plenty of 2 men. Many women think they're 2s, because of the cultural stereotype that women should give. Most mothers need to be a bit 2-seeming, but real 2s have difficulty dropping the caring, nurturing role. They are often devastated when their kids go to college or people no longer need them. To no longer have a giving role is awful. To be rejected is hell. To watch others give to the one you love can bring feelings of jealousy and rejection to the fore. You're upset with yourself if you can't please and upset with others if you can't win them over.

# Positive Traits of the Type

2s are cheerleaders for happiness. You're sunny, generous, and attentive, particularly when life is good and you have a receptive person who appreciates you. You're positive, uplifting, and love to delight others. You'll work to alleviate excessive pain and make others feel great, look good, and be happy. You're here to make the world brighter. You tune in empathically with care and delight in others' successes.

2s are upbeat and see the glass as half full. You'll put in the necessary time and attention to plan a great party, make sure the project is successful, and greet customers with a smile. You want your waiter/waitress to definitely be a 2! 2s keep the energy up to produce a great result and point out everyone's best traits. Need a hostess with the mostest? 2s are into beauty, making and creating attractive environments. Party planners for sure.

You network and promote others who need to be recognized for a worthy or success-driven service or product. Being an Image type, you want people to feel good around you. 2s are attentive, relate personally, and aim to please.

In a nutshell, positive traits of 2s include …

- Being able to attract success
- Charm
- Generosity
- Being action-oriented for others
- A loving, affectionate nature
- Being supportive

> **Insights**
>
> Famous 2s include Leo Busca-glia, Kelly Ripa, Ann Landers, Richard Simmons, Jerry Lewis, Dolly Parton, Desmond Tutu, Eleanor Roosevelt, Alan Alda, Monica Lewinsky, and Sally Jessy Raphael.

# Embracing Your Spiritual Side

As a 2 you have a positive view of life and believe the higher forces will support you, if you give. Good things will happen to good people. It's a risk, of course, because 2s bank on their accounts earning interest if others like their giving. 2s need to learn to trust that life works when you let go, give naturally, and allow others to take care of themselves, as well as trusting that the universe will work, whether you give or not.

2s' spirituality focuses on affirmation, the value of healthy dependencies, and main-taining an uplifting spirit. 2s focus on creating beautiful environments and often have art that features angels, Madonna and child, happy people, reunions, and blissful nature scenes. You look toward the bright side of life and help create a universe that is full of life, promise, and joy. You praise others and see the best.

2s' spirituality increases when you surrender to life, see everything as a part of the whole, and accept that your needs will be met as a natural course of events. God will feed the birds of the air, etc. Relinquish control, along with your pride that thinks you know what is best for others. Let go, and let God.

## The Dark Side

2s don't have an exclusive right to giving and helping. It's just that your whole life focus is wrapped up in pleasing others, with the hope of love and validation returned. The Giver has an internal magnet that listens for cues of what people need and is on their doorstep immediately to deliver. You might not stop to consider whether the receiver wants the gift or feels the delivery is too fast or the gift too much.

Giving represents your hidden need for love, so you go overboard and hope others will reciprocate your kindness. If they don't, guilt ensues. Others can feel a demand to respond to your gift or your need for loyalty and bonding. Too much giving can feel like an invasion or setup for expectation or fantasy fulfillment. The clearer your expectations, the more you can build trust and create natural relationships.

2s, like all the types, have hidden defenses. You're giving, but you can give to get. Usually you don't want much on the surface—appreciation, acknowledgement, some attention back. You can want more than is apparent, though. Because you're givers more than receivers, you can be shy or feel overwhelmed and not in control when you receive too much attention. Many 2s have defined expectations, so when gifts come other than within the boundaries of those expectations, you may miss them.

**Lifelines**

Try expressing your needs openly. You may find that others are willing to give. They just need to know what it is you want!

2s who feel deserving might want lots of special attention. You can expect adulation or gifts that are out of proportion to what you give. All this depends on maturity. Developed 2s give with little or no expectation, while more undeveloped 2s expect too much and overrate their giving. 2s are desperate to be loved and you react negatively when you feel unloved.

2s protect against showing needs. You hint at what you need or want and expect others to pick up the hints and become upset if others misinterpret your signals. 2s experience shame around needs and you don't like your worst fear (neediness) exposed. Be more direct! So what's the problem with being a little needy? It's what you thrive on in others.

2s may appear positive to hide the darker emotions of sadness, pain, hurt, fear, anger. It's okay if you have those emotions. People will accept you more for being human. In masking your darker side, 2s can seem good at the topsoil line but be in turmoil with the creepy-crawlies below. 2s project a sunny disposition to overshadow the dark clouds. Let your true feelings out. You can't pretend it's a sunny day when it's pouring! More developed 2s accept the full range of emotions.

Pride is a core feature in the type. It's a 2 job, making others happy, and you want the credit you deserve for doing it. What an impossible challenge! The more the inner tension around this, the less ability you have to give well. Pride gives false strength, protects against intimacy, and prevents getting help for yourself. Humility is the answer. Realize you don't have all the answers and that, like everyone else, you need help at times.

Worst traits of the type include these foibles:

- Giving as a way to get

- Being resentful when expected returns aren't fulfilled

- Hiding your true self and what you need

- Smothering others with love

- Giving advice without permission

# Stress Type

2s generally try to repress anger in an attempt to be nice and caring and good, but go to Type 8, the Director/Powerhouse, when stressed. You can become like 8 and tell others what they need to do, with no ifs, ands, or buts. If they don't follow your advice, you may dole out the consequences. In 8, you can unload your anger, feel righteous, and tell others how ungrateful and bad they are. This is usually set off by a perceived lack of appreciation. You take a direct tack and tell others who's who and what's what! You bypass all the sweetheart stuff and express how hard it is to be with them.

It is advisable for 2s to develop the best traits of 8 and be more direct and basic. To combine your tact and ability with 8's directness and honesty is the best of all possible worlds. Practice being that positive 2/8 mix, and your relationships will be clear, personal, and satisfying.

# Decision-Making

2s make decisions for others more easily than for themselves. As a 2, you feel confident you know what decisions should be made and sometimes these decisions benefit you more than the recipient! You can have a hard time with self-needs and your own decision-making. You may fear that others think you are selfish if you make choices for yourself. Because the helper image is important, you want to please, and the loss of anyone's love is devastating. There are so many people to make happy. You wonder who might withdraw from you if you make the wrong decision.

Best to consciously think of your own outcomes and not put this burden on others. People will feel guilty and beholden to you if everything you do is *for them*. They'd rather you be more self-centered and some see those parts of you, anyway.

# Picking 2s Out of the Crowd

2s are sometimes difficult to detect. Women are often programmed to be givers, when it's not their core trait. *Faux 2s!* Real 2s? You go out of your way to give and hide your own needs, but you may become upset and more selfish when others don't follow your advice or appreciate your attention. You generally show the positive side and don't reveal much of your pain and vulnerabilities. When you do, it's a big deal!

## Nonverbal Cues

2s want to please, so you'll do anything to be the person needed in a particular situation, to the extent of forgetting what might be best for the people involved. It's so automatic. Your self-worth is based on how well you do.

In identifying 2s, look for …

- ◆ A smile.
- ◆ Good eye contact.
- ◆ Confidence in giving.
- ◆ Someone who's looking for hugs by giving hugs.
- ◆ An affectionate nature.
- ◆ Someone dressed colorfully, cheerfully, and to please others.
- ◆ A seductive, inviting nature.
- ◆ Generosity, but sometimes too much.

## Verbal Cues

2s offer advice, say positive things in flattering tones, and talk in a cheery way. There can be a slightly forced tone to keep it positive, against a possible backdrop of pain or displeasure. More developed 2s are totally natural. 2s talk about love, giving, pleasure, and happiness. The language is *can do*, with a refusal to acknowledge the negative, even if the negative is obvious.

Other verbal cues:

- Use language to influence the listener.

- 2s' advice or suggestions are the only way to go.

- 2s speak about the bright side of life, avoiding the negative, but it surfaces if they get negative.

- Tend to be extroverted, engaging, and personal

- Expressions can seem planned or affected

**Lifelines** _____

A female 2 is upset and her mood ruined if she can't get a smile from the male tollbooth attendant or other nonverbal acknowledgement of her attractiveness. Look in your mirror instead and smile at yourself!

## Maturity Within Type

More developed 2s are generous, tuned into what others need, and expect little in return. You know how to give to yourself, are direct with your needs, and realize people's limitations. You delight in relating, giving, and watching others develop. In general, you trust life will be positive, no matter what the ups and downs.

Most 2s give but expect return. You still manipulate to get people to relate to you in ways you want. If you're a 2, you develop by being clear about your expectations and realizing there are many ways people give. You're learning that you have needs too and needn't be ashamed of them. The more honest and relaxed you are, the more you'll have a right balance of giving and receiving.

Undeveloped 2s strongly manipulate to get appreciation. Your gifts may be unwanted and you tend to be angry when recipients aren't grateful. You don't take care of yourself but expect others to. You hold onto people for dear life and forget your own independence.

# Type 2 Childhood

2s are the active pleasers as kids. They help mommy with dinner, bring in the newspaper, do the dishes, perform for others, remember important dates, give gifts and cards, and love the smiles of approval on people's faces. They like the feeling of affecting someone, particularly with immediate results, although they can wait, hoping for returns. They're active, social, helping the down and outs, rescuing birds and cats (hopefully not at the same time!). They repress their bad stuff and try to please in order to be valued.

2 children need to learn not to overly fix things, that they can't please everyone, and should be selective with playmates. They need to choose what feels good, share painful feelings, get help, and accept being attended to. As a parent, praise their giving but don't feed on it. 2s can start parenting you! Let 2 children explore what they want and support them to seek and receive love and attention without trying to get it in underhanded ways.

# Type 2 Parents

As a 2 parent, you can try too hard to please your children. You may also place too much pressure on kids to give positive feedback. Let your kids have their moods and upsets, their independence, and your guidance. Listen to their feelings and problems without *fixing* so strongly. They'll find their own solutions if you resist the urge to fix their problems for them.

> **Warning!**
>
> Be careful of intervening or pressuring your kids to conform to your expectations or need for appreciation. No bribery either—make sure your time and gifts are freely given.

Let go of control or your kids will avoid you! You don't have all the answers, and that's fine! You are an exceptionally generous parent, so appreciate yourself for how much you give. Your kids will naturally give to you when you give them their space. They'll also feel secure when you are giving to yourself and setting limits with them.

# What the 2 Thinks About

If you're a 2, you think about relationships, love, hearts and flowers, clothes, smiles, upsets, being misunderstood, how to affect people, what would work, what you can do to give and get attention, what you want and need, avoiding what you want and need, planning how to give, and imagining positive outcomes. Among the other things 2s think about are the following:

- ◆ I can help you.
- ◆ I hope I look okay.
- ◆ I wish she would appreciate me.

- I'm feeling awful. I wish I could reach out for help.

- I wish I didn't have to focus so much on others.

What 2 adults *wish* they could say:

- I can't help you, but I know someone who can.

- I decided to dress casually today. I feel better that way.

- She's preoccupied. I trust that she appreciates me, whether she says so or not.

- I'm down. Can you listen to me?

- It was fun spending time. It's nice just to hang out.

> **Warning!**
> Take time off to please your-self, get to know yourself, and find your own stability and sense of self. Otherwise your stress will be off the charts!

# Relationships

2s are totally about relationships. You feel responsible for others' happiness and your esteem and pride are wrapped up in it. You struggle with your own independence, and project that others need pleasing 24/7. When balanced, you please yourself equally and it's easier on everyone!

A cue for anyone in a relationship with a 2: 2s will do anything to please you if they've selected you to receive their attention. And 2s are selective, hoping their love will be returned. They alter themselves to satisfy you, and nothing is too much to give if you appreciate them.

Some 2s induce guilt. Their agendas are felt but not necessarily directly expressed, and 2s can withdraw when you don't fall into line. You'll know when they are upset. They withhold their gifts, reject you outright, unleash a blast from the past, or try their best to force you to receive their gifts. Don't buy the guilt if you haven't done anything wrong.

2s can do major push-pulls in relationships. You want the attention but not necessarily the challenges of a real relationship. If others get too close to your vulnerabilities, you can easily move away or blame them for the exposure. Sometimes the chase is what you're most interested in. You can pursue too much, even indirectly, and need to trust that others will pursue you if you back off a little. You don't trust to a natural unfolding of events in a relationship and can be commitment-phobic, which seems odd, given your affinity for pursuit.

Obstacles entice, and overcoming them can draw 2s into a relationship. Having no problems to cure or no people to fix can be a problem! The more developed 2 loves to be in a solid relationship with ongoing happiness, though romance is always desired. Make sure it's the person you want and not the *process* of winning them.

As a 2, you grow in relationships when you see that others may give to you in many different ways beyond your immediate hopes or expectations. Be open to the ways that love expresses itself, even if it doesn't match your expectation. Love requires flexibility, receptivity, and openness. You aren't in charge of the giving game.

2s are romantic to the hilt and love romance in all its guises: cards, flowers, chocolates, special gifts, attention, pursuit. Forgetting Valentine's Day or anniversaries will create severe disappointment. It's the emotional pulls and romantic surges that are wanted—the reconnection and displays of caring and needing. Special ways of loving are relished and displays of giving and special recognition are all desirable.

### Insights

A woman doesn't know what to do with all the gifts she gets from her Type 2 male friend. He comments if she isn't wearing the gifted necklace or sweater. Don't you love me? He stocks her glove compartment with extra candy to sweeten his pursuit.

Some 2s are on target, giving what is needed, while others give what they think is needed or even what they need themselves (giving to self in the guise of giving to others)! For this, 2s expect kudos. More developed 2s are okay with occasional feedback, but most 2s feel criticized if the recipient doesn't want or like the gifts. Be sensitive to how feedback is given and also appreciate the intention, time, and energy from which the 2 gave. Set limits, though, as rooms can fill with goodies that must be displayed!

2s need to see that there are many ways to relate, apart from giving: spending time with friends, receiving, sharing activities, being a student, opening to difficult emotions, sharing vulnerabilities to get help, learning together. Let go of your solid ideas of love or expand them. Be open to love showing up in different and mysterious ways.

# Tough Lessons

2s need to self-focus, spend time alone (not always making connections), identify, and attune to personal needs. Learn to be more direct with others, observe your pleasing, over-involvement, seductive behavior and actions, and notice the tendency to hide real desires and motivations. Instead of convincing others you're helping them, it's best to help yourself. If you are covering up your own needs, people sense your stress and might withdraw from you.

The more honest you are, the more people will trust you. Keep up the positive focus but open to your insecurity and needs. Most people will find your vulnerability appealing. Trust that others can accept your quirks, your before-makeup look, and your humanness. Wipe that smile off your face, on occasion. Don't blame when relationship blunders occur. Relationships are messy affairs at times, and you can't control them by putting on a positive front or thinking you're always in charge.

As a 2, you may manipulate emotionally, affectionately, or sexually to influence and hold onto someone—to get things your way. Special treats, as well as threats of taking away those treats, are tactics you may use. There is a tendency to be possessive, jealous, controlling, and territorial. If you feel others are competing with you for someone's love or loyalty, you'll do almost anything to win. "I am your giver, no one else. You are mine! I need to keep you dependent on me for me to feel okay." Dig deep to explore, as your 2 tendency is to only see the positive motivations and you may feel shame around any part of you that you perceive to be selfish. What's wrong with some selfishness? You have needs too!

# Growth Type

The Growth type for 2 is 4, the Romantic/Depth Seeker. Learn to focus on feelings and individuality and self-reflection, like 4s, and value the dark side of life. 2s are other-focused, and 4s are self-reflective and often self-absorbed with feelings. 2s are afraid of dark feelings and tend not to focus on fear, pain, anger, and self-centered emotions. When 2s go to 4, you accept these feelings, as well as your individuality, can spend time alone to relax, reflect, or create, and take care to give to yourself as much as you give to or want from others.

4s are creative, and 2s integrate when you open up to your own self-expression—art, drama, music, or poetry. Giving is balanced with individuality and self-care. The positive side of 4 is a healthy dose of creativity, self-awareness, and attunement to feelings. Focus inward as much as you focus out.

# Creativity and Development

2s are already creative in abilities to relate and to interconnect with others. Extroverted 2s network easily, set up conference-type atmospheres, and bring people together. It's important for 2s to spend time alone to journal or create art, to discover real, personal interests, and to focus on what really satisfies. As 2s, you often decorate your apartments and homes with beauty. Colorful objects, sunny art prints, and uplifting themes are your style. 2s are among the best dressers of the Enneagram—textured fabrics and unique color combinations that flatter the body are worn with panache.

What do you want to create that reflects your personal self? What do you feel and want? What makes you unique? What are the constants in your personality? What do you stand for? What's as important as pleasing people that will give you the solid feeling you are loved? Are you loved more than just for pleasing someone? These questions, relating to self-discovery and development, will help spark your creativity.

# Work and Career

2s generally choose work and career related to people. You make great receptionists, hostesses, event planners, executive secretaries, entertainers, and real-estate agents. You also work in advertising, sales, and hotel management (more 2s with 3 wings). You do what it takes to make any organization look good, so public relations is your game! You aim to please and create the image needed to accomplish that. You enjoy greeting people and may function well in the complaint department! You're found equally in helping and service professions (more 2s with 1 wings)—counselors, teachers, nurses, hairdressers, and yoga instructors. Your smile is your number 1 asset.

2s, particularly 2s with 3 wings, try to connect to the powerful elite and influence those who can make a difference. You tend to know everyone's personal business and might be too much in the gossip loop and feel left out if you're not in the know. You sometimes need to watch becoming over involved with people. You can take things personally at work, so focus on the task at hand with an outcome-orientation.

# Leadership

2s can be great motivators, cheering on constituents and underlings. 2s inspire others, bringing out their best traits. 2s' approval or disapproval is powerful and others want to be on your approving side. 2 leaders are customer-oriented. You lead less by rules and regulations and more through human interactions and strategic relationships. You encourage managers to get to know their people and to really get to know their customers well and what they want. Interested in personal histories, you try to influence each person, individually. Because you desire positive feedback you'll go out of your way to please. You prefer the subtle approach, selecting stroking, taking someone out to an exclusive restaurant, or offering a special favor or gift over major power moves.

# Digging Deeper into the Type

2s manifest in different ways, depending on wings and subtypes. 2s with a 1 wing have more of a moral focus, while 2s with a 3 wing focus on success. Though all 2s aim to please, subtypes skew the flavoring. Self-Preservation subtypes focus on having a beautiful environment and possessions. Social subtypes have a strong focus on social position and knowing the right people. Sexual subtypes highly focus their 2ness on relationship pursuit and closeness. Get to know many 2s before you feel you know the full range of the types.

## Wings

There are two wings for 2s: the 2 with a 1 wing (2/1) and the 2 with a 3 wing (2/3):

- **2/1: Giving and Service.** This wing is more service-oriented, serious, moralistic, not as success-driven, more into social work, nursing, and therapy as professions. This wing helps the down and out. 2/1 is more perfectionist than 2/3 and not as extroverted. Downside? You can become over involved in trying to be good. You can be critical and controlling, needing validation around giving and goodness.

- **2/3: Giving and Success.** More success-driven, this wing wants to move among successful people and be more in the spotlight. 2/3 is more extroverted, materialistic, very image-oriented, and into glamour. Downside? If someone is in a relationship with this type, they'd better have a full wallet and never make this 2 look bad in public.

| Insights |
| --- |
| One 2/3 would only go out with certified millionaires. She married one and is happy! |

## Instinctual Subtypes

There are three Instinctual subtypes for the 2:

◆ **Self-Preservation subtype: Treat Me Special.** This subtype likes special possessions, beautiful clothes, unique restaurants, and earned gifts—he or she expects attention and reward for love and attention given: "I earned it!" This subtype spends time alone and is more private than other subtypes. Downside? Make sure expectations are clear so that paying or giving more than intended doesn't become a problem.

◆ **Social subtype: The Social Connector/Climber.** A great networker, this subtype likes to be around successful people to enhance personal social value. This subtype is invited to the right events, knows the right people, is treated as one of the in-crowd, and appreciates receiving awards of recognition. Depending on the wing, he or she may be oriented either more toward helping others or wrangling invitations to success-oriented events: "May I have the Oscar nominations, please!" Downside? They are sensitive to image. Never make them look bad in public.

◆ **Sexual subtype: The Seductive Pursuer.** Seductive, alluring, confident, pursuing … this subtype does whatever it takes to win over a desired lover, pleasing beyond measure, being the ideal attractive person. "No one can resist me!" Downside? It's an attractive package, but the pursued better deliver on love and appreciation!

## The Least You Need to Know

◆ 2s look for love by giving love.

◆ 2s tend to love too much, but learning to give appropriately as well as receiving can create a strong, mutual love.

◆ 2s hide their needs, hoping the *other* person will notice and give to them. By being direct, 2s learn that their needs are an important love component.

◆ 2s work to cheer up others but protect their own painful emotions, hiding them deep inside.

◆ 2s need to be with people and are found in people-related professions.

# Type 3: The Success Striver/ Winner

## In This Chapter

- ◆ Win at all costs
- ◆ Who I am—role and image
- ◆ Human being versus human doing
- ◆ The inner life of a 3—where is it?
- ◆ Everything is a goal
- ◆ The star—no second place

Success Striver/Winners want to excel, come in first, and be rewarded for what they accomplish. Always focused on success, the word *failure* doesn't exist for 3s. Image and the right impression are fundamental and essential. Ever-focused on goals and action, 3s produce results.

## Understanding the Type

3s are the Success Strivers, doing whatever it takes to accomplish, win, and cross the finish line first. Whether it's reporting to work at 7 A.M., having the right connections, or looking the part, the 3 will make sure to accomplish the task. Nothing blocks the goal. Obstacles? You'll overcome them—and your speed and efficiency accelerate the process. It doesn't have to be perfect; it just has to work, with *you* being recognized for the win.

**Insights**

Famous 3s include Bill Clinton, John Kerry, Mitt Romney, Tony Robbins, Tom Brady, Dick Clark, Paul McCartney, Tom Cruise, Mick Jagger, Sharon Stone, Jane Pauley, Demi Moore, Vanna White, Bryant Gumbel, and Diane Sawyer.

3s stand out as the models of success. Whatever the family or culture deems worthy of success, 3s are there to accomplish. You'll become a doctor, even if it isn't exactly who you are, because it feels great being admired and reaping the rewards of what is worthy and desired by others. Your worth is what you do, not who you are, though ideally they mesh. Being who you are is secondary to the symbols of success, the money, and the recognition of being the best.

3s are the family heroes, the rags to riches story models, and the stars we admire. 3s are motivated by the dream. In one culture, it's material success; in another it's the equivalent of the Olympic gold medal, the tribal head or shaman, or the president of the student council. Image becomes as important as reality. Your goals are measured by outcomes—the roles, the trophy, the degree. You want people to desire to be like you.

# Positive Traits of the Type

3s will finish the task; people can count on that and also benefit from the 3's efforts. If someone invents a new electronic device, 3s will multiply it so that everyone has one. You'll produce it, market it, sell it, and, of course, reap a reward in the process. The free enterprise system is a perfect fit for 3s. May the best man or woman win! Whoever makes the most widgets in the least amount of time earns the bonus!

3s help others feel successful, too. You work hard, are self-starters, and need no extra motivation beyond the goal. If there's a reward and it looks good, the job's done. Whether it's painting the house, providing the best for your families, bringing home the bacon, or being publicly recognized for a great community project, 3s are committed 100 percent.

3s are positive in thought and deed, have a can-do attitude, and overcome obstacles. Secondary concerns don't sidetrack you. You can target several goals at once and keep everything in order. You see how one goal benefits another. Instead of wasting time thinking, processing, brainstorming, or becoming overwhelmed by too many options, you plunge right in. Efficiency and speed are your trademarks. The success drive keeps your priorities straight. In a nutshell, positive traits of 3s include …

- Having an excellent work ethic.

- Motivating others to be winners.

- Being a positive thinker.

- Getting to the point.

- Having high energy.

When developed, you help others with their goals, inspiring and encouraging them to win their successes. You don't focus on failure. From your viewpoint, anything can be won, if you work hard enough and keep the goal in the forefront. Never short of goals, your can-do spirit inspires.

# Embracing Your Spiritual Side

Spirituality for 3s is in the positive focus on life, the awareness to use your inner resources and the world's outer resources to make things happen. Spirit is experienced more as the energy to do and change the world—amplifying your God-given talents. If a spiritual or religious focus helps in accomplishing a goal, that's great.

3s can make full use of what is good in the world and refuse to believe anything is hopeless. Many 3s support worthy causes. As 3s develop, you tend to choose to use your resources to develop your inner life—for philanthropy, the arts, or spiritual pursuits. Inspirational and charismatic, 3s are often motivational speakers. Spirit is experienced as the fire that makes things happen.

# The Dark Side

In the drive for success and the shortcuts taken to get there, 3s might step on a few backs, forget to stop to smell the roses, and might not attune to relationship needs or others' sensitivities. Fast cars look and feel good, but fast *drivers* may lose touch with reality and forget some of the necessary rules and regulations of the road. You can deceive others and also yourself in your shortcuts for success.

3s identify with role, image, and appearance. What is seen is not necessarily what is. 3s promise a lot and often deliver, but might miss the bugs in the program. 3s are not always detail-oriented, leaving that for others who can slow down the process for quality control. 3s sometimes go for the quick win and do not check out the whole program. As one 3 professes, you sell the sizzle, not the steak!

**Warning!**

In *The Wizard of Oz*, the same actor plays the snake-oil salesman, the mayor of Oz, and the formidable Wizard of Oz. Playing for success, he's a sham, deceiving others. Success is fine, but don't become the Wizard. Keep your integrity, relationships, and worthy goals while you pursue success.

The drive to win can replace integrity, thoroughness, and concern about consequences to others. A used-car salesman might have no qualms about selling a car to a poor person for a higher price than to his rich buddy! 3s are seen on late night infomercials, hawking get-rich-quick or get-gorgeous-now schemes, once in a lifetime real estate opportunities, marketing solutions for your small business, diet pills, exercise machines, beauty products, and motivational tapes. Is the real Wizard of Oz smiling behind the curtain? Keep a moral focus and separate the real from the fake.

Impatient, 3s hate interruptions and may prioritize goals over people. Competitive more than cooperative, your single-minded focus can cause some folks to avoid you, knowing they are product rather than an integral part of your life. It's sometimes hard for others to be close to you, knowing that you measure friends according to how they mesh with your goals. Someone who is not a good fit is really just a drag on your fishing net.

3s avoid feelings that interfere with success. That covers quite a bit of territory. Sadness, fear, anger, guilt, compassion, love, and needs slow down the process. "I'll deal with those when the job is done," thinks the 3. Years pass and the job is never done. Too late to relate!

Processing feelings and long discussions of upsets and differences is not where 3s want to go. It wastes time and not much is accomplished, is what 3s think. But there is a price to be paid: healthy needs for interdependence, the need for listening and attending, sharing time, and relaxation are sacrificed for *The Goal*. This means that others must deal with 3s' unprocessed feelings. Shame and rejection are failure's companions for the 3, so 3s must avoid failure at all costs. Focusing on an immediate win, however, could hurt in the long run—with regard to relationship difficulties, problems surfacing later, and ethical concerns that can arise. Short term gain or long term loss?

3s' esteem is on the line *all the time*. Sales figures have to improve over last year, production must exceed goals, you have to look good. The pressure is on. You are not okay unless you succeed, even if others would rather have you and your time than money or symbols of success.

Worst traits of 3s include these foibles:

+ An elite attitude

+ Feeling stressed, pressured—a definite type A personality

+ Workaholic—no time to relate or play

+ Lacking in empathy if others are not achieving

+ Being vain, superficial, overly materialistic

# Stress Type

The Stress type of 3 is 9, the Harmony Seeker/Accommodator. 3s eventually burn out. The pressure is just too much. 3s move to 9 when life is too stressful and start working on secondary goals. Clean the kitchen, cut the lawn, but don't deal with important priorities. 3s can take on a feeling of failure and experience low esteem when unsuccessful, instead of using the experience as a learning situation.

3s can go hopeless like 9s at times, and not see success and failure as normal ebbs and flows in life. 3s can crash and avoid real living. You kick back, like 9, instead of going to the healthy part of 9 and just taking an appropriate break. The positive side of moving to 9 is learning to relax and having a healthy balance of fun and play and work. There are many ways to be successful, other than material success—hobbies, interests, enjoying life, and good relationships.

# Decision-Making

If you're a 3, you're a *great* decision maker. You know your priorities and want to cut out extraneous garbage. You decide toward action, yet sometimes move too fast. On occasion it's best to process a bit or experiment with temporary solutions and get feedback, before making final decisions. Don't make up your mind too quickly.

You can do quick turnarounds when the goal gets off track or is not working according to plan. Get some feedback from others and slow down enough to plan or get some reinforcements to help the project. Others' opinions can make a difference and, in the long run, create a better outcome. Sometimes the tortoise gets there faster than the hare!

# Picking the 3s Out of the Crowd

Many people try to imitate 3s, the type most imitated in the United States. Many businesses demand a 3 focus: bottom-line results or you're gone. Many people try to be 3s at work but once they get home, they relax and revert to their own type. That's the difference: the real 3s are always 3s.

## Nonverbal Cues

3s project a winning image and the look depends on the people you are trying to impress. What will accomplish the job? What kind of attire? Who's the target person to sell? An Image type, 3s will don the image and action to make that positive impression. First impressions are second nature to 3s! Other clues to spotting the 3:

> **Insights**
>
> I set daily, weekly, monthly, and yearly goals. I have a 5-year plan and a 10-year plan. I make several fresh daily goal lists and love to check off the boxes.
> —John, 35

- Dresses sharply for success—dress for the crowd
- Associates only with winning group, teams
- Has star quality and a competitive streak
- Is charming, engaging
- Prefers short meetings

## Verbal Cues

Results-oriented, you're irritated by too much theory, irrelevant personal stories, and excuses. You like to set the goal and have clear-cut guidelines. You like to be in charge of the conversation or will adapt quickly to the goals of the group. You soon become the star, if possible, talk about your accomplishments to impress and sell, and you can motivate a team. It's difficult for you to deal with individuals and teams that have unclear goals. It's even worse if you have to be a member of such a team. Other verbal cues that show you're a 3 include …

- Talking about your positive traits, success.
- Talking about action steps, can-do, outcomes.
- Engaging in get-to-the-point conversations, which may seem abrupt.
- Being irritated by interruptions.
- Not enjoying small talk, unless it creates successful connection.

## Maturity Within Type

A developed 3 is a paragon of risk-taking and success and can do what is right, no matter what the obstacles. You are committed to the success of any project and put your blood, sweat, and tears into good causes and outcomes. You remain positive, though you can address problems, feelings, differences, and conflict. You can both lead and be part of a team. While enjoying material success and admiration, you also see relationship success as important. Developed 3s don't have to win at everything and can be learners, relax, and have fun. That's what to aim for, if you are a 3.

Most 3s prioritize and fantasize about success in ways that limit growth, with too much concern about looking good. Concern for winning dominates other important needs for enjoyment and finding a balance between work, play, and other interests. 3s can struggle to enjoy others' wins. 3s grow by supporting others' successes, being part of the team, and seeing failure as a learning process and not a reflection of self-worth.

Undeveloped 3s compete at all costs. Winning becomes more important than relationships. Deceit, dishonesty, and image-making can lead to conning and short cuts. Insecurity is hidden behind impressions, competition at all costs, and unconcern for underdogs. The undeveloped 3s need to be on top and look good, while others see through the appearance and turn away from this narcissism.

# Type 3 Childhood

3s are the star children who aim to be the best at whatever they decide to be. Whether to please the parents or get adulation from teachers or peers, 3 kids aim for the top positions of value: the spelling-bee champion, president of the class, the budding tennis star, the champion. They long to be at the top echelon and feel *less* if they can't make it.

3 kids are well-placed in school yearbooks. They want admiration and can feel stressed if they can't get it or lose to an opponent. They either groom for success while generally enjoying the competition or, to please the parent, feel pressured to perform and never reach any real comfort or sustained satisfaction from winning. These kids always have to win one more time and miss out on opportunities for hobbies, lessons, or goals that are more about development and fun.

3 kids pick areas in which they excel and avoid showing the learning process mistakes. They hide their insecurities and have to look good all the time, imagining people might see their flaws. Outside validation is essential, even though others look to them as models. There is confusion between "Am I pleasing me or them?"

# Type 3 Parents

Type 3 parents need to be careful not to groom every child for success or express disapproval if the child is not successful in every endeavor. Motivate as much toward honesty, kindness, fun, and many different forms of creativity. Learn from the type strengths of your child. There are many forms of success, and it's not always grades, awards, or excelling in some major way. Encourage 3s to play, show acceptance, and allow 3 children to spend some time in the middle of the pack, learning *from* others.

**Warning!**

It's vital to encourage your Type 3 children that it's okay to come in second or third or any position. Enjoyment, feeling part of the group, and learning are as important as winning. Otherwise, you'll have a stressed kid who may feel loved for winning only!

Type 3 children need to know they are loved separate from their performances and stardom. At least as an option, encourage hobbies and interests that are not centered on winning. Excelling is great, but back off on pressuring your children to perform and showing disapproval if they don't make the grade. Encourage a focus on developing relationships, attunement to feelings, and relaxation. Find many ways to validate your 3 child, other than competition and winning.

# What the 3 Thinks About

You think about success in all its forms. You are the model for achievement and you pressure yourself to live up to your fantasies of accomplishment and reward. You think of roaring crowds, admiration, and symbols that acknowledge your worth. Whatever you sell, it could be more—gold to platinum! Among the other things 3s think about are the following:

♦ This is what has to get done.

♦ How can I win in this situation?

♦ I'm always getting home from work so late.

♦ I want people to like me.

♦ Let's get going!

What 3 adults *wish* they could say:

- ◆ I'm taking a break now. The job will get done in time.

- ◆ I don't have to win on this one. Coming in second is fine, as long as I do a good job.

- ◆ I've worked enough. I'm starting on my two-week vacation tomorrow.

- ◆ It's okay if people don't like me. Everyone is different.

- ◆ Let's think about this before we act.

# Relationships

3s can see relationships as a means to an end, namely, personal success. As a result, you may miss out on the value of relationships for their own sake. Relationship needs, particularly others' needs, can slow down productivity, point out your inadequacies, and seem exhausting. You can imitate appropriate feelings but sometimes you aren't sure what you really feel or what you want to say:

- ◆ Am I doing it right?

- ◆ Did I make you happy?

- ◆ Stop crying.

- ◆ Get a grip.

3s want to know, "How do I accomplish feelings, empathy, and relationship success?" You have a hard time understanding *being*, just listening, allowing an answer to come, letting something unfold and not rushing the process. 3s like to move it along and solve a problem. Allowing discomfort is difficult, feeling incompetent is worse. It's all about how competent you are or are perceived to be. You become irritated if you aren't good at something. "Why are you putting me in this position?" the 3 asks.

3s generally are good at providing money and material possessions in a relationship, but are lacking in the areas of spending enough time together (you're out making money or succeeding), listening, sharing nongoal activities, and just being with others. You want a goal in whatever you do. Even on vacations, it's a goal—time your mountain climb with a stopwatch, visit five museums in a day, eat at the best restaurant, *do* the symbols of success. You need to listen to what you really want and, of course, listen to *others*.

In relationships, 3s need to slow down, really listen and empathize, go below the surface for real needs, allow some pain and difficult feelings to just be, and give time and attention. Experience fewer goals, just fun, connection, allow for differences, and allow for mistakes. Not all problems can be solved instantly. Accept differences and trust that conflict can be valuable learning.

# Tough Lessons

You miss out satisfying your own needs and wants if image conflicts. In endless doing, there's no time to self-reflect and see if you are satisfying deeper needs. What do you dare not do because you might not be good at it? What would you like to do just for the fun of it? Can you be a learner and not an instant expert? Can you show us your humanness, your struggles, your fear, your doubt? Can you let others lead? Can you trust that answers may come from relaxation as much as from effort or quick responses?

Your concern about being seen well and having to produce is exaggerated. Most people will love you even more for being a bit flawed, for coming in second, and being more cooperative than competitive. They feel uncomfortable comparing themselves to you, the star producer. Let go of the pressure of image.

You don't have to be on top all the time. Your very effort and quick-paced drive could be challenging your health, well-being, and relationship success. Enjoy the results of your laboring, instead of always laboring! Take a break to receive the adulation before the next move toward success.

**Lifelines**

Research shows that taking breaks, being cooperative as well as competitive, eating well, and exercising increase longevity.

# Growth Type

The Growth type of 3 is 6, the Guardian/Questioner, with its positive trait of being part of a team instead of the star. How can you all work together? How can alliances with others benefit you? 6s check out dangers and problems and sometimes don't move until they've got a strategy in place. That's useful, as you tend to move too quickly and then have to backtrack. 6s focus on loyalty, processing feedback, and brainstorming solutions. 6 qualities of security and stability can be valuable contributions to the 3's planning. Otherwise, your too-quick, too-competitive personality might gather many challenges to your stardom.

# Creativity and Development

As a 3, you're creative in your productivity, focusing on endless ways to be successful. You quickly see how a desire can turn into an outcome and you focus until you see the physical result. Visualizing results comes easily to you and action is your creative tool; along with networking, fine-tuning, and a positive attitude. You grow by opening up your creativity and producing for personal satisfaction and not exclusively for money or adulation. Take up a hobby or interest, just for personal enhancement. Pursue it for fun, growth, excitement, or entertainment. Even if you enter your artwork in a juried show, do it to share your art, as much as to win a prize. Share experiences with and learn from others rather than constantly competing with them. See what you have in common. You don't have to win to be loved and to enjoy life.

# Work and Career

Work is the domain of 3s. It's easy to be married to work and surrender your life to it. There's money, reward, and esteem tied up in it, particularly in cultures such as the United States and Japan that value work so highly. 3s tend to be workaholics and influence or cajole those in lesser positions to climb on board. Be careful, as 3s, not to place your demands on others. Not everyone is motivated to work so hard for success as *you* define it.

3s often are managers or leaders, have a natural tendency to be in charge, make things happen, and encourage or push others to support their goals. 3s will work out in the gym, play squash with important people, have strategic lunches, and join the right organizations to influence outcome. Networking, making the right calls, giving the right gifts—3s are lobbyists for results.

3s are career-driven, with as much entrepreneurial spirit as possible (don't want a limit on income!), and welcome challenge. 3s are often in sales, advertising, entertainment, high fashion, marketing, management, and investment, and thrive in professions with high esteem, such as law and medicine. Any profession with showcase quality is a perfect fit for the 3.

Many 3s are entrepreneurs or venture capitalists, where the sky is the limit. They usually rise up in rank, learn the trade, and take on whatever responsibility is required. Image-conscious and concerned about challenges to that image, 3s hide their weaknesses. They might hire a coach or personal trainer to close the perceived gap in expertise.

# Leadership

3s are natural leaders, and you often want to lead before you're ready. You're future-directed, planning your career, outcomes, and bottom lines. You feel deserving of being rewarded and will generally produce the results to earn it. Sometimes, however, you pose as an instant expert and this can backfire. Wait until your experience matches up with your ego.

Your staying power and vision are strong. Always be aware of your tendency toward shortcuts, taking too much credit, and competing in ways that could be damaging, possibly losing support from others. It's essential to create alliances. Long-range leaders work better than short-term winners, who might lose in the long run.

# Digging Deeper into the Type

3s can manifest in many varieties. The 3 with the 2 wing (3/2) can be extroverted and charming (Bill Clinton), while the 3 with the 4 wing (3/4) can be more introverted and serious (John Kerry), suffering with internal feelings and longings that are usually repressed, like the 4. There's also a big difference between a Self-Preservation subtype 3, who is very money and security-oriented, and a Social subtype 3, who mostly is into fame and recognition. Let's delve deeper.

## Wings

There are two wings for 3: the 3 with a 2 wing (3/2) and the 3 with a 4 wing (3/4):

♦ **3/2: The Winner/Charmer.** These extroverts know how to win, play a crowd, and sway the group. Bob Hope, the classic 3/2, entertained millions. He loved the limelight and won every imaginable award. 3/2s are winners and also love to give. You're given the keys to the city. You know how to play the part and can produce excellent results. Downside? You impress so much, it's hard to know if you can deliver as much as you promise. You usually do, unless your desire for image and reward is bigger than your integrity.

♦ **3/4: The Winner/Feeler.** Appearing more serious and more introverted than the 3/2, behind the exterior are deeper feelings, romantic longing, and desire for special attention. 3/4s feel more alone than 3/2s and network with less ease than the 3/2. You keep your noses to the grindstone. There's less image and more hard work. Downside? You can be a bit serious and hidden under the surface. Image is important, though you war inside with other needs for self-understanding and standing up for values.

## Instinctual Subtypes

There are three Instinctual subtypes for the 3:

- **Self-Preservation subtype: Security City.** Loves to have the symbols of success—money, investments, the best furniture, best car, and designer house. You work hard to have a secure future for yourself and loved ones. Name brands and high priced or valued items are important. Overly concerned about loss of lifestyle, you work to accumulate more, just in case. Downside? There's no time to play.

- **Social subtype: The Social Elite.** This subtype is often head of community organizations, on the board of directors, in high-profile positions, or in politics. You know the right people, are invited to the right parties, and are part of the in-crowd. You love recognition and your mantels are laden with trophies. Downside? You're showy, but what's real? You are dependent on adulation from others.

- **Sexual subtype: The Gender Role Model.** This subtype wants to be the model sex symbol. You want to be considered the great catch. You know what sells and do what it takes—work out, primp, have the right credentials—to have the look of success. You want to be wanted and admired, yet may struggle with genuine connection.

## The Least You Need to Know

- 3s are image-driven, focused on appearance at all costs.

- Natural leaders, 3s thrive on competition.

- Goals, results, and the bottom line may prevent 3s from forming deep relationships.

- 3s live the American Dream. It's all about acquiring riches, possessions, and the Gold Ribbon.

# Chapter 6

# Type 4: The Romantic/ Depth Seeker

## In This Chapter

- ◆ Living a life of passion
- ◆ Everyday living versus living on the edge
- ◆ Including pain as part of the mix
- ◆ The agony and the ecstasy
- ◆ Be authentic or die

Romantic/Depth Seekers are characterized by an emotional intensity. Longing for special attention, they want to be perceived as unique, deep, and beautiful, whether female or male. They are looking for love and searching for meaning.

## Understanding the Type

Type 4s are true individualists who do not give in easily to group identity or shallow images. 4s hope their unique qualities will captivate others, draw others to them, and cause others to seek them out. Accept the ordinary?

Never! The very idea is abhorrent to the 4's romantic nature. If you long to be recognized, appreciated, and adored for your beauty (like Narcissus, in Greek mythology, a beautiful youth condemned by Nemesis to pine away for love of his own reflection), depth, creativity, and emotional intensity, welcome to your type. You are a 4!

As a 4, you're attuned to aesthetic and artistic creation, ideally born from the depths of the soul's suffering. Day-to-day reality is difficult, even boring, so you measure life by those special moments that transcend the mundane, where life soars to special heights or plummets to moments of deep despair. 4s are the emotional junkies and emotional roller coasters of the universe, seeking experiential, spiritual, and relationship thrills and spills to make life worth living.

You can give others special attention and teach the other types to feel deeply, to remember we come from spirit, not to give in to normalcy or what others expect of us but rather to live with personality, creativity, romance, drama, and depth.

You believe that sacrifice for these qualities is worth the cost. As a 4, you don't hide or hold back from your own inner exploration of feelings, thoughts, longings, searching. "Let go of family, cultural, or relationship expectations and be your true self," says the 4.

# Positive Traits of the Type

4s want sublime language, special moments, and no missed opportunities for depth, joy, or one of a kind experiences. How you express language—the tone, the nuance, the emphasis—is as important as what is said. You want to live out the most romantic, idealized movies or theater of the mind and heart and be pursued by the sexiest and most mysterious people alive. Who's to say that much of this isn't possible?

> **Insights**
>
> Famous 4s include Prince, Johnny Depp, Judy Garland, Edgar Allan Poe, James Dean, Michael Jackson, Angelina Jolie, Eric Clapton, James Taylor, Francis Ford Coppola, and Judy Collins.

You see life in a deeply emotional way and inspire authentic emotional expression in yourself and others. You are the only type committed to feeling anything and everything, not shying away from pain, loss, despair, joy, or ecstasy. If it's real, you want to feel it. Suffering is part of life as much as the positive and you don't miss a moment. You show what you feel and it takes courage to do that. Most people hide, but you do not. You don't mind being the individual who exposes what is real and can be a role model for others to be true individuals.

In a nutshell, positive traits of 4 include …

- Being empathic and emotionally present when deep experience and honesty are expressed.

- Being expressive.

- Creating beauty.

- Developing a rich, emotional vocabulary.

- Being engaging, entertaining.

- Having a spiritual orientation.

- Supporting individuality.

- Committing yourself to socially relevant causes.

- Transforming pain into depth and beauty.

# Embracing Your Spiritual Side

4s long for more depth and excitement than day-to-day reality provides. Spirituality is a natural fit for the 4. Typically 4s are more drawn to esoteric and unique forms of religion, such as Buddhism, nature worship, *shamanism*, mysticism, and goddess worship. If you're a 4, you might listen to your inner spirit, consult with psychics, read the Tarot, use crystals, and believe that life forms exist beyond our Earth.

## def•i•ni•tion

Shamanism is a belief in the existence of spirits and the practice of mediation between the visible and spirit worlds. This can also include the spirits of living objects—trees, plants and animals—as well as rocks. It is also the belief that the vital principle of organic development is immaterial spirit.

You can feel stuck in a reality that is limited to just what you hear and see. You long for more and want enlightenment experiences, special moments of beauty, or meaningful sunsets. You may believe in past lives and don't think reality stops when the body dies. 4s teach others to be open to the extraordinary, yet also need to see that the ordinary may have special moments, as well.

If life experience doesn't have a deeper meaning, it isn't a life worth living. You are always searching for mystery, origins, the unseen, the seed buried in the ground with potential for life. You are fascinated by death and what happens after death. You are always exploring what is unspoken.

> **Warning!**
>
> 4s often go too deep. Be careful not to self-reflect and process so much that you live solely from your insights and feelings, and not from risks and creative actions. Don't go off the deep end!

You are always seeking your version of God to transform everyday life into one that has more meaning. You value therapy and do your part to support that industry! You look for all manner of venues, classes, and growth experiences to heighten states of awareness and to create new options and special ways of being and deepening who you are.

# The Dark Side

As a 4, you depend on others to love, accept, and value you and are prone to translating lack of attention as feelings of rejection or abandonment. The romantic in you doesn't realize that, no matter what you do, rejection may come, often for reasons unrelated to you. It's difficult to imagine acceptance for simply being who you are, without showcasing or being extra-special. Your inner reality is one of strong imagination and intensification of feeling. Being hypersensitive to criticism, you easily project you aren't good enough or *unique* enough to be acceptable.

4s could be called emotional perfectionists. While this has its positive side, it can also be a problem, as you can become so absorbed in understanding exactly what you're feeling—and why—at any given moment, you lose sight of everything else. It can also lead to a judgment that if a feeling isn't sufficiently intense, it isn't "real" or at least it isn't valuable. 4s may express this by dramatizing stories and feelings if life feels insufficiently intense. Generally 4s do this out of habit, but sometimes also out of fear—if you aren't intense or special enough, you'll be left. Ironically, it's often your very quality of intensity and drama that can distance others from you. Too much drama can cause others to leave the theater!

Often, you don't want to take responsibility for the consequences of your actions and may look to others to bail you out. You may also rely on others for validation. This reliance on deriving a sense of self-worth from others may create fear and anger, as you worry that others judge or devalue you or that you are replaceable. 4s can also easily feel envy and inferiority. Therefore it's important for 4s to see and remember the positive that others are seeing. Downplay the tragedy, trust life's flow more, and realize that many people are not as rejecting as you imagine. Matter of fact, it's more likely you'll be first to become bored and leave a relationship.

4s can justify leaving. Someone doesn't love you enough or can't give you enough quality attention. You can forget that you need to equally give to yourself, that you need to give to hold another's attentions, and that a relationship can only work when both parties have their basic needs met. Many 4s have a strong connection to Type 2, the Giver/Cheerleader, but when the abandonment fear is heightened and your attention is anxiously self-focused on loss, it's hard to pay attention to anything else.

4s tend to be wed to the inward process. You overindulge and swim in intense feelings, personal stories, and self-absorption, hoping others will be fascinated by your subjective experience. To balance, you need to see objectively, pay attention to others, and find a balance between your inner and outer worlds. 4s can think the inner world is the true reality and not see options that could lead to more optimism and real freedom from possible illusions and suffering. Too much inner dialogue and personal drama create removal from day-to-day reality.

Depression is not unusual for 4s. All the intensity and depth and self-exploration and analysis can be too much. Short term or long term, 4s can see suffering as a way of life. Allow depressed feelings to come and go, and more positive feelings will flow as a result! If you focus too much on what's missing, you'll just reinforce the down tendency. Pay attention to everything equally, including the good.

To be fair, we live in a culture that tends to negatively judge intense feelings and personal expression. Often the norm is to be stoic and rational, downplaying and holding in personal emotions. 4s can also be models of courage to express joy, sadness, pain, and whatever is authentic.

Worst traits of the type include …

- Being self-absorbed.

- Focusing too much on emotional pain and personal, repetitive stories.

- Seeming to always be in crisis.

- Obsessing about being abandoned.

- Taking everything personally.

**Lifelines** _____

4s' worst-case scenario of abandonment is felt at the slightest sign of disengagement, lack of interest, or withdrawal. It's more likely that the other person is self-engaged with personal needs but the 4 feels personally rejected. It's self-rejection rather than abandonment by another.

# Stress Type

4s in stress can keep doing 4 traits, such as being more intense, engaging in self-pity, and all manner of attention-getting behaviors. If that doesn't work, 4s go to the worst traits of 2, the Giver/Cheerleader, and become either extremely needy—hoping that their person of interest will attend to them—or withdraw totally. 4s also become very giving, but from their anxious, deprived place and expect the other person to be satisfied and appreciative of these attempts to give. The other person will likely feel manipulated, guilty, and unappreciative, and want to leave!

4s must balance and give from a genuine place of caring, abundance, and appreciation—the good traits of 2. Some 4s do this, and you'll feel happy and balanced if you do. Focusing less on what you are *not* getting and more on what is working helps immensely. Focusing on the positive increases the positive, and is always a good remedy for the 4.

# Decision-Making

Decision-making for 4s too often results from personal reaction and perceived or imagined needs. Learn to take the big picture into account and broaden your perspective. Consider how things can affect others. Think before acting! 4s can do worst-case scenarios and crisis orientation, rather than acting in a measured way.

Decisions are important and have consequences, so if your feelings are overwhelming you, wait. At least get feedback from important friends first. Make sure there are elements in your decisions that do fit your needs for aesthetics, depth, and a dash of drama. Of course, when decisions are simple or without serious consequence, no drama there, please! Deciding what to wear or what movie to watch should not bring you to tears.

# Picking the 4s Out of the Crowd

4s' intensity is not always easily detected. If you're in a relationship with a 4, however, you won't miss it! 4s' exaggeration is often for play and could easily be mistaken for another type, such as 7.

## Nonverbal Cues

If the eyes are truly the mirror of the soul, look deeply into the eyes of the 4 and you will see depth. Also, look for beautiful, fluid hand movements. 4s also express their individuality in unique ways of dressing—black, shades of red, and purple are not unusual, as are scarves and asymmetrical or unconventional patterns in dress. 4s dress for mood and often change clothes as moods change.

Other nonverbal cues to look for include …

♦ Intense mood swings, from joy to despair.

♦ A history of intense relationships—often of short-duration or else long-lasting ones with much drama, emotional demands, breakups, and reengagement.

♦ Passionate expressions.

♦ Push-pull in relationships.

♦ A tendency to cry.

## Verbal Cues

If you're a 4, you can go on and on talking about relationships, your feelings, your need for more engagement and expression from others, what is lacking in others, what is missing in you, what you long for, and what you dream about. If in the throes of love, you talk about how perfect your lover is or isn't.

You use words that stir, themes that excite or cause others to feel intense. You love to talk about life, birth, death, abandonment, reconnection, loss, closeness, the agony, and the ecstasy. You place great importance on being understood and are delighted when you are. You can also magnify slight misunderstandings. One percent misunderstanding represents 100 percent for you. Other verbal cues include …

♦ Dramatic, emphatic words.

♦ Focusing on painful parts, what could go wrong.

♦ Seductive, romantic language.

♦ Storytelling with rich, emotional detail.

♦ Subtle, emotional vocabulary—undertones, hints, nuances.

## Maturity Within Type

Developed 4s have passion, depth, empathy, creativity, appreciation for differences, and support for others' growth and uniqueness. You have an amazing aliveness, with no fear of exploring the dark side of life. You don't over dramatize, yet spice up life and are perfect entertainers, making fun of life's quirks and complexities, while maintaining your center. You see the irony of your own life drama and suffering and even the humor within that in a way no other type does. You can appreciate simplicity and don't use others to satisfy your needs. You are natural givers, your hearts are open, and you are deeply compassionate.

Most 4s struggle between desiring drama with its soaring heights of emotion and the pain of daily life, the pull toward boredom, and *no one* meeting your ideal mate fantasies. The tendency for crisis orientation can easily exhaust you, let alone the rest of us. Most 4s need more understanding than the rest of us can give!

> **Lifelines**
>
> It is often best to act out some of the pain and intensity and drama on real-life stages. Local theaters are perfect places for 4s to work through their emotions and be creative with their lives and stories.

Undeveloped 4s are all story and self-pity, wanting to pull others on stage to act out various parts of anger, sadness, and irresponsibility. You will blame others for causing your pain and could easily attend this play for endless reruns. If this is you, notice how you are creating your own unhappiness and write a better script. Model yourself after others, who can help you out of the mire.

# Type 4 Childhood

The 4 child uses imagination and emotions as a way to cope with discomfort, trauma, abandonment, or even happiness. The 4 is a sensitive child, experiencing sadness, loss, despair, and hopelessness, often at an early age. Major ups and downs are common—one moment very happy and another moment very sad. Life is experienced very dramatically, creating intensity and turmoil, with not much in the middle. Relationship closeness peppered with conflicts is common. 4 children need special attention for their feelings and dramas, and often parents don't know what to do. 4 children can feel sad when friends don't respond well or don't understand them. The hurt can feel unbearable, and yet can also quickly reverse!

> **Insights**
>
> Note written to third-grade teacher by Type 4 student: "I feel lonely. One of my friends is spending more time with another friend and my other friends are in different classes or schools. I don't get chosen when partners are picked."
> —Amy, 8

4 children often are play actors and actresses, performing for the family or community. They need costumes and makeup and they'll act out dramatic characters with flair and romance. Children's theater is perfect for these performers! Some young 4s are

much more introverted and act out their feelings internally, rather than on stage. It's important to encourage these 4s to talk and reveal what is happening or else have a depressed kid with no means of expressing or creating from these inner conflicts. Otherwise, acting out with anger, tantrums, or withdrawals that demand special attention, is common.

Parents of 4s feel at a loss on how to create a happy child. They become frustrated and either blame the child or long for one with a more even keel. 4 children can be fun, if you can be on stage with them a bit, enjoy the playacting, strong expression of feeling, and have the ability to relate to their moods.

4 children just want to be understood, not overly coached, changed, or controlled. They are often happy with the ups and downs of life and feel okay with sadness. Allow that to be. 4 children don't pressure themselves to be positive or happy, and parents can learn from this. These imaginative kids can teach their parents to have a fuller range of feeling, for sure!

# Type 4 Parents

As a 4 parent, you can be caught up in your own life dramas and struggles, making it difficult to give your kids the attention they need and deserve. 4 parents who are not well-developed can force their children to parent them or can become angry with their kids for demanding too much attention. If the parents want as much attention as their kids, this can create major competition.

At the same time, developed 4s can be great parents. You can empathize; you're fun, dramatic, creative, and plenty lively for any child. You teach kids to respect their inner life of thoughts and feelings and desires, as well as their outer life's joys and struggles. You really understand both internal and external strife and listen and talk to your kids. You encourage children to feel whatever is true—pain, sadness, anger, joy—the full range of feelings.

As a 4 parent, share your own process and how you deal with feelings, moods, and changes; tell them how you manage your emotions and deal with being misunderstood. Don't expect your non-4 children to go in your direction. Learn to be more even-toned, direct, detached, whatever your child needs. Do your self-connecting experiences on a daily level, so you can manage your own feelings and not get them entangled with your kids.

# What the 4 Thinks About

4s think about ideals—ideal romance, sex, longing, transformation, love and wanting to be loved, Valentine's Day, moods, pain, suffering, joy, and relationships. You think about how to understand others more, and about how you aren't understood. You feel and analyze what is going on in relationships and what could be better. You focus on what needs to be changed in you, what's wrong with you, and how you could have a richer life. You also think about how much you enjoy yourself, rich sensual textures and colors, subtle fragrances, and visual delights. Among the other things 4s think about are the following:

♦ I'm bored out of my mind.

♦ I feel so rejected by that comment.

♦ I don't feel understood. If only he would listen to me.

♦ This is so deep for me. No one gets it.

♦ There's so much crisis in my life.

> **Insights**
>
> I have a love/hate relationship with being a 4. Many of my closest friends are 4s and we need each other. Other types don't understand or appreciate the amount and type of suffering we experience, particularly around relationships, including my relationship to myself.
> —Melanie, 40

What 4 adults *wish* they could say:

♦ I'm bored. So what? This mood will pass.

♦ I don't take that personally.

♦ It's okay. We can talk about it later when you've had a chance to relax.

♦ I'm just being a drama queen. Nothing's wrong.

♦ Peace and quiet—that's what I really want!

# Relationships

Abandonment is death. Being in love is ecstasy. Being out of love or in a relationship that's not working is agony. Attachment is so strong and it takes a lifetime to leave a relationship. When you are described with words such as *complain*, *dramatize*, *dwell*, *exaggerate*, and *indulge*, it can seem like judgment. Your emotions—empathy, sadness, pain, grief, fear—are perceived, in this culture, as feminine. This can seem like a sexist bias—rationality and stoicism versus overemotionality.

You are attractive often for the same reasons you are seen as unattractive! You speak up for what you feel or want, become openly upset, sulk, demand special attention, or say what others dare not. Your need for expression or to get attention may extend beyond what most people expect. 4s take the risk to be individual and the price sometimes is high, particularly in systems that don't support expressing feelings.

You want authenticity from others, yet at the same time, can amplify your own feelings to such a degree that they can seem inauthentic to others, and your feelings and expressions can seem staged or exaggerated. On the bright side, 4s support authenticity in others. You have a flair that makes life intriguing and engaging. One will never be bored with a 4.

4s can be empathic, particularly if others are taking a risk, have intense emotions, are struggling with a major decision, or are being honest or vulnerable. Pain is totally welcome. Passages in life, complex relationship situations, or courageous acts—all are magnets for 4s.

Joy, ecstasy, and positive feelings are also welcome, but nothing in the boring middle interests the 4. The thought of doing the same old thing day after day is worse than death! "Don't tell me today's boring details. I want to hear how you feel, what you want, what you would live or die for, what upsets you (unless it's about me), what makes you cry, what you really, really want to do."

# Tough Lessons

You grow when you let go of competing for special attention and trust that the love and attention you seek are natural. You will come to what you want more easily by simply being you, both your humdrum daily self, as well as your special self. You grow when you see that your intensified thoughts and feelings might be creating much of your unwanted reality.

Managing your inner life in a more grounded way has a great deal to do with positive outcomes. Too much adrenaline from drama will blow out your system. Daily practices of meditation, journaling, yoga, or *centering*, can help immensely in grounding yourself and living more in the middle.

## def•i•ni•tion

**Centering** is a way to connect to yourself, to go inside, to feel grounded, clear, and unscattered. People often center with practices such as breathing techniques, visualization, and meditation. Simply close your eyes and connect more to your individual, higher, or universal self, removed from day-to-day problems.

When you see that your needs do not have to take priority, it's a welcome relief. You sometimes miss others' needs, if they are not strongly expressed or you're too absorbed in your own process and upsets. When you allow feelings to come and go, it's a sign of great growth and a more stable life.

### Lifelines

Self-love is an essential solution to the pain of longing for another. The healing for 4s is to realize that only you, not another, can fully satisfy the longing you have!

Don't make your experience more special than others' experiences, and you'll be accepted even more. You're often scared of stability, mistaking it for boredom; yet 4s long for security, ease, and fulfillment. 4s tend to see life symbolically, talking in metaphor. Growth for the 4 comes in realizing that not everything has deep meaning or is personal. Focus on self-love, appreciating what is, and what you have, as much as what you don't.

# Growth Type

4s often tend to move toward Type 2, the Giver/Cheerleader, to give, both from generosity, as well as from desperation and neediness if abandonment fears get kicked in from not being attended to. 4s can also move to the Growth type 1, the Perfectionist/Improver, to be more objective, to see the truth of just what is, and not make everything a personal story. The focus here is more on ethics and right action.

Developed 1s adhere to what is right as objective truth beyond the personal spin. They accept time-honored principles and guidelines for living. In adding the higher side of 1, 4s see that everyone struggles. You are not alone, and you can join others to live, not only the tragic and the comic, but also the joy of everyday events.

# Creativity and Development

4s create beauty. You like to be surrounded by beauty, dress uniquely, and talk about beauty. You'll decorate your apartments or homes with art or special objects—unusual arrangements of dried or fresh flowers, or black roses! 4s love color and nuance and objects that elicit special memories.

4s need to be creative to survive. Transforming painful or exhilarating feelings into beautiful objects and productions is a major focus for growth and transformations for this type. 4s teach us to put our own individual mark on reality and make it more beautiful than it was. Don't let special moments die.

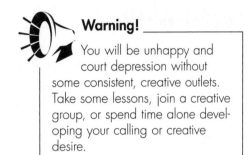

**Warning!**

You will be unhappy and court depression without some consistent, creative outlets. Take some lessons, join a creative group, or spend time alone developing your calling or creative desire.

Strongly attracted to and by beauty, you love the outpouring of soul, hard work, or risk-taking that creates it. As a 4, you admire people who devote themselves to creating art and only feel satisfied if you create as well, whether in the traditional realms of music, poetry, drama, film, dance, sculpture, acting, and theater, or in the realms of teaching, counseling, social movements, and creative science.

# Work and Career

Typically 4s are in careers and work settings that satisfy needs for individuality, creativity, and aesthetics. Their work should match up with important personal values, have special meaning, and contribute to personal happiness. Because our culture is more focused on business and money, it's not easy to make a living from individuality and personal expression. 4s are often waiters or waitresses, part-time musicians, computer programmers, and substitute teachers, hoping for an opportunity to get on stage or be recognized. Many 4s are entrepreneurs, hoping a unique boutique, documentary film, or one-person show will succeed and pay the rent. You can find 4s working as professors, psychotherapists, and art teachers. Factory jobs or meaningless office work is out, for sure. You need to feel your individuality in any setting and don't do well if you can't create it—decorate your office, do projects that have meaning, have flextime. Work values have to fit personal values.

4s often struggle to find work that is personally fulfilling and lucrative. There are fewer well-paid jobs in the arts, so competition is high and many introverted 4s, not liking competition, can withdraw from the fray. Some 4s can struggle to eke out an existence.

# Leadership

4s are natural leaders, transforming problems into creative, beautiful, and meaningful solutions. You love to challenge people to see their world in a new way. 4s see problems as symbols for bigger issues, and work to change not just the particular issue but transform its core, as well. In organizations, it's not just changing rules and regulations. It's about changing the way you think and the whole purpose of what you are doing. 4 leaders support others' individuality. No homogeneous environment or expected conformity to rules and regulations! Do what is new or different or relates to your personal values.

---

### Insights

The world needs 4 leaders. Your passion, creativity, emotional depth, and aesthetic sense are essential to help others live in their heart and develop their spiritual awareness and attunement to beauty.

---

# Digging Deeper into the Type

4s can have radically different subcategories within the type. The 4 with a 3 wing is success-driven and is often mistyped for a 3. It's easier to be a 3 in this culture than a 4—business people are more rewarded than artists! The 4 with a 5 wing is more introverted, analytical, and inwardly directed.

## Wings

Wings for the 4 include the 4 with a 3 wing (4/3) and the 4 with a 5 wing (4/5):

◆ **4/3: The Love Goddess/God.** You love to express yourself in a unique way—really out there—and you dress for success and beauty. You tend to be dramatic, one of a kind, extroverted. The 4/3 fits more into the culture of action, attraction, and looking good. Typically successful, which can cover up the 4 qualities, the 4/3 still longs for love and romance, high drama, and special moments. The 4/3 fits into U.S. culture more easily than the 4/5. Downside? Intensity City, but fully alive!

◆ **4/5: The Creative Gypsy.** More introverted than the 4/3, the 4/5 struggles
with success and tends to get more focused on the inner life. The 4/5 is less
image-oriented than the 4/3 and more prone to be drawn into subcultures.
You have loner qualities, are less mainstream, and also are less image-oriented.
Because 4s and 5s are both individualistic, 4/5 is even more analytical than 4/3.
You long to be discovered for special qualities and may live in fantasy worlds.
There is a strong artistic bent. Sometimes the 4/5 successfully bridges the
worlds between feeling and thinking. Downside? The 4/5 can be depressed and
then not have an outlet for creativity.

## Instinctual Subtypes

There are three Instinctual subtypes for the 4:

◆ **Self-Preservation subtype: Beautiful Surroundings/Risk Taking.** This subtype has two versions:

The **Beautiful Surroundings** subtype creates special physical environments
of security and beauty as a shield against the storms of life. Special objects that
create a feeling of deep personal connection, timeless value, and beauty surround your living quarters. Meaningful, personal, or antique art objects substitute for needs and longings.

The **Risk-Taking** subtype can live on the edge, taking major financial risks, as
a way to intensify feelings regarding security. You may go back and forth with
security, wanting it and creating it, yet being willing to lose it. If you're more
developed, you risk less and protect your investments and possessions. You like
security.

◆ **Social subtype: Discover My Specialness.** This subtype plays out 4ness in
the social arena. Am I included or excluded from a group? Can I contribute
something special to this group? Will I be recognized? Can my individuality be
experienced in social or work settings? Fantasies are played out regarding social
worth and social 4s can feel competitive (better than, less than) others. 4s want
to join in and be accepted and at the same time want to be different and stand
out. You play out your intense longing and self esteem issues in social rank concerns and the need for special attention.

 ◆ **Sexual subtype: The Special Lover.** Highly focused on romance and relation-ships, this subtype has high expectations for a partner to fit specific romantic and sexual longings. Prone to intense feelings of love, fantasy, jealousy, envy, and desire, the Special Lover creates high drama and passion and wants a part-ner to satisfy those needs to entertain, engage, and communicate authentically. Willing to be very personal, this subtype loves deep sharing and revs the motors of sex, passion, and desire.

## The Least You Need to Know

 ◆ Type 4 focuses on being unique to be valued and loved.

 ◆ 4s need to be emotionally and creatively seen and appreciated.

 ◆ 4s are searching for an identity and end up with searching and longing as that identity.

 ◆ 4s live for meaning and depth and true individuality, yet want to enjoy day to day reality and be accepted.

 ◆ 4s need support to simplify life and find meaning and acceptance with the here and now.

 ◆ 4s teach all of us to fully live and experience life from more than the mundane—to live from one's spiritual depth and the personal gift of one's unique expression.

# Type 5: The Observer/ Knowledge Seeker

## In This Chapter

- ◆ It's all in your head
- ◆ I heard you the first time
- ◆ Of course I love you—let's talk about astronomy
- ◆ Intimacy—let's read together
- ◆ Have you heard the one about the physicist and the aeronautical engineer?

Detached, objective, analytical, and rational, Observer/Knowledge Seekers don't want to be overwhelmed with feelings, personal sharing, or high expectations from others. A knowledge seeker *par excellence*, you're happiest spending your time researching the subjects in which you want to become an expert.

## Understanding the Type

5s crave the learning experience. Do you tear something apart and put it back together again just to see how it works? Do you study cause-and-effect relationships and develop theories about them? Do you see yourself as an observer, wondering what is really true and what is conjecture? If objectivity defines you, and you tend not to take things personally, welcome to your type. You're a 5!

5s are reflective. You love the process of analysis and may have a strong scientific or technical bent. Repeat the experiment to check accuracy? Yes, sir! Let's think and not get emotional about it. A healthy skepticism is welcome, and while you approve of tried and true methods, you are also open to new approaches and methods.

> **Insights**
>
> Famous 5s include Albert Einstein, Stephen Hawking, Bill Gates, Descartes, Friedrich Nietzsche, Karl Marx, Thomas Edison, Sigmund Freud, Georgia O'Keeffe, Jane Goodall, Jodie Foster, George Lucas, Emily Dickinson, and Bobby Fischer.

Innovations, new perspectives on old ideas, or combining ideas or fields of interest to create new realities are your cup of tea. You use your brain's creative power to unfold new possibilities and then test them with as much proof or logic as possible. 5s are rational and don't fall prey to whimsical thought or personal impulses, though growth includes trusting your intuition as information.

# Positive Traits of the Type

5s are objective, independent thinkers. You improve the quality of life for the rest of us. Science beckons you, and technology is your playing field, though you will enter the art world to explore it with objectivity and experimentation. You manage quite nicely on your own. You value yourself and don't need approval from others, but it's nice when you're appreciated for your creative thinking. Codependent relationships are the farthest from your mind. You don't glom onto others or expect others to compensate for your shortcomings. You want to see the world from a dry place—no personal spins. Show you the truth—you can take it!

5s don't like small talk—it wastes time. You want to spend your time in substantial learning. *The Big Idea* beckons. NASA employees, inventors, and advanced-degree professors are 5s, driven to pursue and teach the latest creative thinking.

You might not be a brilliant conversationalist, but you engage in brilliant conversations. It's a challenge to join in for the rest of us! You protect your personal space and don't dump your personal self or emotions onto others. You respect privacy, yet listen if others want to share.

5s don't get caught in emotional reactivity, though inner emotions can get stirred. You observe emotional states and learn from them. What do they represent? How can I change them? Curiosity at its height, 5s constantly explore. You see people buffeted by the storms of personal reactions, and you want to make life work better. 5s don't repeat what doesn't work.

In a nutshell, positive traits of 5 include …

- ◆ Mental brilliance and thorough thinking.
- ◆ Supporting others' individuality.
- ◆ Objectivity and not taking things personally.
- ◆ Independence with no expectation to be taken care of.
- ◆ Constant exploration and curiosity.

# Embracing Your Spiritual Side

5s are skeptics. While 5s may have the highest percentage of agnostics or atheists of all the types, 5s respect the universe and are awed by the possibilities of studying it. Constantly curious, 5s create theories and integrate disciplines, analyze and classify, and develop concepts on how the universe works. How are physics and chemistry and biology related? How are the components of cells similar to components of stars? 5s ask the big questions and are always seeking the answers. The Big Bang theory, quantum physics, natural selection, and the theory of relativity—all about origins and deeper levels of reality—were invented by 5s. Natural philosophers, 5s create frames of understanding on the nature of reality. The mind has a spiritual focus, too— excitement abounds.

> **Lifelines** _____
>
> 5s teach others and teach well. One 5 teaches a group on energy awareness—how to use mind and body awareness to experiment with ways to consciously shift subtle sensations in the body for more control and happiness.

# The Dark Side

5s generally don't mind exploring the dark side of life, actually a positive trait. You are fascinated by everything—what is to be avoided or dark to one person is interesting to another. Dark is self-defined and exploring what is unknown becomes less dark. 5s can be curious when others shy away. Violence, future predictions, science fiction, dinosaurs, viruses? Fascinating!

5s can detach and see the mind as a mechanism to study. For instance, some 5s can watch scary movies or even romantic movies and not be affected emotionally. Instead, you can observe what is going on and investigate it. 5s can analyze people and not seem personally engaged or empathic. You don't necessarily show the signs of caring or concern, yet can care. You observe life from a distance, trying not to be personally affected. Yet, you are affected more than others think.

5s withdraw, as a norm. You need time and space to think, and so you protect the private self. Sometimes, you are afraid to feel too much emotion, and you disengage. This protects you from pain, from revealing needs, and from feeling too attached to others. Because your tendency is not to react, you can be hard to read, and don't give many clues as to what's happening inside. It's easy for others to project you are thinking poorly of them, because you give few signs of excitement, pleasure, or agreement. You're checking things out and playing your cards close to the chest, or mind!

> **Warning!**
>
> When dealing with a 5, it's best to explain what you're feeling and make your expectations clear. 5s don't like unidentified flying emotions and will withdraw from you if you react too much!

As a 5, you don't often reveal personal needs, even to yourself. You're comfortable keeping things a bit distant. You're amused by private thoughts and conclusions, by what you detect in yourself, as well as in others.

5s can seek vicarious thrills, and may even be sexual voyeurs. Observation is easier than taking the risk of personal involvement, so others' desires or emotions can excite 5s. You are fairly spacious with accepting others' uniqueness, so judgments are limited. You do make judgments if you perceive someone isn't smart or hasn't researched well.

You isolate to such a degree that you avoid reality; evading the trials and tribulations of relationships. You like to keep life focused on a mental frame and tend to avoid the body, social needs, and emotional states such as jealousy, competition, and rejection. Albeit a paradox, you want to understand before you act, but once you understand, there's no need to act!

It's hard work, drawing you out of your isolation and into relationships. 5s resist the emotional context of mutual sharing and revelation and see this disclosure as a loss of control. Because 5s live in the mind, comprehension can *seem* like the end product for 5s, so others may give up and go elsewhere for a relationship. Of course, this just reinforces the emotional isolation for 5s. Many 5s do connect to emotions, the body, and spirit, realizing that there's more to existence than just the mind and ideas!

Worst traits of the type include these foibles:

◆ Being overly private and isolated

◆ Communication from the mind and less from the body, emotions, and spirit

◆ Tendency to withdraw without explanation

◆ Avoidance of feelings and personal expression

◆ Can seem cold, blunt, superior, and insensitive, with focus on knowledge with no feeling

# Stress Type

The Stress type of 5 is 7, the Optimist/Fun Lover. When 5s are stressed for a period of time, thinking becomes scattered, like a 7. You sample a bit of everything, but tend not to go that deeply into anything. You feel ungrounded, are easily distracted, and can't make decisions. You then seem jumpy—the mind is revved up and can't stop. Subjects change quickly. It's not so much a brain*storm* as a brain *tornado*. The positive side of 7 can be developed, too—more play and experience without having to get too lost in thinking. Have a good time, laugh, and be silly. 5s can seem serious with study and the move to 7 can lighten things up.

# Decision-Making

Decision-making for 5s is an exercise in careful consideration and logical analysis of all options. You don't want to be rushed. Once you've processed everything, you'll arrive at an independent decision. There's no place for personal desires and agendas, so you distrust others' input.

Your objectivity can be useful in a crisis. You keep your head, listen to constructive feedback, and don't swing from one emotional pole to another. You remain stable.

If you're working with 5s, be prepared for an information-evaluation process, rather than a quick decision. You may feel left out. Push the 5 to share the process, as well as the result. If you must challenge a decision, use a logical approach. You'll need good evidence as backup.

# Picking the 5s Out of the Crowd

5s can be one of the easier types to pick out of a crowd, particularly if they're engaged in conversation. 5s focus on knowledge as their primary interest. Gestures are more limited and there's little, if any, small talk. There can be a detached quality, particularly in men, that seems removed of heart or feeling. 5s usually spend lots of time alone.

## Nonverbal Cues

5s offer fewer nonverbal cues than other types. They gesture less frequently, and when they do, their gestures are often around the head area, where the type excitement is expressed. Listen well when they talk, as they won't repeat themselves!

**Warning!**

As a 5 you tend to avoid small talk, but you may be losing out by tuning out. Sometimes small talk sets up the stage for deeper conversations. And who knows, that good conversationalist might be conducting research on the social interactions of people at parties!

Other nonverbal cues:

♦ Most 5s dress for ease more than fashion.

♦ 5s can stare when listening but don't have much eye contact when talking.

♦ Some 5s, particularly men, can seem disembodied, as if walking, talking heads. Many 5 men and women are thin, feeding the mind more than the body.

♦ 5s can miss or be oblivious to important social cues.

## Verbal Cues

5s tend to talk about what they are studying—the mind, politics, sciences, fifth century B.C.E. Etruscan pottery! Social venues are astronomy meetings, chess clubs, political discussion groups, classical music gatherings, and mathematics clubs. They talk about subjects that might be over your head. Often the subject of 5s' talk is their area of research, but they can also be intellectual innovators. They are skeptical, on average, and you may see them on television as the hired scientific experts—debunkers of television psychics, for example. Yet if the information seems accurate and provable, 5s may explore astrology, psychic awareness, and other esoteric arts.

Other verbal cues:

◆ Fairly quiet and generally respond to questions rather than offer personal information.

◆ Voice tone is neutral, though excitement rises with an interesting topic of
learning.

◆ Sophisticated, though truncated, use of language. They actually know the
meaning of *truncated*!

◆ They teach only what they know—not instant experts.

◆ While 5s typically speak less than other types, they can talk your head off on
topics of interest, particularly if you seem receptive.

## Maturity Within Type

Developed 5s use heart and mind. In attunement with the body, you engage in life,
rather than withdraw and detach. You trust intuition, as well as analysis, and are giving and nonjudgmental. Gifted with intelligence, developed 5s understand that others
have gifts as well: musical ability, athletic talent, and virtuosity in the arts.

Most 5s wage a struggle between feeling distanced from the world and seeking inclusion in it. Your analysis and categorizing take precedence over involving yourself in
life. You can be open to new ways of thinking, so long as there's proof the new ways
have validity. Relationships can be compartmentalized and distanced and emotions
repressed. The heart needs to deepen, with an allowance for being affected by the
need for connection over the tendency to isolate.

Undeveloped 5s tend to isolate themselves, living in the private world of the mind,
not getting much feedback. Other people can seem strange, with their petty concerns
and need for people or power. You try to be competent in a special field of knowledge
but don't necessarily share that competence. The world can seem like a dangerous
place, and 5s can isolate further, possibly wanting to connect, but not being able to.

# Type 5 Childhood

5 children typically retreat to live in their own private worlds. They develop knowledge-
related interests that may or not be supported by the family and they spend time alone,
developing their interests. Science toys, computers, and books on how things work are

some of the gifts 5 children might appreciate. Observer children typically spend more time learning than participating in team sports, dance classes, or social skill building. The world can seem a bit daunting and 5s would just as soon spend time alone practicing an instrument, studying, or spending time with a special friend. Emotional and social expectations are generally difficult for the 5 child to comprehend.

Parents of a 5 may pressure the child to socialize, thinking something is wrong with a child who tends to spend so much time alone. 5 children don't seek the social spotlight, though they might be the brightest kids at school. Other kids may envy their smartness or may label them as nerds, misfits, or social wallflowers.

5s don't necessarily adapt well to school systems, as they are often bored. More intelligent than many of their peers and sometimes more intelligent than their teachers, 5s grow up to be lifetime students, whether on their own or in established settings that allow them to grow and learn. Many 5s pursue advanced degrees.

> **Insights**
>
> As a child, I wasn't lonely. I didn't want to do what the other kids wanted to do. I was an outsider. Skipping rope, hopscotch, schoolyard games, parties, and talking about each other was not interesting to me. I was interested in climbing trees, writing poetry, and collecting tadpoles.
> —Maureen, 52

5 children need help with social skill building, group engagements, and group sports—if they are interested. 5s are almost always introverted and shy away from groups and even being called on in class, even though they often know the answers. They can be picked on for being different, as they're not too concerned with dress, image, or adulation. If and when they talk, it might not be about the most popular subjects—rather, natural science, science fiction, politics, or philosophy. These kids are independent and okay alone but could use help in connecting with others.

# Type 5 Parents

Type 5 parents are often overwhelmed, particularly with young kids. One 5 woman was used to reading 20 books a month before she became a mother; she didn't read a single book for years while raising her three children. Many 5s are not used to picking up on the emotional needs of children—the need to talk and listen, the need for attention, the need for special caring.

5s can be overwhelmed with a needy child who's all over them. Children are irrational, and that's the bane of 5s. One moment wanting this, another moment wanting that, crying, competing. There's a lot to learn, and as another 5 mom said, "That's the time to read a book on parenting."

5s usually figure out some of what's going on, but because you are used to logic and learning, it's a challenge. 5s need to ferret out previously unknown needs and feelings. Most 5 parents provide an opportunity for children to learn and grow—lots of books and encyclopedias, computers, and classes. 5s can teach and have knowledgeable conversations with their kids and hopefully learn to explain things in ways that work.

5 parents tend to prepare their kids for the real world—for example, how to read people and what to watch out for with people's motivations. 5s don't hide the truth and tend to provide guidelines, rather than strong rules. 5s promote independence in a child.

> ### Insights
>
> It's hard for me when my kids have emotional reactions or tantrums. They seem so illogical. It's also hard for me when my child hangs all over me—when she needs so much reassurance and touch. My personal boundaries feel violated.
>
> —Alice, 34

5s parents can be hard to read, often due to limited facial expressions, which can increase anxiety in a child. Avoiding or limiting hugs and touch can be difficult for children. Having constant physical expression and excitement can be too much for many parents, but especially 5s, who prefer either quiet or mental stimulation.

# What the 5 Thinks About

5s are more interested in learning than in what to eat, what to wear, and the details of daily life. You pursue thinking about and deepening your knowledge about current reality and topics you want to understand. The mind focuses on new pathways and discoveries. Among the other things 5s think about are the following:

◆ This new book is great—exactly what I've been looking for—the latest research on bird migration.

◆ I don't want to go to the party. I can't stand being around people who aren't smart.

◆ Who needs sleep? I'll be up on the Internet most of the night researching or playing games.

◆ Emotional people are such a drain.

◆ If I skip lunch, I can go online with my quantum physics chat group.

What 5 adults *wish* they could say:

- ◆ I'm interested to know what you think of this book.

- ◆ Let's go out tonight.

- ◆ There's nothing I'd rather do right now than take a nice long nap. I'll wake up so refreshed!

- ◆ "I love you."

- ◆ I'd like to get to know you better. Would you like to go to lunch?

# Relationships

5s can feel socially awkward. Typically you learn from the mind and might not pick up body cues or the complexity of social cues, what is appropriate to do socially, or how to read individuals in terms of preferences, defensive states, or hidden meanings. People can be fairly hard to read and may reject you or be upset if you read wrong. Understanding other people is not so systematic as studying bugs or rocks or scientific or philosophical theory! You can be overwhelmed or angry at expectations that make no sense or seem too much. Why expose your confusion and enter the world of emotions?

5s like measured relationships. You protect your own needs, even from yourself, and feel out of control if desire, fear, anger, sadness, or joy is too strong. Control is important for you, and a partner with too many needs takes you to unfamiliar and uncomfortable terrain. Relationships expose irrationality, projections, misunderstanding, and chaos. Your response is to distance yourself and study the situation through your analytical mind filter. You feel safer alone, but your partner feels rejected.

**Warning!**

If you can't learn to share the emotional side of life, you may be in for some rocky, short-lived relationships. Talk about what you're feeling, as well as what you're thinking.

You certainly can listen and often listen well, as listening is safer than sharing. You'd rather have others lead the discussion. More misinterpretation and hurt feelings arise if people don't listen well and interpret correctly. You give critical analysis and feedback, often useful. Sometimes, though, you can miss the mark, if you haven't had enough emotional experience in your background. You read others as more detached than they are and are surprised that people seem so reactive. Isn't information and talk enough?

A 5's privacy and lack of effusiveness can be torture for types that thrive on revelation, sharing, juicy tidbits, and emotional depth. People often have to guess what is going on for the 5 and would be shocked by what the 5 is actually thinking. Share their process as it is happening, instead of merely revealing conclusions that can be painfully mysterious for others.

Want to know what's happening with a 5? Be direct! 5s often don't forward information unless asked. 5s need to know it is okay to explore feelings without having to overdefine them. In relationships, give 5s as much advance notice as possible, even if they don't do likewise. 5s like to prepare and are threatened when caught off guard with sudden emotions, expectations, changed plans, or new input that requires instant attention or decisions.

 **Lifelines**

If you are the partner of a 5, educate your 5 that you make choices and have feelings that may be other than rational—that relate to your past, to spontaneous impressions that arise. Intuition isn't based upon analysis!

# Tough Lessons

You like to control life by keeping it intellectual and analytical. You like to put things in categories, keep it objective, and not have the messiness of emotions, needs, upsets, illogic, and expectations placed on you. You learn when you see that life is often irrational and beyond your control. Reactions, selfishness, power, control, and manipulations are all part of the dance.

There's a lot to learn, so keep up the curiosity and have the courage to face other ways of learning that are even more challenging. Use your strengths to explore and don't mind some confusion, fear, overwhelming, or uncontrolled feelings. You can study them too!

You definitely are not an eat, drink, and be merry type. Though with the comforts of the mind—books and a desire to have unlimited free time to study and explore— the sky's the limit. Set up your life to have that free time and see that all learning is valuable, even the chaos of relating, conflict, and stress.

# Growth Type

The Growth type for 5 is 8, the Director/Powerhouse, a Body type that is direct with communication, impulsive in actions, and trusting of the animal instinct, all good traits you go to when you develop yourself. It's good to balance your brilliant mind with body intuition, act from your natural feeling instead of overthinking, and also go into action, trusting that you'll figure it out along the way. You don't need so much preparation, anyway.

The 8 integration protects you from mental obsessions, drives you to be more in your body (play sports, listen to what your body needs, eat well, exercise), and gives you permission to be more spontaneous. Live more in your body and you will be more powerful, your ideas will have more of a punch, and you will speak with more determination and strength. Some 5s are very 8-like in that they're more direct and have a heavier body build.

# Creativity and Development

5s are mentally creative, always up for new learning and integration of knowledge. Repetition and outdated information makes you crazy. You're often a wiz at computer games, Scrabble, word games, and chess. You're relentless in your pursuit of new knowledge, often building intuitively on previous information.

# Work and Career

5s are drawn to fields of work characterized by data gathering, data analysis, technology, and theoretical research. You'll find 5s populating the computer field, engineering, the hard sciences (physics, chemistry, mathematics), library science, and R&D (research and development).

5s take research to the next level to create new products. Many film editors, animators, graphics wizards, screenwriters, book writers, and musicians are 5s. You'll also find them in art and science museums, creating exhibits, or as directors. 5s are analysts, political columnists, and commentators. 5s need to have work environments with as much autonomy and privacy and as few interruptions as possible. Power struggles and office politics leave them cold. They often have unbounded imaginations. Reading tastes may lean toward science fiction and writers such as Isaac Asimov.

> **Insights**
>
> Archaeologists, often 5s, use hidden clues to unearth the secrets of the past. This is the kind of dirt 5s like to dig!

# Leadership

5s aren't initially drawn to leadership in the traditional sense. You give office politics a wide berth and being in charge of a department or corporation may give you cold sweats. You tend to take on positions of leadership by default due to your expertise. You would prefer others do the leadership—with you in charge of knowledge-oriented goals or projects. "I'd rather work with peers as a sole contributor," is a typical comment from a 5.

You'd rather not lead. All those people, with all their *needs*, getting in the way of your private time. Then there's the blame game—it's not appealing to be singled out for the blame if things go wrong. Influencing people, swaying opinions, giving special attention to other power players, constantly monitoring others, dealing with people issues, and managing conflicts—these are not what you want to do.

> **Insights**
>
> I like to work in a collaborative, egalitarian atmosphere and be held in esteem for my contributions. I like to work with data and smart people in a data-rich environment. I don't like going to dinners and socializing after work.
> —Erik, 33

Everyone should be self-directed, independent, self-motivated—just like you! Knowledge-based learning is what's important. Your needs for intimacy, image, and connection are less pronounced than in other types. Motivations related to image, money, and social needs usually are secondary to the your drive for security, privacy, and time to learn. Money, like image and other outward symbols of success, serves a deeper purpose that relates to learning and related experiences. Money buys the ability to control your own time.

5s' leadership strengths include the ability to detach, delegate responsibilities to others, support independence, and strategically plan. You are experts at what you do and can lead from a position of knowledge. From your observation post, you can select competent professionals to help you in your own leadership process and development.

**Lifelines** _____

> A 5 heads a book discussion group but gets frustrated at members who don't read the books and who would rather talk about shopping and hairstyles, subjects of no interest to the 5. Give some space for nonlearning, too. Just guide the conversation to topics beyond shopping, hairstyles, and nail color.

5s will take on leadership to fill a void or to forward important knowledge-based goals. 5s manage best if others help to network, market, handle conflicts, and deal with politics. 5s can create connections with small groups but may find large group settings difficult.

5s need to develop being spontaneous, as your managerial style tends toward over-preparation. You grow when you trust your own abilities, develop people skills, and stay engaged without retreating to your ivory tower. Share your thinking to keep your constituents involved.

# Digging Deeper into the Type

5s can differ greatly within the type. 5s with the stronger 4 wing can be the individualists, preferring to have a touch of creativity and emotional awareness in the process. 5s with the 6 wing are more systemic in the thinking process and are less about their own individuality and more interested in forwarding knowledge about how systems work. The Self-Preservation subtype is the most private of the subtypes. The Social subtype can be quite social around knowledge gathering and sharing. The Sexual subtype can be very engaging in a close relationship, revealing personal information and interested in yours, as well.

## Wings

There are two wings for 5: the 5 with a 4 wing (5/4) and the 5 with a 6 wing (5/6):

- **5/4: The Mental Artist.** If this is your wing, you like to be on your own, creating projects and mental worlds that have your own personal flair. Both the 5 and 4 are individualistic and don't fit into any traditional mode. You listen to your own drum beat, creating books, science projects, art projects, or nature-oriented learning with a flavor of feeling and panache. Downside? By operating strictly on your own you miss important feedback others could offer.

- **5/6: The Commentator.** You take a broader sweep to talk and write about what you see. You analyze the political landscape, explore intricate ways in which the mind works, use computers to extend your learning, and, as researcher, study the interconnectedness of individual parts. You can explore DNA in minute detail and perform data excavations that are mind-blowing and revolutionary. You are into systems and how they work and your commentary is brilliant. Downside? You can be detached, so make sure your commentary also has a personal, people element.

# Instinctual Subtypes

There are three Instinctual subtypes for the 5:

◆ **Self-Preservation subtype: The Castle.** You are on your own and like it. Hours and days go by with little or no contact and you are fine. A machine answers the phone and a good day is reading, thinking, and puttering around doing what you need to. You may have more than a few friends but tend to protect your time and space. You may have one person you relate to and shared intimacy may consist of both of you reading together and occasionally discussing your insights or bits of knowledge. Not too much though, unless it's intriguing. Downside? You're hard to get to know because you mostly share when prompted. You underestimate how interesting your thoughts may actually be to others.

| Insights |
| --- |
| It's difficult to share what is going on with me. I need a moat between me and the rest of the world where I can retreat behind. —Erik, 33 |

◆ **Social subtype: Sharing Your Mind.** This subtype doesn't mind social gatherings, clubs, discussion groups, and public lectures if they're interesting or challenging. Astronomy clubs, animal tracking groups, brain chemistry conferences, and political discussions are filled with social 5s who talk about their favorite subjects and are all ears, if you can share some interesting tidbits or integrative knowledge. No idle discussion here—bright conversations abound. Downside? If you don't extend the mind's passion to other areas of life—the emotional, artistic, and physical—you won't experience all that passion has to offer.

◆ **Sexual subtype: Still Waters Run Deep.** This subtype deeply pursues the personal self. You don't mind getting to know others' personal thoughts, desires, and passions—needing the stimulation of knowing their heart and sharing yours, even more so if you're a 5/4. Still, much of the conversation is about knowledge-based subjects. That's where the passion lies, though you don't mind extending beyond. Some intensity excites you. Downside? Sometimes you back away after these intense engagements, leaving people confused. Stay in touch!

## The Least You Need to Know

◆ 5s want to understand all of life but are afraid of the emotional underground.

◆ Ask a 5 specific questions that trigger a vein and you'll get a response.

◆ The fantasy marriage proposal setting for a 5 is on an active volcano studying lava flows.

◆ 5s are seduced with new information—they'll follow you anywhere.

◆ 5s feel no need to make small talk unless a knowledge vein is tapped.

◆ There's more going on than meets the eye—the 5 brain is constantly stirring a rich brew of new ideas and learning.

# Type 6: The Guardian/ Questioner

## In This Chapter

- ◆ Fight or flight: fears both real and imagined

- ◆ *You* are the authority

- ◆ Be prepared!

- ◆ Nothing in this life is certain—can you handle it?

- ◆ I have a question!

Guardian/Questioners scan for danger. You can't always trust what is apparently so; you'd better check for deeper motivations and determine what is real. Once tested, 6s tend to be loyal to the max and expect the same from others.

## Understanding the Type

All of us are fearful and vigilant, at times, in the face of real or imagined dangers, but 6s live in that state as a preset condition. As a 6, you are wired to prepare for worst-case possibilities. Security comes when you have planned enough and feel ready. But can you tell the difference between real dangers and concerns generated in the mind? If this describes how you think, welcome to your type. You're a 6!

6s have a million questions to ask. You notice the positive, but your mind generates limitless negative possibilities, so your attention is *focused* on problems and problem-solving. Issues of trust, doubting, and fear abound, so you are always on guard, scanning the environment for dangers.

> ### Insights
>
> Famous 6s include Robert Kennedy, Spike Lee, Phil Donahue, Joseph McCarthy, Diane Keaton, Julia Roberts, Mary Tyler Moore, Princess Diana, Evel Kneivel, Johnny Carson, and George H. W. Bush.

Let's get real—6s need to prepare! Forget about fantasy and romance and imagination for a moment. There's no time to live in an imagined world. You never know what's around the corner, so it's important to plan for contingencies—constantly. Crisis mode becomes your *modus operandi*. The problem is you don't see that living in a hyper-aroused state of adrenaline, in case an enemy shows, is just as unrealistic as being totally *un*prepared. Just in case, however, should the enemy appear, you are ready!

You test for danger and may never trust completely. Why should you? You can go back and forth, for and against, for and against. Amidst nature's uncertainties—global warming, earthquakes, snowstorms, outages, avalanches, hurricanes, tornadoes, forest fires, floods, disease—there is no end to danger. And people cause just as much distress: betrayal, death, lies … can anything or anyone be trusted?

You look for certainty in an uncertain world and hope another person or situation can create the solid ground you seek. Once you have found that person, group, or cause, your loyalty knows no bounds. 6 is a Head type. You overmanage in the mind to protect yourselves and those you care about. You forget to use your bodies to feel secure.

6s are the only type that  divided into two categories:

- *Phobic* 6s run from their fears, which are often irrational. Something is lurking in the shadows! Better get home quick and turn the lights on!

- *Counterphobic* 6s outwardly challenge their real or imagined fears and concerns, either confronting others with probing questions or challenging themselves by meeting their fears head on. Attacking the fear creates a surge of feeling more secure. These are the folks who jump out of airplanes to conquer their fear of heights.

Actually most 6s are a bit of both, but some can be quite one or the other. Think of trial lawyers and stunt men and women as possible counterphobics and lab technicians and insurance analysts as probable phobics.

# Positive Traits of the Type

6s are the guardians and protectors. You are there to offer advice and to help in any storm. And you know your storms! The Weather Channel is one of your favorite TV channels. You also are ready with safety gear and are well-versed in the latest rescue techniques. You know building codes, you have spare safety equipment in your cars and homes, and your security alarms are ready to catch any intruder. You've practiced fire-exit drills and have your second floor window ladder ready. It's quite likely that 6s founded the Boy Scouts and Girl Scouts. You also probably thought up the 911 emergency response system. You wear your bike helmet and always use hand sanitizer. Not all 6s are this prepared, but you want to be!

As a 6, you thrive in crisis situations. Problems? No problem! You have solutions, options, and strategic plans to target, change, or solve what is ailing. You know the competition and what they are up to. Generally you are a team player, and you like cooperation and mutual support; yet you can compete to win. You sacrifice for the sake of your loyal group, whether family, friends, work, nation, or group members. 6s love OSHA, the Occupational Safety and Health Administration.

You support the underdog and rally under stress. You are motivated by challenges and do anything to support equality and fairness, to help a worthy person win, and to do what is right. You don't have to be the star.

> **Insights**
>
> As a dedicated observer of people's idiosyncrasies and motivations, 6s often have a great sense of humor. Famous 6 comedians or comedy stars include David Letterman, Jay Leno, George Carlin, Meg Ryan, and Rosie Perez. 6s can also be great moviemakers. Woody Allen, a phobic 6, creates comedy, making fun of people's neuroses, and Mel Gibson, a counterphobic 6, challenges conventional ideas.

You are a thorough researcher. You'll only make purchases after reading *Consumer Reports*, checking the Better Business Bureau, and talking to friends. The research may take a while but ultimately you'll make a good decision. You aren't fooled by appearances. You go for what is solid underneath. Where's the foundation? Even foundations can fail—check for radon (a colorless, odorless, radioactive, gas element found in rock and soil that can be highly damaging to lung tissue) and mold in the basement, where these substances can concentrate. Better to be safe than sorry.

In a nutshell, positive traits of 6 include …

- ◆ Protectiveness.
- ◆ Being reliable and loyal.
- ◆ Being prepared and organized.
- ◆ Skilled in strategic planning and analysis.
- ◆ Being team players.
- ◆ Able to sacrifice for the right cause.

# Embracing Your Spiritual Side

6s' spirituality relates to trusting group consciousness and believing what is tried and true. 6s attend meetings of self-help groups, perform ancestral ceremonies, and join political organizations. You believe in God as a protector and believe we must bond together in groups and communities to survive and grow. You appreciate the sacrifices others have made for your well-being.

> **Insights**
>
> Many 6s feel comfortable working through 12-step programs. These programs have stood the test of time, are egalitarian, have rules, but offer flexibility, too.

You see the bad and need to believe in the good, so you look to have trust in others and hope for a higher power. You need to have faith there is something more reliable than your fears, dangers, and concerns—faith in life itself, authorities that really care, people motivated to do good. Your hope is that other people are also motivated by higher traits and qualities.

6s are both loyal congregational members, as well as questioners for the truth. Is the minister trustworthy? What are the real motivations of committee members? Are we promoting the right things? Are people really committed and really honest about what they are thinking? You're willing to work through the challenges to build more trust and bonding. You are the sentinels for security for yourself and others.

# The Dark Side

You search out the dark side and want to know the dirt. The dirtier the better, if it's true! 6s are activated positively by looking for the dark side. You want to know the truth and you trust those who know their own dark side and who are honest about their own greed or power dynamics. You look for the hidden problems and like to call a spade a spade.

Looking to uncover others, you sometimes don't see the worst in yourself. Best to uncover yourself, as much as exposing the emperor's clothes. In grilling others for truth, include yourself or you'll spend your time blaming, attacking, and preaching against other evils and dangers as a projection. It's not that you make yourself out to be good. It's more that you don't expose what's off in you, so as not to be attacked by the mob!

> **Insights**
>
> A lot of my life is spent looking for and ferreting out potential problems, before they become catastrophic. Head 'em off at the pass.
> —June, 53

Investigative reporter, investigate yourself! You are so focused on what others are hiding that you might not explore yourself. Hold yourself to the same flashlight with which you look at others. Know your own fears, insecurities, and doubts and expose them on occasion so others might empathize, reassure, or assist you. If you're blind to your own indirectness and dark side, others won't trust you.

You often are worried, anxious, and nervous. This is contagious! Fairly soon, it's Worry City. Don't imagine your fears as always true. Be careful not to blame others for your self-generated fears. Sure, maybe there's some truth in your fears or projections, but it's your job to calm yourself down either way and see what's true.

Skepticism can be healthy, but if the evidence goes against your fears or preconceived notions, be open to it. Challenging just for the sake of challenging is tiresome after a while. Not everyone likes debate or opposition. Live less in the world of *what ifs*!

Worst traits of the type include these foibles:

◆ Having a tendency toward worry, anxiety, and second-guessing

◆ Projecting your fears onto others

◆ Questioning others to reveal while hiding yourself

- Being passive-aggressive

- Expecting others to make you feel secure

- Being critical and thinking in black-or-white terms

# Stress Type

Your Stress type is 3, the Success Striver/Winner. You rev up for action and completion but don't feel centered. Make sure you need to accomplish something first and don't run around doing actions that have no base. Sometimes just enjoy, be quiet, rest. Best to spend some time alone to self-connect and figure out what to do, and then act with less anxiety. Get some feedback, if necessary, but don't let others decide for you. Go to the high side of 3, clarify goals, do the action steps and picture the positive happening. Sometimes your fear tells you that success will expose you to envy and competition from others. Just as likely, you'll enjoy it and others will support you.

# Decision-Making

You tie with 9s for being the most reluctant decision makers. Ambivalence abounds or certainty-doubt, and more certainty-doubt. Decisions can be risky but so is not making any. Do your research, and then take your chances. Make some test decisions that have lesser consequences. You'll learn, either way.

> **Warning!**
>
> In wanting to be decisive, sometimes 6s make decisions too hastily, wanting to get rid of the stress around deciding wrongly. Take your time and decide based on your best interests. Trust yourself!

Just don't sell your belongings, marry a stranger, and move to a new city. It's unlikely, but sometimes you get fed up with the procrastination and make decisions too hastily. It's normal to have some doubt—no need to freak! Think of best-case scenarios, too. Your indecisiveness reflects worst-case scenario thinking, and your real life, thank God, isn't as bad as your mind may think it is.

# Picking the 6s Out of the Crowd

Of all the types, 6s like to be typed the least, a real cue to typing a 6. Fear is a core feature. You might be perceived as negative with danger and worst-case thinking as traits.

6s ask lots of questions and may appear anxious and fretful. If danger is approaching, look for the person with the road flares, first aid/snakebite kit, and other sorts of safety equipment at the ready—he or she is likely a 6.

## Nonverbal Cues

6s tend to challenge assumptions, can interrupt with questions, have a nervous energy, look for definition from others, and have issues with authority. 6s can be black and white and judgmental, like 1s. Judgments are not grounded as much in morality like 1s, but are concerns for the safest outcomes. When secure, 6s can be great listeners. When not, you challenge everything others say. You can have strong opinions, mostly to ensure security. Other nonverbal cues include ...

- Hesitancy to act.

- Listening intently for problems.

- Appearing uncomfortable when compelled to make a decision.

- Testing your loyalty and honesty.

## Verbal Cues

6s are always trying to define things, achieve certainty, or at least clarify what is uncertain. 6s talk in a questioning, doubting tone, wanting others to be more definite, even if you are not. 6s can corner someone to question what is true or real.

- Yes, but ... what if ... what about this, what about that ...

- Labeling, needing to define things, not leaving a lot of space for differences or complexity?—then go to the other side!

- What about your credentials?

- With an argumentative, questioning tone—prove it to me.

## Maturity Within Type

Developed 6s are wonderful. You question, but not too much. You realize life is complex and accept the gray tones. You need no more definition from others than from yourself. You are protective, empathic, caring, and allow people their individuality.

You work hard for the causes you believe in and need no special attention. You fight for the underdog and justice and you understand psychological dynamics. You are not easily fooled.

Most 6s worry, focus too much on fear, and miss out paying equal attention to what is good. Relationships are important, and you expect too much from people who have their own problems. You look for security outside yourself and need to focus more on providing it for yourself. You want others to be committed to you or as committed as you. Make sure you are committed yourself, providing what people really need, not what you think they need. Make sure you can let in the good that builds feelings of security. Trust yourself on how to be in the moment.

Undeveloped 6s can be paranoid, living in worst case as a norm, and don't trust the good. Everyone is suspect and the weather can turn at any moment. Everything is an emergency and the adrenaline is affecting your health. Practice thinking positive thoughts and using your knowledge to develop trust.

# Type 6 Childhood

6 children notice the difference between what adults say and what they do—causing a major mistrust with adults and parents who don't follow through or live up to what is said. They're always trying to figure out what is real and are hyper-alert for problems, dangers, and what to trust or not. Some non-6 kids might go through a hurricane, for instance, and not be traumatized. They might even find it exciting. 6s remember the experience and realize life is dangerous and can turn at any moment, so they may overprepare for problems and dangers, knowing that one danger may breed another. If your childhood overalerted you, best to realize that current reality might be safer.

**Lifelines**

Remember what it was like, being a child with big adults who often decided your fate? It's even harder for a Type 6 child. Follow through on actions promised or else don't promise!

6 children need reassurance, advance preparation, and as much explanation as possible. Talk to their level and realize children have their real concerns and need to understand what is happening. It's best to repeat and overexplain than underexplain. The more information you can give them, the more security and less anxiety they have.

Parents of 6s need to nurture, rather than toughen up, though it's okay to talk in real terms. Fantasy talk can cause even more fear. Encourage your 6 children to ask questions and be patient. The worst thing to do is to discourage or cut off questions. Your child will live in a state of more fear, creating endless bad-ending stories. Teach your child the difference between what is real and what is imagined.

# Type 6 Parents

As a 6 parent it's important to not overprotect or share every fear you have with your kid. Children who aren't 6s probably don't share your fears. Let them stay that way. A little unawareness or best-case thinking can be helpful. Offer an umbrella, but don't demand they take it on a cloudy day. Encourage the hats and mittens but realize you can't be with them all the time. Remind them of negative consequences, if necessary, but don't terrify them.

Ask some questions but not to the degree of causing irritation, withdrawal, or fighting if your children don't see the danger. You are a caring, concerned parent. Teach some survival skills, to watch out for strangers and the usual concerns, and let go. Check in with your children on occasion to see what their concerns are independent of yours. Have fun, lighten up, look at the bright side, affirm what is good, and reinforce there are many forces that support the positive.

# What the 6 Thinks About

6s think about planning, what ifs, relationship difficulties, preparing for the future, and security. You think about the news and what could happen. You have fearful, angry thoughts about unfairness, injustice, liars, and thieves. You have a mind scanner for inconsistencies and deception, false images, and the bad guys. Other things 6s think about include …

- I wish I could predict the future!
- What did he mean by that?
- I see a difference between what you say and what you do.
- She always does it this way. Why did she do it differently this time?
- What's really true? What isn't he telling me?

What 6 adults *wish* they could say:

◆ I feel secure. I am ready for whatever comes.

◆ I understand what you're saying. No, I don't have any questions.

◆ It's okay. It'll make sense in time.

◆ Oh, you changed your mind. I understand. No problem.

◆ Let's discuss it.

# Relationships

Relationships are essential for 6s. You are a trustworthy partner and friend, yet others don't seem as accountable as you. Why did they do that? How can you say something and not do it, or at least not tell me? Why aren't you totally honest with me? Don't I deserve that? Questions like this abound, and you need to make sure you are being as honest, too. Are you revealing as much as you want others to reveal?

> **Insights**
>
> I want to stay. I want to leave. I can't deal with the gray. My partner doesn't make me feel secure. He's too private and withdraws from me. Drives me crazy. I want security but often feel ambivalent.
> —Sandra, 47

Ambivalence and doubt plague you. You like relationships, yet being too close brings up fear. It feels as if others have power over you, particularly if you like them. You are concerned if you share too much, or if they don't share enough. It's hard when people have different values and ideas from yours.

You are psychologically sophisticated. You tune into motivations, reasons for, and what is happening below the surface. You realize people and life situations are complex; yet you don't want to be fooled.

You are a sleuthhound: you look for clues and feel more secure when you figure things out. Sometimes you make things too simple, though, in your need for security and exact explanations. Your detective qualities are both a boon and a bust and some people feel intruded on, examined, and overexplored. Please, no more questions!

Are your questions related to general concerns or are you testing? Others are cautious of your questions, which touch on challenge, rather than caring or curiosity. Are your questions direct or do they cause more confusion? Is it okay that people are different and self-centered? Because you are more other-focused, maybe you need to take care of yourself more and be less concerned about others' motivations. Your direct honesty can be a model for others, rather than expecting others to lead first.

You are a great model for sacrifice in a relationship. You understand crises and challenges and can stay resolved and committed during difficult times. Having a problem to fix is a catalyst for action and connection. It's also as important to be steady and relaxed during times of ease and solidity. Don't fill your mind with potential problems. Enjoy life and have some comfort for now.

# Tough Lessons

You are family-oriented and your definition of family is extensive, embracing friends and groups. You value bonding and contribute greatly. Realize, though, that things change and you need to manage and adapt to change. You want solidity and consistency but the only true solidity is within yourself. Don't push others for definition, when they have their own confusion. Balance yourself with play, adventure, tolerance for others' independent process, and more acceptance of change.

You want consistency or at least the truth in others but don't always provide it yourself, as you can be private. In general you are solid as a rock, but your inner questioning can cause you to go back and forth on important decisions related to relationships, work choices, and money issues. You need to communicate more of your truth, which includes your ambivalence, confusion, and difficulty with choice and imagined loss.

People can never be as consistent, reliable, and as solid as you like. One of your lessons is to put more trust in yourself and less in demanding that others make you feel secure. Everyone has differing needs and no one can devote his or her life to you to make you feel secure. That's your job. Let go of the ideal of a perfect protector and your life will be more flexible and realistic. Don't provide something to others (loyalty, devotion) thinking they will give you the same in return. People give what they know to give and not what you expect. If there's a contract, make it clear.

**Lifelines**

You might be looking for a parent figure to count on, and it's too late for that! Let go of searching for a parent substitute. No one wants that burden placed on him or her. You are your own parent now and you have a better shot at it, being grown up!

Focus more on providing for yourself—self-esteem, safety, security, loyalty, compassion, understanding, etc. Be your own authority figure and let go of some of the needs for approval from others. Trust yourself as your foundation, rather than obsessing about whether to trust another or not.

## def•i•ni•tion

Affirmations are positive statements or judgments, something declared to be true. Affirmations offer us a method to affirm the future in order to create that future.

Because a good chunk of your fear is mind-created, it's important to discipline yourself. Consciously think of positive things that happen, say *affirmations*, and notice worst-case thinking and stop it. Redirect your attention to activities or interests. Your mind is your main culprit. Don't let it dominate you!

# Growth Type

The Growth type for 6 is 9, the Harmony Seeker/Accommodator. 9s know how to relax, tend to be positive, and imagine people and life being nice, rather than dangerous. All these qualities are balance points for 6. As a 6 you stress yourself out with worry and fear and need stress management. Any relaxation helps and also trusting in things you can count on. 9s rest, take breaks, and enjoy the simple things in life, exactly what the doctor ordered for 6s who generally need to slow down.

6s see the bad side of life a bit too much, while 9s avoid the bad and are gullible, not wanting to see evil and corruption. Find the balance in between where you see the good and the bad, and hold both in mind at the same time. 6s need to create security based less on the environment and more from their own resources and those they trust, as well as the basic goodness of life, the 9 perspective. Search out the good people and forgive them their faults.

# Creativity and Development

6s' creativity reflects the ability to see the dark side of life and still have the courage to operate. More than any other type, 6s know that anything can go haywire, and that bad things really do happen. You have an amazing ability to plan for contingencies and can hold all the information together. You access everyone's weaknesses and strengths and accept their humanness, if people are honest.

6s come up with creative solutions to problems and provide many options. You pick up on psychological subtleties and complexities in others and in life situations, particularly when you develop yourself. You ask creative and thought-provoking questions, bringing the unconscious to a conscious level. 6s' keen insights and observations contribute to problem-solving. If there's a noise in the basement, a 6 will figure it out, and get excited by the search for the answer! 6s have played instrumental roles in all the protection systems we have—dykes, weather alerts, storm surge walls, pumping stations, scanning devices, and disease control. 6s' attention to detail can help artistically with jewelry making, drawing, painting, crafts, sculpture, or any of the other creative arts.

# Work and Career

6s are great at anything that requires attention to detail and solving problems. 6s do well in detective work, pathology, auto claims, accident investigations, and research. You want safety, but are often drawn to danger. Insurance industry employees, military personnel, CIA agents, FBI agents, firefighters, paramedics, police, stunt men and women, emergency personnel, and meteorologists have a higher than average chance of being 6s. Great psychotherapists, 6s analyze below the surface and tie in the past with the present. 6s are often social-service workers, protecting the rights of the innocent.

You are drawn to prediction, planning, safety standards, science, and administration. You like rules and standards and rebel against them if they are unfair. You want security and react, often strongly, if things aren't secure. You want a clear sense of expectations and guidelines that others provide, but you'll attack them if they are unfairly used.

> ### Insights
>
> Many revolutionaries are 6s, most likely counterphobic 6s. You fight for what is right. Both types of 6s are on the line marching, organizing labor unions, righting wrongs, seeking justice and fairness, stopping the bad guys.

# Leadership

Many 6s tend to shy away from leadership, but will assume the role if it is for the good of the group. Usually, if others initiate, you'll respond by either going with or against, instead of striving to be number one. Others often choose you to lead because of your knowledge, your commitment to the organization or group cause, and your protective nature. You're concerned that others will dump on you as the authority figure, so you'll take on the task with some anxiety, wanting alliances and backup. You see leadership as a team effort.

You are an anxious leader, scanning for dangers, problems, and what could go wrong. You might spend too much time solving problems rather than forwarding positive agendas. With security the issue, sometimes more than development or inclusion, allies and enemies are the focus. You need research and evidence to make decisions. This might create solidity but also irritates staff, who want to move faster. Explain yourself to others. Secrecy will incite other 6s to challenge you! You can be good at allowing trusted others co-leadership positions. Create best-case scenarios to encourage others.

# Digging Deeper into the Type

6s have a great variety within the type. The phobic and counterphobic 6 type differences could almost be split into two types. The 6 with the 5 wing is quite serious and intellectual. The 6 with the 7 wing is lighter and chummier. The Sexual subtype challenges a mate, the Social subtype creates alliances, and the Self-Preservation subtype will do anything for security, taking fewer risks.

## Wings

There are two wings for 6: the 6 with a 5 wing (6/5) and the 6 with a 7 wing (6/7):

- **6/5: The Protector/Intellect.** You protect what you believe in and analyze things to death or life! You are a systems person and a thorough researcher. You're a bit serious, even cynical, and yet you know what you're talking about. You try to create solidity but are always questioning and seeing the cracks in the granite. You defend what you believe in. You are traditional, but will start a new tradition. Downside? You can get too isolated, not trusting feedback from others. You are too much in your head and theoretical.

- **6/7: The Protector/Friend.** You are relationship-oriented, solid as can be, and lighter in tone than the 6/5. You like jokes, self-deprecating humor, and are more extroverted. Liking a bit of fun, you're a natural comedian, making fun of your insecurity. Downside? Sometimes it's hard to tell if you are secure or insecure. Reveal your insecurities and let your buddies help.

## Instinctual Subtypes

There are three Instinctual subtypes for the 6:

◆ **Self-Preservation subtype: Securing Your Turf.** You are a solid citizen and expect others to be also. You pay your taxes and your mortgage on time. You work hard, worry about emergencies, and plan for every contingency on earth. You are to be counted on but might miss some fun, being so worried about survival. Move out of your financial blueprint a bit, and trust that it will work out. People see you as solid, so don't worry. Downside? You can be a bit too concerned about survival. Have more fun and survive in other ways.

◆ **Social subtype: The Group Loyalist.** You create bonds with friends, family, or groups—alliances, mutual trades, and being there for others in emergencies—and you expect the same in return. You are dutiful at work and with groups and alliances that are important. You often participate in social or political causes and form your identity from your group commitments and responsibilities. You create acceptance and inclusion, unless someone attacks your values and allegiances. Downside? You might expect too much for your group commitments. Make sure they benefit you and realize that loyalty is not a priority for some people.

◆ **Sexual subtype: The Strong Protector.** You want to be strong, attractive, and smart for your potential or real mate. If you're strong or can attract attention or admiration, you'll have some power. You take risks, are seductive, or are at the top in your field, at least in terms of smarts—so that people won't mess with you. Your worth is your attractiveness collateral and others' value of you has a lot to do with it. Downside? Make sure you are as attractive to yourself as you need to be for others. Trust that people appreciate your real strengths.

## The Least You Need to Know

◆ 6s are loyal and can be trusted, testing others for the same.

◆ 6s are overly prepared for emergencies.

◆ Tending to shy away from leadership, 6s will be anxious in that position, if forced to assume it.

◆ Psychologically sophisticated, 6s understand life's complexities.

◆ 6s are ever on the alert, scanning the horizons for dangers.

# Type 7: The Optimist/ Fun Lover

## In This Chapter

- ◆ It's party time!
- ◆ Keep the energy high
- ◆ Ride the waves—please, no turbulence
- ◆ Freedom is my middle name
- ◆ Positive ideas cure anything
- ◆ The best is yet to come

Always looking on the bright side and seekers of excitement, Optimist/Fun Lovers are always up for something new. 7s don't tolerate painful scenarios. This energized type is chipper, charming, and always up for the latest venture, whether it's sports, gala parties and events, or a new and exciting challenge!

# Understanding the Type

7s are the quintessential positive thinkers. Life is what you make it, and 7s choose to make it great! Sure there are challenges, but you can overcome them. You just have to work at it. The mind can conquer all adversity. Do you refuse to spend much time with the negative side of life—pain, discomfort, bad feelings, or boredom? Do you believe people cause their own misery by having bad attitudes? If this is how you think, welcome to your type. You are a 7!

7 is a Head type, so it's all about *attitude*. You're confident you can think your way out of anything, as long as you keep that affirmative mindset. For 7s, thinking is doing. A good idea, particularly one that's upbeat, can save the day. Unfortunately ideas aren't executions, and 7s are criticized for trying to merge the two.

Enjoyment, excitement, and adventure are at the heart of 7s. If there's no pleasure in it, why do it? You don't see pain, obstacles, or major difficulties as inevitable parts of the process; rather, they're signs of something major being wrong. Of course, as a 7, you have creative ways of making even pain less painful. Your favorite expressions include …

- Let's look at it this way instead.
- It's a learning experience.
- Let's move on.
- It's just a temporary setback.

7s stay stimulated or highly engaged with life, partially to not focus on the bad stuff. As a 7, you can acknowledge pain, but there's no lingering on it, that's for sure. If you focus on what's good, deny what's bad, or reframe your thinking, the pain will lessen or disappear. There's always more fun to be had, thank God, so life is *always* good.

"I have to feel free in order to commit," says the 7. Freedom comes first. It's the foundation of your type. Defined limits cause pain. You need options, the freedom of your individuality, and liberation from limited or dysfunctional situations. More developed 7s realize that limits and some life-ache are just normal parts of life and growth, and not a reflection of something wrong.

You are generally extroverted, social, and engaging, loving to both entertain and be entertained. You know hordes of people but prefer to keep the connecting light. Conversations can be deep, at times, but changing the subject is easy for you, and if things get too serious, well, it's just too serious. Introverted 7s do exist, and the excitement with them may remain in the head as ideas, shared with fewer people.

You have tons of energy and many interests. You not only think but act, though it's hard to complete everything when your interests are so diverse! You remind us to see the glass as half full.

> **Insights**
>
> Famous 7s include Leonardo da Vinci, Timothy Leary, Ram Dass, Mozart, Goldie Hawn, Robin Williams, Elton John, Jim Carrey, Regis Philbin, Jack Nicholson, Steven Spielberg, Carol Burnett, and Lily Tomlin.

# Positive Traits of the Type

Your bright mind, cheerful nature, and ready smile get others smiling, too. You've got a good repertoire of jokes and enjoy being the life of the party. You're a storyteller with considerable life experience.

Your quick mind easily comes up with all kinds of solutions to problems and an endless supply of ideas and ways of looking at whatever topic needs to be expanded. If anyone needs a brainstorming session, you're available! Future visioning? You've got some thoughts on that.

Most likely you have traveled extensively and are already planning your next trip. Whether you actually carry out your plans, dreams, and schemes is less important than the thrill of thinking about what you *might* do. Planning a trip is almost as much fun as taking it. Studying restaurant menus, reading vacation brochures, and listening to stories from fellow travelers are terribly exciting. New hobbies, new jobs, new places to live, and new ways of experiencing life—there's no end to the possibilities.

You have boundless energy, are resourceful, and are a Jack- (or Jill-) of-all-trades. You know a bit about everything. You might know five languages, have written books on a number of topics, and have a storehouse of information for solving myriad problems.

You are good at multitasking. Switching gears is easy for you and you rather like it. You have high energy, and are lively and responsive. You can be intensely focused when you're doing something you enjoy.

You are often giving and helpful, generous with love and support for others in need. Your attitude is contagious. 7s who have lost limbs in an accident or who have been in the midst of the devastation of war retain a positive outlook. Whatever trouble befalls you, things could have been worse, and you make the best of the situation. You reach out to those who do have it worse than you. Life is good, independent of what happens, and what's past is past. Let it go. Inspiring indeed!

In a nutshell, positive traits of 7 include …

- A bright, cheerful attitude

- Adaptability to change

- Seeing and focusing on the positive side of life

- Boundless energy

- Resourceful ideas and solutions

# Embracing Your Spiritual Side

Concepts of God relate to receiving the abundance of the universe. You enjoy the bounty of the earth and appreciate life deeply. Whatever an individual 7's spiritual perspective, many 7s believe the world doesn't end with the physical form. Life is expansive, so why should it end here? Many 7s even video their death process, throw parties to say goodbye, and prepare for even more joy beyond. There is an inherent faith in the future, and who says you have to be in a body? 7s trust that even the unknown is good. 7s, caught up in the material world overly much, might not be as optimistic about the afterlife, and may even need support from other 7s around this topic.

> **Insights**
>
> A Type 7 hospice volunteer picks out new drapes and decorates a room to be cheerful for her terminally ill patients. He or she speaks about what heaven or the afterlife might be like from a positive perspective.

You enjoy the material world and want others to enjoy it as well. Even difficulties are seen as positive. You often surround yourself with good food, fun gadgets, colorful clothes, jewelry, and unique experiences. Travel is often essential. The Unity Church, which espouses constant positive affirmation, is the essence of 7 religion. Upbeat and rah-rah, the congregation repeats affirmations and sings songs of joy. The minister preaches about God's glorious desire for all his creatures to be richly blessed.

> **Insights**
>
> People create problems, conflicts, and separation, just as a way to have fun. We are all spiritual beings, but without distinctions, we don't experience ourselves as individuals, and without that, we don't experience our divinity.
> —Neale Donald Walsch, a well-known spiritual teacher

# The Dark Side

7s avoid the dark side, as if it doesn't exist. Why darkness, when everything is light and good already? From a 7 perspective, it's just a distorted mind that's the problem. Make all things bright by the power of your thoughts! Thoughts can't cure everything, though. Pain still exists, however good the thoughts!

7s sometimes deny the bad that is happening to them or others—either through ignoring obvious pain and hurt or reframing the good too quickly. "Well, I'll acknowledge the pain. Okay, let's feel it deeply and quickly and be over it. We definitely don't want to get mired in the swamp of despair."

7s tend to focus too much on the bright side. Avoidance protects against repressed anger, greed, and insecurity surfacing. "No, I don't want to talk about that. Why do you keep bringing up things that are painful to me?" Everyone else either has to pretend all is well or deal with the consequences you deal out.

> **Lifelines**
>
> Some 7s play a game to briefly visualize or feel pain. Feel the worst for 15 minutes. Okay. That's done. Now, let's get on with something positive. It's an in and out strategy—but maybe pain has a lesson to teach that can't be taught so quickly!

You live at one extreme of the pendulum—the happy place. But life seeks its balance in the middle, where truth and reality hang out. When you go to one extreme, the other extreme is always there, pulling at you. You blame others for raining on your parade, when, for you, there are no options, other than constant parades. It seems that others are being negative, when it's your avoidance of your feeling that's causing the problem. Fear, sadness, and anger are normal emotions—relationships and life can't go deep without them!

7s can have a real issue with commitment. Giving up freedom runs counter to your nature, so you avoid options that might actually offer you deeper gain. Freedom is often more about possibilities than reality. Limiting yourself may be painful, yet there's the lesson—temporary discomfort for something that gives you more happiness in the long run. It's a gamble. You can commit to work, relationships, and interests, when you see that freedom is relative and sometimes even an obstacle to the joy of real growth and fulfillment.

Worst traits of the type include these foibles:

♦ Avoiding pain and discomfort

♦ Expecting others to always be positive

♦ Avoiding limits and deeper commitment

♦ Starting projects but not completing them

♦ Jumping from subject to subject

♦ Denying what is genuinely a problem

# Stress Type

The Stress type of 7 is 1, the Perfectionist/Improver. You can be angry and controlling, like 1s, when people limit your options or *force* you to do something boring or constrained. You act out and vent your anger or complaint or alternatively try to control others, limiting their freedom. If people are constricting *you*, you'll constrict *them*. You go back and forth.

You can also be a perfectionist, but it's *your* version of perfection. Instead of having a balance between options and rules, you go to the opposite extreme and become rule-bound yourself. You realize you aren't accomplishing enough with your *in the moment* way of being and reel yourself back in. Develop the positive side of 1—being more serious and committed, valuing order and guidelines, yet not being too rule-bound.

# Decision-Making

7s can be indecisive. You want all the options and hate to close any down. You can't have it all. Instead of three parties in a night, go to one. If you spread yourself too thin, you'll miss out on deeper connections and developing interests in a more expert way. Let go of the concern about missing out and see what takes more priority. Decide what benefits you and others the most and go for that. Choose quality over quantity!

**Warning!**

You worry about missing out, but you'll miss even more if you run around tasting everything but miss the main meal in the process. Look to a deeper and more sustaining experience of living.

Get help with decisions to see what your priorities are. Look at your values—fun, excitement, desire to learn, wanting to develop a skill, learning how to compromise and decide from those values and others as much as from titillation and fun. Sometimes it's okay to be a bit more serious and have goals that might limit your typical 7 agenda. Trust yourself that you'll always have a good time and not miss too much. After all, that's who you are.

With so many activities and interests that drive you and often decide for you, you mostly decide from what feels good, which could make you feel bad later. Be more in charge and think before you act. Prioritize what's important and envision your future by outcomes you want, even if this means some limits.

# Picking the 7s Out of the Crowd

7s generally are easy to spot. You are fun and often speedy in talk and movement, with your drive for excitement and love of a good time. Sometimes you're a bit wild! You are often boisterous, charismatic, or even clownish, and you love to tell stories. Your sunny disposition is hard to miss.

## Nonverbal Cues

You dress colorfully, sometimes as if on constant vacation. You bring the energy up and do your best never to be down. You're positive, but a tad defensively, as if it's a sin not to be. It's almost a veneer.

Other nonverbal cues:

♦ You avoid pain and conflict, when possible.

♦ You adapt easily to change.

♦ You don't necessarily finish what you start.

♦ Almost everything fascinates you.

♦ You have an excited, childlike demeanor. Let's play another game!

♦ You catch on quickly and are irritated by slow people.

♦ A Renaissance person and generalist, you have a wide range of interests.

♦ You fidget! You're always moving about.

## Verbal Cues

You love to learn and love to talk about what you've learned. Ideas and options come quickly, so you jump from subject to subject with ease. Hobbies, people, sex, travel—whatever the topic, you're prepared to shed some new light. Your mind loves to be entertained and generally you'll entertain others with your learning. Other verbal cues:

♦ You love to tell jokes or stories.

♦ You're always ready to talk about new ideas and experiences.

♦ Your excitement shows in your voice.

♦ You listen, but if the conversation is lagging, you'll jump right in to bring up the excitement level.

## Maturity Within Type

Developed 7s are absolute delights. You see difficulties as part of the mix and learn from them, while you also refuse to have anything but the good life. There is nothing you can't accomplish! You are up for any challenge and see the value of commitment. You are an inspiration to others, generous with your ideas and help. You can be serious and may even welcome pain for the experience it can provide on your life's journey.

Most 7s enjoy life immensely but can get irritable with limits. You might run away from important feedback and refuse to feel too hemmed in. You might leave relationships or jobs prematurely, when conflicts arise, rather than facing and resolving the problems. You want your freedom but also like it when others are more committed to you. You can siphon off energy from the stronger commitment and groundedness of others—liking their solidity, yet reacting negatively to their rules or demands.

Undeveloped 7s try to stay in constant stimulation and activity to have fun and avoid pain. Pain creeps in and haunts you, sometimes causing depression. You get bored but yet never feel fully satisfied. You're missing something and aren't sure what it is. You become increasingly angry with people who are limiting you. Others leave you because of your irritation and self-centeredness.

# Type 7 Childhood

However difficult the childhood, the 7 strategy is enjoyment. 7s relate to life with play, activity, and refreshing their minds with positive thoughts. 7 children can entertain themselves. Their positive attitude is a great way to deal with stress. Acting, board games, dancing, physical activities, talking, lessons, and endless activities—7s can make a game out of anything.

Parenting a 7 is both enjoyable and difficult. 7 children are always up for exploration and fun, but, at the same time, there can be a denial of pain. Children of divorce can pretend nothing is wrong, protecting against hurt. Confronting 7 children can be challenging, as they either deny the problem, go toward play, or wish the problem away.

> **Insights**
>
> I can always make people happy. It bothers me if people are negative. I like it when my friends focus on what they want rather than complain.
> —Katja, 11

# Type 7 Parents

Type 7 parents need to realize their children might not want as much stimulation as they do. While most kids will love your more zany, fun energy, the quiet child might become overwhelmed by it. Also, you might have issues with setting limits. Children need healthy limits to feel secure. Your upbeat perspective is great, but your children might feel forced to be happy when they aren't.

Make sure you can nurture your kids, whether they're happy or not, and accept their sadness, hurt, fear, and anger as much as their joy. Don't bring them out of a difficult-feeling experience too early, just because it hurts you to watch them. Continue to heal yourself, by allowing them their feelings. Be careful of an over-positive atmosphere that causes repression. "Only positive allowed" protects you more than the child. Of course, all kids are different, and it's your job to adapt to parenting from their worldview, as much as yours.

> **Insights**
>
> The hard part is not knowing sometimes if she's hurting about some difficult situation. She seems to be not really in contact with these more intense emotions (pain, sadness), although I know they are there.
> —Joan, 45, mother of a 7 child

# What the 7 Thinks About

You think about future options, what could happen, what you might do—all with a positive focus. You think about ways that are limiting you and how you can shift that. You look at what's happening that you like and plan more options, spinning out pleasant stories. You think about people and activities and ways you can attend parties, book signings, whitewater trips, balloon rides, or yoga. They're endless—the possibilities.

You also think about …

- ♦ I can't stand to listen to complaints or negative feelings.

- ♦ It bothers me that she's always complaining.

- ♦ I love to come up with ideas and solutions.

- ♦ People are so uptight and controlling.

- ♦ How can I get to three events in four hours?

What 7 adults *wish* they could say:

- ♦ I'm sick of running away from what's negative. I'm ready to feel it and face it.

- ♦ Tell me how you're feeling and I'll just listen. Take as much time as you need.

- ♦ I know it'll take time to solve this problem. I don't have an easy solution, but we'll figure it out in time.

- ♦ Thanks for confronting me. I like to see all parts of myself, particularly if it's hurting you.

- ♦ Maybe I'll just go to one party tonight. I'll meet more people that way.

# Relationships

You love relationships, but you want to make everyone a 7. You demand everyone be happy, look at the bright side, and not complain about much—a tall order for anyone but another 7. Most people can't pull it off, and your criticism of non-7ness can also be a complaint and rejection. Your demand for happiness can be a pressure on you and others!

7s can be great in relationships. You can follow or lead, being egalitarian. You're for whatever works—not needing the *whatever* to be overly defined. When you develop yourself, you are more sensitive to others' feelings, whether those feelings are easy or difficult. You can be supportive and helpful to others and love to see smiles on their faces from your giving. Your cheerfulness and joy bring joy to other's lives. You are playful and spontaneous and ready to engage in life. You enjoy yourself and make sure others do, too!

It's hard for you to listen, sometimes, as your mind is speeding along, thinking of other things. Pay closer attention when your friend or partner is talking about difficulties. Listen for others' needs, even those that are below the surface, as much as you focus on your own. Listening is as valuable as solutions are. Prioritize empathy over excitement.

If someone repeats too much, which you hate, say you got it the first time and only need to hear it once—but say it with a smile! If you show real interest and patience, people will be less likely to repeat themselves. On one hand, be a bit more patient; on the other, tell people how to talk to you so you'll listen better.

When others are talking, be careful about changing the subject to bring attention back to you or to a more exciting topic. Listen as much to others' emotional needs as you do to stimulating ideas or fascinating details. Do some detective work!

You can be a challenge for others when it comes to really sticking it out to solve a real problem. You love the quick fix, but the nitty-gritty details of fixing things that take time, unless they are relevant or interesting, bore you. You need a few lessons in persistence and fortitude to learn that solving some problems requires time and real change. The more developed you are, the more you are committed to commitment and relating in-depth.

Everyone has different interests; so don't be disappointed if your interests and those of your partner don't mesh at times. Generally you have others to share with and are okay with differences, but you do like to have fun with your partner. Independent, you prefer other independent people. Sometimes it can feel as if others are attaching themselves to you with glue, so let them know you want to help but don't want strong dependence, unless you do.

# Tough Lessons

Lessons for you include slowing down, focusing on fewer things, accepting the negative as part of life, and facing feedback about limits. You can't make everyone and everything positive. Not everyone chooses happy, excited feelings as a number-one priority. Your way is no more right than others.

If there is danger or hurt or obstacles or a bad mood or whatever, they are real, and you can't wish or think them away. Accept what is, rather than how it could be. You are future oriented and miss out sometimes on the value of what is *now*. Be more fully present to this moment, whatever it is, positive or negative.

Even though you are giving and often empathic, you sometimes lack heart sensitivity. Compassion and connection often happen at a slower pace, when you resonate with the emotional experience of another. Let go of trying to solve problems too quickly and just *be* with another, accepting their difficulties. Listen well before bringing in attitudes, affirmations, and right actions.

Face pain and difficulties. Cry when sad, express anger when necessary, and be aware of your fear. Notice guilty feelings. Don't bypass your inner experience, in your attempt to get back to fun and pleasure. Don't dwell in pain, which is unlikely, but feel enough not to avoid what is real. Sometimes you get depressed, because you've been holding back a wall of feelings. The more you allow yourself to feel, the more you heal and provide protection from depression.

Your tendency is to start something and not necessarily finish. Realize that completion can be fulfilling and don't stop just because you get bored or the details become tedious. It's temporary and the excitement will return again, if it's the right project or situation for you. Just hang in there and get some help with what's hanging you up. If you get down on occasion, not to worry!

# Growth Type

The Growth type of 7 is 5, the Observer/Knowledge Seeker. 5s explore in depth. Instead of dabbling in everything, become an expert in a few things that really interest you. 7s grow when you get a bit more serious and commit to what you believe in, work hard to develop those traits, and aren't afraid of some struggle. Determine to be good at what you do, whatever the cost. The 5 journey is introverted and less about outer stimulation than the inner stimulation of a job thoroughly done with deep learning. Spend some time with self-reflection, like 5.

# Creativity and Development

7s are creative and love to move between realities. There's no end to the subjects that 7s can combine or intermarry. 7s can explore and define the interrelationships between modern politics and religion, or the differences between religion and spirituality, or sex and spirituality. New music, new spirituality, new anything! 7s love to arrange and rearrange, synthesize, and intuit new possibilities.

7s seldom say no to the unknown. 7s are into mind play, work games, art themes. Many 7s create new food combinations and dishes, new ways to express sexuality, travel, and work roles. 7s adapt, create change, and are trendsetters for clothes, electronics, adventure travel, and sports. Let's work for cultural exchanges among nations! There's so much to learn and share.

> **Insights**
>
> One 7 workshop leader uses theater as a medium to create "playshops" for children and adults, to support play in life. Themes include shamanism, connecting with the earth, creating communal connection, and promoting world peace.

# Work and Career

7s are found in travel, entertainment, and movie industries and are comedians, musicians, and magicians. You prefer jobs and careers that provide plenty of freedom. A locked-in job with a hovering or controlling boss is a no-go or short-term stay.

Perhaps you're an entrepreneur. Many 7s are. You have great ideas, though you may struggle with the follow-through. 7s often start ventures and pass them on to others to develop. Boring details are torture. Many 7s have five, six, or more major careers throughout a lifetime. Even in a regular job, 7s prefer to wear different hats.

# Leadership

7s lead by inspiration, motivation, and holding a positive vision. You usually are excellent speakers and can keep the energy up when things show signs of flagging. Strong on innovation, you need to energize others to stay interested and excited. You can create an organization of team players, as you know you can't do it alone. You encourage egalitarianism and want everyone to be energized on his or her own but can be negative toward complainers or too-practical people who fearfully hold back the process or stop the ball rolling for research or future concerns.

As a 7, you want to move on, yet you sometimes need help with action steps. You may act without a clear and consistent focus. You want others to act out your ideas, thinking ideas are the main catalyst for action. Sometimes you're too confident, not expecting the obstacles. "Don't they see that this could work?" Other times you'll just make obstacles fun.

# Digging Deeper into the Type

There are different kinds of 7s. 7s with 6 wings alter more for harmony in relationship and 7s with an 8 wing are more independent and assertive. 7s are positive to a fault, but anyone, when stressed, becomes different. Some 7s can be irritable and controlling when obstacles become too great. It's hard to be cheerful all the time, especially when a positive attitude alone doesn't produce results.

## Wings

There are two wings for 7: the 7 with a 6 wing (7/6) and the 7 with an 8 wing (7/8).

- **7/6: The Fun Relater.** This wing is more relational and more willing to compromise than the 7/8. With some of the caution of a 6, the 7/6 wing is still mostly spontaneous and trusting. Fun Relaters are entertaining, connecting, and witty. If you're a 7/6 you can be scattered, take off on tangents, and lose focus.

- **7/8: The Fun Driver.** This wing is more realistic, independent, and materialistic, focusing more on the goal. If you're a 7/8 you're outspoken and less concerned with conflict, even being a bit callous, if folks get in the way. You tend to be outrageous and less concerned about people's responses.

## Instinctual Subtypes

There are three Instinctual subtypes for the 7:

- **Self-Preservation subtype: The Gadget Collector.** This subtype likes to have the latest gadgets and keeps up with current trends, such as iPods or Blackberries. Acquiring unique items found in antique shops and planning for fun ventures are all part of feeling secure. If this is your subtype, you might grow a garden or buy that one-of-a-kind breakfast table. You love yard sales and talking about and swapping items with friends. Make sure you have enough money to play and collect unique experiences, too. Downside? Is what you have what you really want? How long will you keep or use what you have?

- **Social subtype: The Partier.** This is an Auntie Mame-type character, a larger-than-life eccentric who collects people to play with, has a large social network, and throws parties. If this is your subtype, you are the life of any party. You're involved in groups and social networks but at times feel restrained by rules or expectations of others. You want to feel free and hope people are available for *your* play and needs for entertainment. Storyteller and jokester, you make sure everyone has a good time. Downside? Have fun and realize some restraints are useful. Fun has a price, too. Let go of the pressure to make people happy.

> **Insights**
>
> Home is where I lay my hat at the end of the day. It's not the center of my life. I am very externally oriented and prefer intense engagements one to one with people who fascinate me.
> —Alice, age 40

◆ **Sexual subtype: The Charmer.** This subtype can convince anyone of anything. If this is your subtype, you tend to be seductive, fall in and out of love easily, and become infatuated and fascinated by new people and situations. You love intensity in relationships and are interested in unique people. Excited by newness and excited by possibilities of someone new, you need to know what's fantasy and what's real. You can cheer up your mate and light up anyone! Downside? Watch out. People can't always bring up new, exciting feelings. What about commitment and follow-through over time?

## The Least You Need to Know

◆ 7s think, live, and breathe positively. The mind can overcome all adversity.

◆ With more interests than time to develop any one of them, 7s are bundles of energy.

◆ 7s tend to begin more projects than you ever finish.

◆ Wanting to keep things light, 7s may shy away from limiting commitments.

◆ 7s move quickly, and slow people and slow scenarios are major irritants.

# Type 8: The Director/ Powerhouse

## In This Chapter

- ◆ Live and let live? I don't think so
- ◆ The generator: step aside, I'm energized
- ◆ Be reasonable—do it my way!
- ◆ In charge on the outside, insecure on the inside
- ◆ Sorry! I didn't mean to step on you

Director/Powerhouses can light up a city with a drive for doing and taking action. Short on patience, what you see is what you get. The most body-instinctive type, 8s tend not to take *no* for an answer. If there's an obstacle in the way, slowing down progress, call an 8 for guaranteed action.

## Understanding the Type

Preferring action to inaction and driven by impulse, Director/Powerhouses have energy to burn and can't stand to wait. No brakes, please. 8s feel easily controlled and are on the alert for that possibility. It's all about the green light and taking charge, so as not to be taken charge of by others. If you test people the way you'd test a new car and push your agenda hard, welcome to your type. You're an 8!

### Insights

In 1859, Charles Darwin published *The Origin of Species* and introduced the idea that only the fittest of any species survive. He called this *natural selection*. 8s, with their dominant and aggressive behaviors, fit this model perfectly.

Strength is power. You do whatever it takes to be strong or at least project a strength you may not feel. You hide any weakness, for fear you'll be taken advantage of if you don't. If you're tough with others and yourself, you can manage. Charles Darwin was right—life's a struggle for survival and only the fittest prevail. You have to constantly prove, challenge, and confront.

Who's afraid of a little conflict? Certainly not the 8! You even like conflict, if it brings out the truth. You want everything brought to the surface. Unlike the 6, who *mentally* challenges, you *physically* challenge, if needed. You live in your body and are ready to leap, pounce, jump, push, shove—whatever it takes to protect yourself and anyone important to you. You live by your instincts and are the most purely physical of all the types.

You shoot from the hip and lip and only think later, unaware of your power to affect others. You're simply trying to get to the truth and are surprised when others are hurt by your directness. You are being more playful and excited than some people can handle. Bear cubs play rough!

You pull your own weight—so should everyone else! You don't like insecurity, doubt, fear, and weakness of any kind. Open on one hand, guarded on another, you usually are generous when people are straight with you and particularly need help, but dismissive and confrontational if people are shirking or taking advantage of you.

# Positive Traits of the Type

Delayed gratification? No way! You work hard at what needs to be done and don't want to wait for your pleasure or reward. Your energy knows no limits—neither do your plans, dreams, and schemes. You deserve all the good things in life. After all, your hard work makes them happen. Subtlety is not a game you play. There's nothing hidden. With 8s, what you see is what you get.

Why put things off? You inspire others. You're not a talker, but a doer. Action makes it happen. Geared for action and focused on results, you don't let anything get in your way.

You are generous. When someone is down and out, you'll give anything to help. You protect the vulnerable and fight for justice and freedom. You watch out for bullies and face them. You're the one who speaks up in the boardroom or office meeting, and your honesty is either a breath of fresh air or a hurricane flattening everyone in its path. With you, there's no middle ground. Hurricanes can create urban renewal!

> **Insights**
>
> Famous 8s include Martin Luther King, Jr., Donald Trump, Rosie O'Donnell, Geraldo Rivera, Rosanne Barr, Danny DeVito, Muhammad Ali, Barbara Walters, George Patton, Winston Churchill, Richard Burton, John Wayne, Johnny Cash, and Debra Winger.

You are independent, trusting your decisions. You don't need approval before acting. Self-motivated, you accept that life is tough and you're ready, either alone or on a team, to withstand an enemy, troubles, or storms.

Your humor tends toward the bawdy and you appreciate the rawness of life. A good stout ale, a long and full-out walk in the snow-filled woods, raising a houseful of kids, or raising cane. You're okay with the basics of life and not afraid to talk about them—food, sex, elimination, going for what you want. Euphemisms are affectations. You call a spade a spade (or maybe a shovel).

In a nutshell, positive traits of the type 8 include …

- Being direct and clear.
- Trusting your instincts.
- An ability to lead and inspire others.
- Passion and energy.
- Being in charge of your life.
- Your ability to face conflict and challenge.

# Embracing Your Spiritual Side

Your spirituality is appreciating that which gives life. You don't back off from life and you appreciate and use what you've been given. Some people ask God for guidance.

You do too, but you also realize it's up to you to do the work. You can surrender to a higher force, but barring a bad connection, you realize that higher force is within you. Most 8s do too much alone. Developed 8s work with others to accomplish their goals.

8s' spiritual growth is to feel part of the whole, instead of controlling the whole. You tend not to trust the flow of events and rather push the timing of things. More allowance, more tolerance, and awareness of limitations will greatly help in your evolutionary process. When developed you are a model to guide the world to what is good. You protect those who would be misled or hurt by others.

# The Dark Side

When you are sad or afraid or stressed or guilty, it's likely to come out as anger. Anger is easy for you to feel and put across, an expression of not getting what you want, feeling held back, or being misunderstood. Anger is relieved when you express it or get what you want.

> **Warning!**
>
> Others can be intimidated by your anger, which blows over more easily for you than for them. Others will remember the intimidation and control they felt when you unloaded your demands or fury. Best to watch this!

Instead of trusting to a natural unfolding of events and believing people will support you and accept you, you tend to overprotect and control—just in case! You tend to feel it's better to take charge and make the first move than to be on the receiving end. You sometimes think the worst in regard to people's motivations, yet you're open to the good when you see it.

Your recklessness can get you into trouble, and you may need to apologize when the consequences of your rapid actions don't pan out the way you'd intended. You tend to leap instead of treading lightly. It's best to wait until the time is right or take things in stages. Float some ideas first, get some feedback, and think about the future before acting.

You tend to rebel. You are the bad boy/bad girl of the Enneagram and don't like to follow rules, though you can demand that others follow yours. You want fairness but can treat others unfairly if you're upset. You can stick a firecracker in the mud and light it, just to see how big a hole it will make!

Excess is an interesting trait of 8s. You may drive too fast, drink too much, overeat, or party till dawn when you want no stops and fast action. You have a hard time with limits and see no need for them, unless you develop enough to value them. Should others try to set limits for you, look out!

Worst traits of the type include these foibles:

◆ Uncontrolled anger and bluntness

◆ Lack of impulse control

◆ Not following the rules you make for others

◆ Taking charge when others need to lead

◆ Taking action when waiting is required

# Stress Type

The Stress type of 8 is 5, the Observer/Knowledge Seeker. When things go bad, you hurt and go into retreat to lick your wounds. It's hard for you to talk about your pain. You become more private and struggle to share what is happening and what you want, including your vulnerability. Your physical energy lessens and you read, brood, or stay hurt. Typically, you wait for the feelings to subside and then reemerge. Notice if you are retreating too much and get help.

The positive side of 5 can be developed, too—be more objective, study the situation more thoroughly, wait till the timing is right, and be less outspoken. Keep developing the 5 to be detached, more thorough in your thinking, and less impulsive. Objectivity and seeing others' positions puts a stop on *heavy on the pedal* action.

# Decision-Making

You are decisive, often to the extreme. You trust your first impulse, partially to avoid any wavering thoughts or feelings. You don't like the slightest edge of ambivalence. You thrive on black or white, strong or weak, right or wrong. Any decision is better than no decision! Watching time pass without a decision is a real stressor. Inaction would suit you well, at times, so that decisions are thought through.

8s often decide for others, which obviously can cause conflict. Waiting or being inconvenienced by others is not in your game plan, so you'll speed things along,

**Insights**

Decision-making is what life is about. I make my best decisions from pure intuition.

—Bill, 48

running over the slower or indecisive types in the process. You don't know what is best for others, and you'll either get resistance or anger projected toward you if you control or dominate. Try the velvet glove approach. Give decision-making support or nudge others in your direction.

# Picking the 8s Out of the Crowd

8s are one of the easier types to spot. 8s are strong, opinionated, sometimes jovial, and can use language that tends to startle or bypass the norms. You don't mind some reactions. Your energy is bigger than most people's and you easily slip into take-charge mode. Some 8s, however, have a softer tone, are more introverted, and only speak when it's necessary.

## Nonverbal Cues

8s can show their independence in dress, actions, or beliefs. 8s are not hiding or trying to create an image to impress. It's more of a take-it-or-leave-it attitude. 8s can speak bluntly and might not realize how others will be affected. Practical jokes are fine with 8s, particularly if the 8 is the initiator! Other nonverbal cues:

◆ 8s can handle challenge and confrontation.

◆ 8s have a commanding presence.

◆ 8s do what they do full tilt—they play hard, work hard, and go after what they want 100 percent.

◆ 8s often are strong with big builds—strong chests and shoulders.

◆ 8s often enjoy a good belly laugh.

## Verbal Cues

8s love to talk about subjects most people don't touch—sex, politics, and religion—and are willing to disagree with others. Sometimes you challenge just to test. Not much is forbidden, if it gets a rise or the truth out of people. You like language that affects.

- ◆ 8s are more than happy to complain to a manager or owner.

- ◆ 8s have a hard time filtering what they say.

- ◆ 8s share opinions as facts.

- ◆ 8s can say "no" easily.

- ◆ 8s talk in a strong or aggressive tone but also can have a teddy-bear heart.

- ◆ 8s use aggressive words such as "kill, destroy, demolish, slap, choke, push." Curse words are not unusual!

## Maturity Within Type

A developed 8 is inspirational. Martin Luther King, Jr., a natural leader, led by example—sharing and encouraging the leadership and bravery of others. Not everything had to be his way. He kept a higher and more mature vision for others to follow. A developed 8 is direct, yet compassionate; self-aware, yet generous; strong, yet open to the comments of others. Inclusive, kind, and grounded on solid principles, 8s are the top of the line, when developed.

Most 8s are strong, but if this is your type, you may overprotect your weaknesses. Needing at times to dominate others and feel a sense of ego, you might not realize you're making some enemies along the way. You may miss out on the beauty and value of your own sensitivities and seeing your own subtler strengths and those of others. Still seeing the world from power plays and stand-offs, instead of cooperation and power-sharing, most 8s miss out on support, on bonding through vulnerability, and having a good blend of strength and openness.

Undeveloped 8s are bullies. They have to win at all costs and are insensitive to the hurts and needs of others. Protecting their insecurities is their main focus. They're always on guard, projecting that others are trying to dominate them. If someone invades their turf, or they think someone is challenging them, revenge is swift.

> **Insights**
>
> In the political tyrant arena, undeveloped 8s include Henry VIII, Saddam Hussein, Idi Amin, Benito Mussolini, and Attila the Hun. More positive 8 leaders include Winston Churchill, Rudy Giuliani, Geronimo, Mikhail Gorbachev, Lyndon Johnson, Jesse Jackson, and Indira Gandhi.

# Type 8 Childhood

8 children fight back if they are bullied or controlled. Whether parents, teachers, or peers are the source of their distress, 8 kids are on guard to protect themselves and others. 8s lead and are the rallying point for friends, protecting them. They expect allegiance and are hurt or angry if one of *their people* pulls away from them. Leadership gives them a role and they like it. 8 children don't like adults telling them what to do when it makes no sense. They can't wait to grow up and be on their own. 8s decide what they want to do, do it, and steel their defenses if their parents resist or punish them. If there's strife, running away is an option. Otherwise, they can enjoy childhood and have opportunities to develop their interests. If 8 children are supported, childhood is a blast with fun and challenges to absorb their energy.

8 kids are a challenge for others, as they can be loud and overly independent. They go after what they want, or think they want, and don't look for feedback. Others may admire their strength and spirit. Sometimes 8s will be oppositional just to prove a point. If they trust others' intentions, there is less to rebel against.

# Type 8 Parents

As an 8 parent, you can be too strong and definite. You sound out your commands and lack patience. Be less dictatorial and controlling, and your children will both trust you more and be more responsive to you. Be careful not to instill fear in your children by cutting off options, barking, or being too demanding. Make sure your children have opportunities to speak their opinions and wants and try not to decide for them, unless necessary. Support their independence.

You are a protective parent and will do anything for your children. You are protective of others' kids, too, and watch out for danger. You teach your children to be strong and independent, as well as generous, particularly with people who genuinely need help. When you are happy, you model laughter, that the world is your showboat, and that you can do anything you want.

**Warning!**

If you are too controlling with your children or bully them, they can grow up to avoid you or hate you. It's so important to be more moderate, even tender with many kids.

You are an inspiring model for living a self-directed life without fear, but you don't always know what is right. Be patient, process before any quick actions, and let your children have their own pace. Your own is so quick, it can overwhelm children, even more than it does adults. Remind yourself to constantly *slow it down* if necessary. Develop yourself and you'll find the right balance between being yourself and growing as a parent. Be open to feedback from your children and be willing to apologize.

# What the 8 Thinks About

You think a lot about protection, control, who has the power, who's a jerk, who's trustworthy, and what actions need to be taken. You think about what you want and how to get there. Occasionally you feel guilty for overstepping your bounds. You look at scenarios on how to influence and effect the changes you want. You think about your fears and go right back to solutions. You think about how to be strong.

What else your type thinks about:

- I wish I hadn't blurted that out.

- How could someone not know what they want?

- I wish I could stop eating.

- God, they are slow.

- This is the quick and right solution.

What 8 adults *wish* they could say:

- I apologize for what I said. I spoke too hastily.

- That's fine. Your way is as good as mine. There really isn't one right way.

- Let me slow down when I eat and stop before I'm full.

- I'm really not feeling as brave as I sound. I'm actually not sure what the right thing to do might be.

- Let me hear their side. Let's find a compromise here.

# Relationships

Relationships are important to you and also a bit scary. You like people and can be loyal, but you hate that relationships bring up fears and insecurities and you struggle with differences between people. You wish people could see things your way and don't understand why they can't. You wonder why others are being stubborn and don't see that the stubborn one is you!

### Insights

My 8ness led to the demise of my closest friendship. I was self-absorbed, not focusing on her. I talked about me too much. I was waiting for her to be more assertive.
—Toby, 61

You think there is a right way to end this conflict and you convince and convince, yet don't see your need to compromise. Recognizing the validity of different approaches is essential for your relationship health and protecting against others withdrawing from your one-sided views. Best to take a course of negotiation and communication. Yet, when you feel good, and if someone has a good position or desire, and it makes sense, you go for it immediately. Why waste time thinking about it?

You really struggle when others are withdrawn, indirect, or manipulative, and you'll hound them until they speak straight. Realize there are many forces that encourage indirectness, hinting, and roundabout ways of communication that may cause challenge and conflict. There are valid reasons why others choose a less direct route than you do.

You are wonderful in relationship, as you are full of life, create all manner of positive things in the world, and don't accept excuses for why things can't happen or change. You challenge your partners to act, be courageous, and don't take no for an answer. You support a can-do spirit and don't like whining, helplessness, or depression.

# Tough Lessons

You are powerful, yet hide your feelings of powerlessness even from yourself. You don't realize that insecurity and doubt and mixed feelings are natural and have a place. Too-quick action can cause blunders and corrections and bad relationships, actually slowing down positive change. You make things happen too much from pushing and pure effort and daunting relentlessness, yet don't know the power of letting go, creating alliances, and that things sometimes need to build from a natural pace.

People give into you, sometimes, because they are afraid or overwhelmed by your demand or drive or it's just too much effort to fight you. You bank on that, but why have a fighting stance in the first place? Why not focus on cooperation as much as contention?

Sometimes you don't know what you want. What really is your deeper desire or truth? Are you doing and fulfilling what you need? You may fight the good fight, but make sure it's a fight you want good outcomes from. Fighting adrenalizes the system and gives a boost, but is it the energy you are looking for or the result? Don't stop at your first impulse; keep exploring what you personally want!

You are as insecure and afraid as the next person. Why spend so much time hiding it? It takes more effort. Sure, some people will reject your feelings, but it's more likely people will see your softer side and like it. They will trust you more and you can relax and not have to be so much in control.

Be open to different ways and options that others may reveal to you. Go with what works more than having to win, control, or be right. Who cares who's right, when everyone can win? A little compromise can go a long way.

# Growth Type

The Growth type of 8 is 2, the Giver/Cheerleader. You are already giving, but this move to the high side of 2 deepens your caring and sensitivity to all people. You see that others are vulnerable and searching, and your heart reaches out to more people. You see past the defenses of manipulation, indirectness, and surface explanations and see that all humanity is *suffering*. Your heart stretches and connects and your gifts are generous and personal and touch those in need. You are nothing short of magnanimous when you are open and connected. You become personal, let go of the need for power, and are safe to be with.

Your power supports your giving. You see the crooks and the greedy forces that limit giving to those in real need and so you do what you can to oil the conduits and speak the truth, so that the wheels move in the right direction. You understand that even the greedy ones are needy, deep down.

**Lifelines**

The Buddhist philosophy that all life is suffering is hard for an 8 to accept. 8s think anything can be fixed with will. Yet suffering occurs and 8s need to accept their own suffering, which is part of the human experience.

You fight injustice and the bad in the world, as you develop and use your power wisely. First you lock up the takers and the criminals and then do your best to help them, misguided as they are.

# Creativity and Development

You create from pure will. You make things happen and generally accomplish whatever you set out to do. In your own growth balance, you network to create a better world, help others, right wrongs, and serve as an inspiration. Develop your creative side for relaxation, aesthetic pleasure, and for your nurturing. Make sure you have time to draw, paint, sing, or whatever pleases your fancy. 8s can be great at sports, trusting their bodies to guide them. Martial arts, challenging sports such as racing, football, hockey, and basketball are filled with 8s, driven to excel and use their bodies as creative works of expression.

# Work and Career

8s are movers and shakers at work. Often in charge of others, you prefer jobs with quick turnarounds and quick results. You hate ambivalence. Long-range outcomes, detailed strategic plans, endless meetings, and fruitless conversations are difficult. Let's be honest, they are torture! You hate being the follower and don't like micromanagement one iota, unless you are the manager. You'll leave people alone, if they get the job done, unless you are a major control 8 and then you can't lay off telling people how to do it right. You value independence, yet struggle with supporting it in others if your beliefs and theirs cross in ways that interfere with business.

You do well in outdoor ventures and tend to own, manage, or work in companies related to this—construction, landscaping, firefighting, sports, logging, coaching football, running a moving company, or commercial fishing. You're drawn to danger and may put yourself in harm's way in your profession. You like the intensity of facing life head on.

> **Insights**
>
> One 8 has written several books on advocating for a 30-hour workweek, using solar power, economic equality, protecting the wilderness, and understanding personality types based on the periodic chemistry table!

# Leadership

You are a natural leader. Slowpokes, stalling, and underhanded tactics directed against you have no place in your world. Rules are meant to be broken, unless they are your rules. You like clear definitions, to-the-point conversations, and clarity around differences. You are known for rash actions, many of which work, at least in the short run! You might create enemies along the way though, which could slow down your projects. Best to balance, by teaming up with other power players. You're honest, yet can deceive (tell only your side of the truth and exaggerate it) to win, particularly if confronted with perceived enemies.

Often CEOs or managers, you build conglomerates and have a bit of the tycoon in you. You are found in the military, police, and other establishments, directing traffic and giving the orders. You quit jobs that irritate you too much or are happy to tell off the boss. If you *are* the boss, you don't mind some confrontation, as long as your authority is respected. You prefer to know what's up! Donald Trump is an excellent 8 example. Winning is fun and firing those who don't produce is fun, too! No slackers here.

**Lifelines**

In leadership positions, it's best to include others in decisions, and be concerned about how you engage in conflicts. You'll be followed more readily if you do!

# Digging Deeper into the Type

8s can show up in many versions. The 8 with the 7 wing is more stereotypical of how many people imagine 8s—strong, loud, and direct. The 8 with the 9 wing is softer and usually more introverted, though with strong reserved energy. Maturity levels in 8s create major differences in this type. 8s often get feedback that causes them to hold back their directness and be more other-centered. You could easily mistype those quieter 8s for other types. Let's look at the variations.

## Wings

There are two wings for 8: the 8 with a 7 wing (8/7) and the 8 with a 9 wing (8/9):

♦ **8/7: The Power Energizer.** This is the most dynamic of all the wing types. With energy to burn, the 8/7 is direct and also geared to fun, play, and adventure. You need projects, exercise, and ventures just to bleed off some energy. You tend to be impulsive, fast, and love to be in charge. You can't help it! Downside? With all that energy, mischief and conflict are sure to follow.

♦ **8/9: The Bull Moose.** This wing is softer in tone. Ready to be strong when needed, you are more reserved. You enjoy some downtime and quiet time, and you measure out your energy in doses. You are geared toward truth but also require some peace. You engage less in conflict but take on challenges easily. You like to lead but are more collaborative and surrendering than the 8/7.

Downside? You can go back and forth between strength and ease. This might be hard for some people to read.

## Instinctual Subtypes

There are three Instinctual subtypes for the 8:

- **Self-Preservation subtype: The Territorial Defender.** You guard your home and castle; supply it with all the necessities, including emergency supplies, and invite people to share what you've earned, though you don't allow anyone to take advantage of you. You fought hard for your security and you fortify your surroundings in case an enemy intrudes. You are generous to those who respect your boundaries. You have adequate supplies of food, drink, and comforts, and either rough subsistence-type living or surroundings of more wealth suit your style. Downside? Protection could take up too much of your energy.

> **Insights**
>
> A female Social subtype 8 was offered a proposal in marriage by a Type 5 male. She said yes, but only if he were okay if a friend in need, even in the middle of the night, would take precedence over everything, including him. Being a 5, he said, "Fine. I like some alone time!"

- **Social subtype: The Friendship Connection.** You have a group of loyal friends you have nurtured over time and will do anything to keep your group together. You test, but deliver your loyalty and bond. You corral social gatherings for your special flock with lots of laughter, food, and good times. You are there for your friends as much as you are for your mate. Downside? If you are a social 8's mate, be prepared for friends invading your home on a regular basis or your mate being out regularly with a bunch of buddies.

- **Sexual subtype: Control and Connect.** You are driven to both control and connect deeply to your mate or chosen partner. You want to know everything there is to know about your pursued mate, but you expect complete loyalty and devotion. You can be possessive and jealous and are prone to fighting and great sex afterward! You give attention, yet might not listen to the subtle cues of what your partner is looking for. Downside? As an 8 mate, are you up for such intensity and expectations?

## The Least You Need to Know

- ◆ 8s fight for justice.

- ◆ 8s are the strongest-appearing type on the Enneagram, yet have a soft, vulnerable side within.

- ◆ 8s are the natural leaders of the Enneagram. You champion causes, fight for the underdog, and take on—with relish—whatever challenges come your way.

- ◆ 8s don't ask for permission to act.

- ◆ 8s are highly independent and tend to dominate the situation you're in, along with the people involved.

# Chapter 11

# Type 9: The Harmony Seeker/ Accommodator

## In This Chapter

- ◆ Standing up for yourself
- ◆ Developing a separate identity
- ◆ What lies beneath the *nice* guy or gal
- ◆ Find your power and your passion

You value peace and harmony above all else, and you want everyone to like you and be nice to you. Your identity changes often, according to the situation at hand and what you perceive others expect from you. Sound familiar? If you've caught tantalizing glimpses of yourself in each of the previous types, but none were an exact fit, welcome to your type. 9s identify who they are by identifying with others. You are a 9!

## Understanding the Type

To understand the world of the 9, it's important to know that 9s adapt to the wants of others, accommodate others, and go out of their way to create either real or imagined peace, at least from the 9 perspective. As a 9, you're generally positive, optimistic, and trusting, although you can get down if you can't create peace. You love life and look for the best in all people and situations.

Sometimes, however, your trust borders on a childlike naiveté, and this can cause you problems. Not everyone wants peace, and not everyone's motives are pure or good. As an accommodator, you're sincere and value relationships, so you tend to go along with what others want. However, some may see you as gullible and may take advantage of you, especially because you are easy to talk to, kind, compassionate, welcoming, giving, and agreeable. You defer your own plans and adapt your ideas and wants to those of others. You may seem okay on the surface, but always putting other people first causes your stress level and resentment to build. When you reach your limit, you slam on the brakes or run for your life. People get confused as to why such an agreeable person is suddenly not so agreeable.

# Positive Traits of the Type

9s are people most people want to know. You are the salt of earth, accepting, forgiving, and generous—the basic, good person. There is no guile. You are generally easy to be with and have a high tolerance for differences in people. You'll easily sacrifice self for the unity of the whole, going out of your way to create harmony and connection. You're happy for the successes of others and are willing to learn from them.

| Insights |
| --- |
| Famous 9s include Abraham Lincoln, the Dalai Lama, Laura Bush, Tipper Gore, Dwight Eisenhower, Walter Cronkite, Norman Rockwell, Tony Bennett, George Burns, Jimmy Stewart, Rosalyn Carter, and Jennifer Aniston. |

In a nutshell, positive traits of 9 include being ...

- Grateful for simple pleasures.
- Spiritually oriented.
- Empathic.
- Even-tempered.
- Skilled at mediation.
- Flexible.

# Embracing Your Spiritual Side

You are not one of the skeptics—that's for sure! You have a clear sense of how life should be lived. As a 9, you see life as good and believe human greed and selfishness are aberrations. You may attend church or belong to groups that emphasize the spiritual aspects of life. Many mystics and psychics are 9s. You understand the inter-relatedness of all life and want to make the world a better place for everyone. The Golden Rule guides your actions, and you *do* go out of your way to help people in need and don't require special recognition for your efforts.

# The Dark Side

There wouldn't be a good without a bad, a positive without a negative. This applies to everything we assign a value to, and it also includes our Enneagram type. At the worst, 9s lose all sense of personal identity, sacrifice everything to another, and then self-esteem goes out the window. Best to find and maintain your individuality, or you will feel lost and at the beck and call of everyone's command or whim. Unfortunately, if you don't keep moving forward, life will put you under a rock, which rarely moves and puts you under an awful lot of pressure.

When you retreat from reality and stress, distracting yourself with comfort or addictions—whatever feels good—you're practicing risk avoidance and repressing your *self.* Avoiding conflict creates internal conflict and more avoidance. If you've ever resorted to cleaning out your sock drawer instead of addressing what's really troubling you, you've practiced avoidance. Handle your first priority, instead of your fifth!

Beyond avoidance, 9s can be plagued by repressed anger and resentment. How does this surface? *Passive-aggressive* behaviors are the tool of choice. 9s disown their anger. Instead of saying no or expressing some self-interest, you get stubborn, delay, forget, avoid, and can even get more agreeable, yet with no action. When someone asks what's wrong, you respond that everything is fine. Of course everything *isn't* fine, and you can't break through your veneer of nice to explain.

## def•i•ni•tion

**Passive-aggressive** refers to behaviors that are anger-based. These behaviors come out in passive, resistant, or indirect ways such as avoidance, withdrawal, delay, or forgetfulness; and more anger expressions such as negative comments, criticism, or negative comparisons.

Each Enneagram type protects itself from stress and the uncomfortable aspects of people and life. Each defense makes sense, once you understand the type. 9s, how-ever, work at cross-purposes and actually increase their stress, holding it inside, instead of releasing. As a 9, your inclination is to downplay and minimize your own needs—hence making "molehills out of mountains." This creates repressed anger that eventually might blow to make Vesuvius look tame! Take care of problems when they happen, not later. Being direct now prevents later explosions.

Worst traits of the type include these foibles:

- Avoidance of dealing with problems
- Avoidance of identifying wants, needs, anger
- Major avoidance of confrontation
- Being unclear, confused
- Indecisiveness
- Agreeableness that masks inner conflict
- Lethargy

# Stress Type

The Stress type for 9 is 6, the Guardian/Questioner. This type manifests itself in a tendency to be frozen in fear, unable to act, obsessive, and even paranoid! The 9 is a Body type and needs to reconnect to the body when in fear, not ruminate to worst-case scenarios in the mind, like the Head type 6. Focus on action and bring the fear along, if need be. Trust your intuition, not your mind torture. When in high stress, go back to 9 and find your relaxation. Focus on balancing with the positive side of 6, being more self-protective, realistic, and seeing the selfish side of others or even of yourself.

# Decision-Making

Feeling indecisive? Your tendency to see all sides of an issue, and not have much of a core self to strengthen you, makes decision-making difficult. Everything seems fairly equal in value and weight. So you freeze up and often wait until the last minute to let someone else or even fate decide for you.

Who am I, really? There's the quintessential question, for you. As a 9, you struggle with establishing your unique identity. This is difficult, as your natural tendency is to mold yourself to fit whomever you're with. This is hard work. It's tiring and counter-productive, as well. Now you've got a conflicted inner reality to deal with, as well as situations to handle and decisions to make. Help!

It's hard to trust that you can be in control of your life and decide for yourself and not have to take care of or pacify others. It's a full time job keeping peace, particularly when you are the main person needing it. Good decision-making comes from understanding that you are an individual, with individual wants and needs. Trying to place the traits of your type upon everyone else, to make peace for the rest of the world, is a task doomed to failure.

True peace is about a decision and commitment to act on your values, even in the face of a very nonpeaceful and conflicted situation. To grow, 9s need to face the realities of competition, selfishness, and strife and still help others and the world with acceptance, unity, and peace. Of course, unless you can make your own decisions based on personal values, it's difficult to help the world!

| Insights |
| --- |
| It's like being a chameleon. I almost always try to fit into every situation. It's like I'm an actor, waiting for someone to give me a role. —Paul, 53 |

# Picking the 9s Out of the Crowd

Because 9s can imitate any type, it can be a challenge to spot a 9, as they can effortlessly alter to adapt to you. The consistent theme is conflict avoidance, with occasional anger eruptions, when 9s have repressed themselves too much. 9s struggle to have a strong and consistent sense of self. Watch for the nonverbal cues to detect the 9. Never consistently like any other type, 9s are the nice guys of the universe.

## Nonverbal Cues

Look for hand gestures that are slower, with both hands balanced and rounded. This relates to seeing the world in a unified, inclusive way. When stressed, 9s push their hands out like a stop sign or press them down to dampen or stop intensity, conflict, or loud noises. They nod their heads in agreement. They take breaks. There are other signs to look for:

- Slouchy posture—leaning against a wall
- Appearing a bit sleepy, droopy, spacey
- Dressing for comfort more than fashion
- Imitating others' body postures and gestures
- Overall sense of innocence, sweetness

## Verbal Cues

9s have some interesting verbal habits. They will agree with you. They tend to repeat themselves over and over, both because they are uncertain you are hearing them and also just because it feels good to talk about pleasant matters. They avoid getting to the point and will verbally meander. Their words are often low-key, trailing off at the end. They can easily buzz out or change the subject when others bring up unpleasant topics.

Other verbal cues:

◆ Slower speech patterns, even-toned or monotone

◆ Conversations are agreeable; using expressions such as "That's so true," "I understand," "I agree"

◆ Voice tone of others is imitated

◆ Changing the topic to something everyone can agree on

## Maturity Within Type

Developed 9s have learned to be individuals, speaking up when necessary and managing conflict, while still being beacons for peace and equanimity. If you're developed, you've taken the necessary risks in life to grow and integrate those traits. You show your individuality and passion, and you'll go after what you want, while still yielding to find balance with others.

Most 9s still struggle with being assertive. If you're like most 9s, you have difficulty going after what you want or even identifying what that may be.

Undeveloped 9s are doormats, living in constant fear of upsetting people and feeling extremely stuck in life, not making any moves to disturb the apple cart. If you're undeveloped, others don't know where you stand, nor do you. You kind of drift through life like a falling leaf, at the beck and call of the wind.

# Type 9 Childhood

Childhood is a time to explore your individuality, to grow, and learn. But for the 9, childhood is also about accommodating the wishes of the parents. Adaptable, obedient, and sweet, the 9 child frequently serves as the family mediator who wants everyone to get along. Sometimes 9 children can act out family drama and anger in fantasy, hoping for change. They'll adapt to do what is expected, to the point of unwilling boys playing war games, even if it feels uncomfortable. They'll even try assertiveness, if that's what mommy and daddy want, but this doesn't last long. It's just not in their nature.

Getting along with parents is the 9 child's first priority and then, if possible, with siblings or friends. Avoiding aggressive children is difficult, as most children seek 9s out because of their acceptance of everyone. 9s attract the loners and are also perfect targets for bullies. If there is too much conflict, the peace-seeker child first tries to make peace. If unsuccessful, the 9 child hides away, reads a book, or takes a walk in the woods.

Nature lovers, generally, 9 children look for solitude or fun games to play, ideally, with less-aggressive kids. If 9s win too much, they feel bad. This adds to their stress, so they feel obligated to make sure others win, too. Generally they're cautious of stepping on bugs and don't kill animals for sport. God forbid! However, the seed of the adult is in the child, and the 9 child's passive-aggressive side lurks within.

9 children think they should be sweet and nice, never angry; get along with everyone; share toys; and in general be good girls and boys.

> **Lifelines** _____
> Encourage your 9 child to be assertive, more self-centered, to set goals, and handle conflict. Model those qualities— yet be gentle.

# Type 9 Parents

The 9 parent wants a peaceful home. Too much conflict is a major stressor, causing anxiety or depression in the parent. As a 9 parent, you encourage your children to be peaceful, caring, and sharing. This works great, *if* your children are also 9s. Develop your own individuality and strengths, so you can understand and bring out the natural type traits of your children. Accept children who aren't as peaceful as you and maybe even learn from them. Adapting to each of your children's types will help you develop and also help you engage more directly with your children. If there's some intensity in your children's types, so much the better!

# What the 9 Thinks About

9s, like all the types, have an inner dialogue going on that reflects the type values. Often, with 9s, what is seen on your calm surface is not an accurate indicator of the conflict that simmers beneath. 9s struggle with an inner life that scares you to share, yet communicating what you want is essential for growth. 9s need to accept your thinking and have the courage to use that thinking to speak out what you dare not say!

What else your type thinks about:

♦ It's best to compromise.

♦ I need to get those two to stop arguing.

♦ I don't like being around negative people.

♦ Selfishness makes me so angry!

♦ I can't figure out what I want. It's hard to know what to do.

What 9 adults *wish* they could say:

♦ I'm willing to work out a win/win on this, but I have some needs that are important, too.

♦ Could you lower your voice? I hear you.

♦ I'm not interested in talking to you now.

♦ You're asking for more than I can give.

♦ I'm angry about this. It's not working for me.

# Relationships

What do you want in a relationship? As a 9, you're often in one! You tend to build your sense of self by going along with or against others, instead of being the initiator. The same qualities—understanding, empathy, acceptance, a forgiving nature, tolerance, inclusiveness—that draw people into relationships with you, can also drive them away. The problem is not so much that you're holding back. It's just that you know what you *don't* want more than what you *do*. Clarify what you want. Be more selfish!

You avoid conflict so much that you often stay in highly unsatisfying relationships for many years. It's just too threatening to see your self-centered desires or emotions known or revealed, even to you. Only seeing the good, while you hide your needs or problems, is a recipe for disaster. If you seek change, you risk conflict. So you go on. And on. And on.

Because your tendency is to avoid setting self-goals that may cause conflict with others, you end up going nowhere fast and run the risk of suffocating a relationship, along with your passion for life. Kind of goes against the grain, doesn't it? On one hand you love life, but on the other you retreat from it. Go more for what you want and take the risks that actually might spark the relationship. Don't avoid by watching TV all day or treading water, when conflict is too overwhelming. Listen carefully to your inner signals and seek some support when extreme fear or surfacing anger calls for it.

9s are generally laid back but often attract those with opposite qualities for relationships—more direct, or anger-oriented types—to bring out their own! When you accept your own anger and are more direct, you can consciously choose whom you want to relate to! Keep seeing yourself as the powerful person that you are and make the choices that suit *you*.

> **Insights**
>
> It's hard being a 9. I can't speak up about what I want, if someone wants something else. I tend to go along and just stay upset inside.
> —Alice, 42

## Tough Lessons

To be honest, there isn't a strong individual self in the 9, and that's the challenge—learning to develop one. Life is about growth. Your journey, as a 9, is to discover who you are as an individual and let go of conforming so much to others' real or imagined expectations. Accept the challenges of life as opportunities to develop the qualities you are lacking. Sacrifice some comfort for strength-building.

Focus your energy more toward independence, direct expression, and a strong sense of self in your interactions. All of these increase relationship success. When fully developed, you're assertive, self-directed, action-oriented, individualistic, passionate, clear, and inspiring in your communication—hard-won qualities. While many people strive for these qualities, for you it's a constant challenge to manifest qualities opposite your natural tendencies.

## Growth Type

9s' Growth type is 3, the Success Striver/Winner. It's a natural evolution, if 9s are growing, to be more success-oriented and self-focused and achieve through goals and action—like 3s. It's tough to reach success if you are too other-oriented or divert your attention to please or avoid. The balance for 9s is to clarify what you want, put on some horse blinders, go for the goal, enjoy receiving accolades, and not settle for anything less than completion. The world needs productive 9s!

# Creativity and Development

Develop your individuality, skills, and creative pursuits and build self-esteem and confidence through those creative endeavors. It's easy to settle for what you've been taught or conform to hobbies or interests that others expect you to pursue. As a 9, tune in to be your unique self, even if others don't understand or like it. Stick with important pursuits, even when they are challenging or uncomfortable.

You may find that, as a 9, you are drawn to communal activities, are often good with arts and crafts, enjoy anything related to nature, and like music. Being a Body type, you are often physically coordinated, and this comes in handy for sports. It's good to challenge yourself and be competitive for fun and for personal development, knowing, of course, it's not fun to win too much if it means others must lose.

# Work and Career

Because you're highly adaptable, you have more varied work and career options than any other type, although you're often working in human services and related service industries. It's not unusual to see 9s as counselors, mediators, child educators, massage therapists, forest rangers, landscapers, or naturalists. Anything related to healing, unity, or nature draws 9s like honey. Often, you prefer a peaceful environment to the actual job description and are generally stressed in work situations with constant deadlines, high competition, and office politics. You do best when you prioritize what you want out of a job or career and stick to your guns. You need to speak up at work about your own priorities, such as ways to improve team communication through harmony-based incentives. These ideas won't see the light of day if you hold back due to fear of conflict.

# Leadership

The more conscious of self the 9 is, the more there is a deep commitment to real peace, and 9s can be leaders for that purpose. 9s can run from their own conflicts, but many developed 9s are active in the world, creating and leading for peace and unity and being an example for others to follow. 9s often are supporters and protestors for peace, but even more importantly, 9s are actively making peace happen, as mediation specialists, negotiators, and advocates for children or animals. 9s integrate their greatest strengths when they stand strong in their commitment to make the world a safer, more inclusive, loving world.

**Lifelines**

The world needs 9 leaders, the only type *naturally* invested in seeing that everyone wins. Take a stand in a world that needs your special traits!

# Digging Deeper into the Type

Like all the types, 9s have two different wings and three instinctual subtypes, each of which has a unique description and flavors the core 9. The 9 with an 8 wing, for instance, may seem unusual, in that the qualities of 9 and 8 are seemingly opposite, with 9s being indirect and 8s being direct. This type leads with peace, yet is generally more outspoken than a 9 with a 1 wing. 9s are generally mellow, but the Sexual subtype 9 is more emotionally intense than other 9 subtypes, being driven to merge with a lover in order to have a relationship work.

## Wings

There are two wings for 9: the 9 with an 8 wing (9/8) and the 9 with a 1 wing (9/1):

- **9/8: Be nice but strong.** Liking comfort and usually more extroverted than the 9/1, the 9/8 has an edge of strength, is impulsive at times, and has an ability to say *no* on occasion. You're more easily angered than a 9/1, though you still have a long fuse. Like the 8, you little devil, the 9/8 has a lust for pleasure and an eat-drink-and-be-merry attitude, with more of a body focus. But there is a price to be paid. Downside? You are more prone to weight gain than the 9/1!

- **9/1: Be nice but with order and values.** You like peace and also order. You're more introverted, reserved, and less prone to speak up until you've got things figured out. You're generally more disciplined than the 9/8, hold in your stress more, and are less impulsive. Downside? While you act from values of right and wrong, as a 9/1 you can be stifled by values you don't personally choose.

# Instinctual Subtypes

There are three Instinctual subtypes for the 9:

- ◆ **Self-Preservation subtype: The Comfort Seeker.** Soft pillows and cozy fireplaces ... you value comfort and don't like to be disturbed from your set routines, habits, and interests. You're stressed by change and require stability. You like a comfortable chair and a cup of tea, while you knit a sweater, with cat in lap. Very reliable, anyone can count on the comfort seeker to give them comfort, too. Downside? Comfort Seekers can use routine and comfort to avoid self-goals. Risk takers? Not hardly!

- ◆ **Social subtype: All in the Family.** You like to be part of a family, family of friends, or club or group of any kind. Easygoing, you look out for people who feel excluded and invite them in. A happy-go-lucky kind of person, you may lead the group or just like to listen or chat and feel a sense of belonging. You hate to be excluded from a group you like and find it nearly impossible to sever former ties. Downside? All in the Family subtypes also avoid self-focus. Easily taken advantage of, they can be just *too* nice! They'll cut your grass or help you move, even at risk of causing stress to their own spouses.

- ◆ **Sexual subtype: The Merger.** If you're a Merger, you form tight bonds with a mate or someone close to you, and identify with and idealize them, as well. You'd rather focus on being close and pleasing your partner, than risk the discomfort of talking straight about your differences. Because you tend to live through your partner, you really don't see yourselves as two separate individuals. Downside? If you mold into someone else, you can avoid being your individual self. But because you like *some* intensity, you often have close relationships with people who are more self-centered than you are. Of course that's what you're unconsciously trying to develop in yourself, more oomph!

# The Least You Need to Know

- ◆ 9s try to create peace and avoid conflict.
- ◆ 9s may cause more conflict by avoiding it. Facing the struggles allows 9s to develop.
- ◆ 9s identify with and imitate others to find themselves.
- ◆ 9s see life as good and try to look for the best in everyone.

# Part 3

## What's Your Enneagram Type and Others' Types?

So, now that you've seen the descriptions, do you know what type you are? These chapters explain how to find your core type and subtypes, and also those of others you're curious about. You'll learn what questions to ask and what behaviors to observe. You'll see how to identify the growth struggles for each type and how to distinguish types that tend to look alike. As you discover how to manage the complexities of typing, you'll begin to understand people with more ease. You'll also see how your family and your personal history influence your type.

# Chapter 12

# The ABCs of Typing

## In This Chapter

- A journey toward understanding yourself and others
- Getting help from your friends
- Trusting your gut instincts
- Distinguishing between type look-alikes
- Looking at gender and type
- Sins of the types

Why is knowing your type so important? Knowing your type helps you recognize and understand the deeper truth and motivational drive of who you are. Whether it's clarification or verification you seek, keep exploring until you feel secure knowing your core type. It has to feel right to be right. In this chapter you'll learn the basics of typing. First, you'll discover your core tendency—the main perspective, from which you think, see, and act. Then you'll hone in on your subtypes and wing. Ready? Of course you are!

## It's You to the Core!

Determining your core type is a bit like weeding a garden. You know the flowers are in there, but there's a lot of other stuff blocking your access to them. So you get to work. You pull out some plants and leave others where they are. It's a sorting process and if the job is a big one, you may want some help. Typing works the same way. Some people can accurately type themselves, but many of us need help.

There are nine core types and you may be unsure which, among several possibilities, is your core. As you continue to examine and question, you'll discover one of them is part of your basic nature, like your heartbeat or breath.

Your type tends to show itself early in life, usually by age 8 and often before. It can manifest itself later, in the teenage years, but it's rare to see it emerge later than that. A guideline is to consider how you are or were in your 20s. This is usually a time where the type is strong, before you realize that something isn't working and you try to change it. No type works perfectly, because each type is missing the best parts of the others. The more you grow, the more you want to change what isn't working for you. You want to be complete.

> **Insights**
>
> Parents often say, "One of my kids came out screaming and hasn't stopped yet. The other one was quiet and still is." For many people, type begins at the beginning.

Why is the type so strongly set in us? There's a million-dollar question for you, and we don't have the answer. One thing's for certain, though—set in us, it surely is!

A cautionary note: as you begin to type yourself, don't go for the type you'd *like* to be or for what you are *growing toward*. Your type is your preset tendency, not something you have to work at or change. It's your basic nature. Even as you grow, there's still that inclination to return to what is familiar. Being your type requires no effort. Changing aspects of your type requires great effort! It's the insight into your type's strengths and limits that gives you the awareness to change and grow.

# A Little Help from Your Friends

Typing yourself can be difficult, especially if all you do is just read about the types. Your friends, however, along with your romantic partner, past loves, and others who know you well can help you out here. How do you do this? Just ask how you are different from others. Give the type descriptions and ask which one is more *you*. It's valuable to use both general questions, as well as questions that reference each separate type's concerns. You'll find a list of these questions in Appendixes B and C, respectively.

You can use these questions once you've narrowed it down to two or three types or to do a check, if you think you've determined the type. If you answer in the affirmative to most or all of the questions regarding type characteristics, you are most likely on target. Quick responses, empathic responses, or humorous responses are indications that you're on the mark.

We often carry a picture of ourselves that isn't accurate. We may think we're one type, but everyone else thinks differently. Generally, the group is right. For example, many people would like to think they are a 9, the Harmony Seeker/Accommodator, but their assertiveness pegs them as an 8, the Director/Powerhouse. In this case, they're probably an 8 with a 9 wing!

 **Lifelines**

If you are typing someone, don't worry about getting it *right*. See it as fun and an exercise in gathering information. If someone, including you, is learning from the process, it's a success.

In counseling or coaching or workshop sessions or over dinner, let your spouse or significant other type you. Seldom are they wrong and, even if they are, they've usually identified a secondary type, usually a wing or a Stress or Growth type that's currently more on display than your core.

When you answer the questions, reflect on your whole life, and consider what's most important to you. What are your deepest values? What is the part of you that remains, no matter what you try to change? What is the strongest lens through which you view life? Filter out what you've been taught to be. Who are you—really?

Why is it so important to be correct? Because you'll be more honest about what is driving you. Your type informs you about what is true, and there's no need to deny any aspect of yourself that *is* true. Also, if you are honest, you'll understand the possible defenses that protect you, have more options for change, and be open to be the best of all the types. Otherwise? You spend endless energy protecting yourself from that truth and the joy of life.

# Explore the Deeper Motivation

Type is about motivation. A 1 and a 3 might complete the same project and have the same outcome, but the 1 will focus more on detail and perfection, while the 3 will hone in on speed and efficiency and winning. There are behaviors that indicate type, but until you know *why* people do what they do, you can't be sure. Your environment plays a major role in developing these behaviors. If you have been shamed or invalidated for your motivations, you may have learned not to reveal your motivations to others or even to yourself. If you've been accepted for who you are and what you do, it's easier.

# Sorting It All Out

Here are some tips for when you're trying to distinguish between two types and can't decide which is dominant. A person may have characteristics of both, but you need to look for the bottom layer of the cake. This bottom layer supports the others—it's the main stage—it's the type. Gotta meet those type needs first, before moving on.

- **1 and 2**—1s give because it's the right thing to do, while 2s give in order to be loved and to please. 2s are more image-oriented, positive, and smiley. Both give advice for different reasons. 1s are more preachy and serious.

- **1 and 3**—Both like efficiency, hard work, and success. 1s aim for perfection, which can slow progress, and 3s work fast and target winning, which can affect quality.

- **1 and 4**—1 is a quality, detail, and moral perfectionist, and 4 is an emotional and aesthetic perfectionist, though the two types can trade back and forth on these qualities. 1s are honest to a *t*, and 4s create high intensity and drama, way beyond the *t*. 1s create or follow the rules and rebel fretfully. 4s rebel often, as individualists, and look for special attention. 4s want to define standards *personally*, but 1s look for rightness and universal standards.

- **1 and 5**—5s are perfectionists with matters pertaining to knowledge and information, but believe in individuality. 1s, as moral perfectionists, think there are universal values to which everyone should conform. Not true for 5s at all, who are individualistic.

- **1 and 6**—Both are detail-oriented and hard workers, but 6s are fear-based and more concerned about safety and security and danger. 1s just want to do the job right—they already feel safe.

- **1 and 7**—1s are serious and control their desires. 7s are fun and light and tend to easily fulfill their desires. 1s, when secure, go to 7 and are more playful but not consistently like 7s. 7s go to 1, when stressed, and become critical.

- **1 and 8**—1s and 8s both like control and power. 1s check their values, morality, and right actions before they act. 8s already trust their instincts and act quickly.

- **1 and 9**—1s are hard workers, need perfection, demand high standards, and are often critical. 9s want comfort and ease and are highly tolerant of differences. The 9/1 can seem like a 1, but peace takes priority over perfection. They are not similar, though the 1 wing of a 9 can imitate some traits of the 1.

- **2 and 3**—2s and 3s are both positive and achievement-oriented. 2s help and please people to be loved and 3s complete tasks and win to be loved and appreciated.

- **2 and 4**—2s are into positive emotions. 4s can handle that, in addition to any emotion, and the darker the better. 2s smile and 4s may frown. 2s give attention and 4s both give and seek it. Both are very relationship-oriented. 4s can be giving but self-absorbed in their own process, and 2s bank on focusing on others' needs as their means to security and affirmation. Both are emotional and when 2s are struggling with negative emotions, they can feel like a 4. Some 4s are very giving. Both are highly relational and romantic.

- **2 and 5**—5s are intellectual and detached. 2s are more emotional and personal. 2s are looking for love and are codependent, and 5s are independent, looking for knowledge.

- **2 and 6**—6s can be giving, too, but for the sake of security. 2s don't worry so much about security. 2s are upbeat and 6s are worried. 6s are happy only as relief, before the next worry.

- **2 and 7**—Both are positive, but 2 is more dependent on others' responses. 7s are more independent and self-oriented.

- **2 and 8**—2s are image-oriented and will alter to please. 8s are solid with who they are. 8s speak up, are more independent, and less concerned about consequences.

- **2 and 9**—9s can seem like 2s. Both types are giving, though 9s give as a way of joining and seeking harmony, rather than for pleasing and needing personal appreciation. 2s are generally more selective in their giving.

- **3 and 4**—4s want to be successful in both their inner and outer lives, while 3s will see too much inner process as a deterrent to outer success. 3s are more easily satisfied with outer success, while 4s want more depth, feeling, and an ideal love.

- **3 and 5**—3s are image and impression-oriented. 5s are more knowledge-oriented. Though both 3s and 5s love competence, 3s prefer a winning edge.

3s crave attention and praise for their production success, whereas 5s are more okay alone, though they don't mind some acknowledgement for their intellectual competence.

♦ **3 and 6**—3s go into action, without much concern for dangers and problems. 6s stop to think and plan before they act. 3s don't mind being in charge, whereas 6s hesitate. 6s in stress try to achieve like 3s but with anxiety and 3s, when secure, are like 6s, more team oriented and group identified.

♦ **3 and 7**—3s complete what they start, even if it's tedious. 7s don't always finish what they start, particularly if it's not fun. 3s need reward. 7s are rewarded in the moment by their own pleasure.

♦ **3 and 8**—Both like to achieve. 3s are image-oriented and 8s like to explode images. 8s are directly honest and confrontational. 3s are not as brash.

♦ **3 and 9**—9s prefer comfort and avoidance of conflict. Action is secondary. For 3, goals and action take the forefront. 9s are cozy and accommodating. 9s can be goal focused and productive (like 3s in a 3-type environment), in order to conform. 9s take breaks and 3s don't have time!

♦ **4 and 5**—5s perceive life primarily through the mind; 4s through the heart and emotions. 5s hold back; 4s tell their story. 4/5 wing and 5/4 wing can seem a bit similar on occasion.

♦ **4 and 6**—4s and 6s both explore the dark side of life and both easily feel abandoned, but 6 more from the vantage point of safety and security needs not being met and 4 more from a lack of emotional connection and intensity. 6s look at life from the outside in (environment has to be safe) and 4s do both.

♦ **4 and 7**—4s include pain and can over-focus on it. 7s tend to avoid emotional pain or have quick remedies to get over it to focus on the fun side of life. 7s are lighter; 4s are sometimes both dark and light. Both love intensity, excitement and change.

♦ **4 and 8**—4s like emotional depth. 8s like direct honesty, which seems deep, but is actually about acting on body instinct. On the surface, 4s can feel either insecure or secure, and 8s almost always appear secure. 8s protect their insecurity more. 4s struggle with it or can't hide it! Both are intense!

♦ **4 and 9**—9s focus on others to create harmony and try to find their own identity through them. 4s try to find their identity through their inner feelings and being seen as special. 9s easily conform and 4s don't. The Sexual subtype 9, the

Merger, can seem like a 4, with a strong desire to merge and a higher tolerance for intensity than the two other 9 subtypes. 4s maintain their individuality, while 9s blend and merge. Both are very spiritually oriented.

◆ **5 and 6**—5 and 6 are head and knowledge based. 5 is more detached, independent, private, and concerned about too much bonding. 6 is more relationship-oriented and anxious, wanting to be included, and afraid of abandonment.

◆ **5 and 7**—5s are private. 7s generally are more social, lighter in tone, and motivated by fun and excitement. 5s are more motivated by serious pursuit of knowledge. 7s pursue knowledge, too, but with a lighter touch. 5s generally are depth; 7s are breadth. Both are intellectual and love to integrate knowledge.

◆ **5 and 8**—5s are in their heads and 8s in their bodies. 5s mostly speak out when relating to learning. 8s speak out most all the time. 5s are private; 8s have loud speakers, though introvert 8s can seem 5ish.

◆ **5 and 9**—5s and 9s can be look-alikes. Both can be withdrawn. 5s want solitude for thinking and integrating knowledge, 9s for escaping intensity and conflict and for comfort. 9s merge with others, are more peace-seeking and body-oriented; 5s are more self-oriented, independent, protective, and in their heads.

◆ **6 and 7**—6s are more serious, anxious, and worried. 7s just want to have fun. 6s go below the surface, and 7s are on the surface. 7s like to start things, and 6s like to excavate things. 6/7 or 7/6 can blend a bit.

◆ **6 and 8**—6s and 8s tend to challenge. 6s mentally challenge and 8s add the physical component to the challenge. 6s examine anything related to their concerns, and 8s go to the source of the problem. 6s doubt themselves—8s don't.

◆ **6 and 9**—6 is the stress point of 9, so 9s in stress can look like 6s, stay in fear, feel frozen, think about worst-case scenarios, have obsessive thinking, and forget they even have bodies. On a day-to-day basis, 6s scan the environment for danger, while 9s are more prone to overlook it and are too trusting. 9s generally are more relaxed and easygoing.

◆ **7 and 8**—Both are full of life and energized; 7s more for fun and 8s with more control, though 7/8 is more direct and can appear as an 8. 7s are less confrontational, on average, than 8s. 7s are egalitarian; and 8s are as well, but only if they are in charge!

◆ **7 and 9**—Both can be fun-oriented, but a 7 is more self-oriented than the 9 and tends to jump from one activity to the next. 7s are more hyper and 9s are more even-keeled, generally less animated, and very other centered.

◆ **8s are seldom mistaken for 9s, but a 9/8 wing can resemble an 8 at times and be fairly strong.** The 8 can almost always speak up easily, where 9 hesitates. 8s are direct in their communication, and 9s tend to beat around the bush.

# Taking the Typing Tests

Test anxiety? Not here! While Enneagram typing tests and assessments can be valuable, they are only one of the tools available. It's easy to mistype yourself, if you rely solely on Enneagram assessments. You might take the test with your best or idealized self in mind or only consider traits you've developed. Begin from the perspective of what your natural tendencies are, not the ones you'd like to have or are working to cultivate. Then, include Enneagram readings and workshops, friends' assessments, a teacher typing session, intuition, and self-reflection to help you decide correctly.

# No Worries!

If you don't determine your type immediately, or if it's taking longer than you want, not to worry. Just be honest and keep learning about yourself. If you are afraid to see yourself clearly, have the courage to see the truth. Don't be ashamed of who you are. You have a right to be the individual you are and may actually be somewhere *between* types. You are more than one, though one type generally is dominant. We are all interesting mixes. Take your time and, in the meantime, see the value in learning about others' types.

## All Good Things Come in Due Time

If you don't find your type immediately, remember that you are on a journey, and you will come to clarity of your type in time. Some people spend months, or even years, before the destination becomes clear. But when they do arrive, they can see why it took so long: they didn't *want* to see. Many people have all kinds of defenses in place. Some people lead with their wing or use another type to protect their own. Does your world accept your type tendencies? Some people lead with their secure or stress type, on the outside. And occasionally, a few people transcend their type and live in their growth type or become enlightened and more *typeless*, but that's rare. The journey, though, is what it's all about, actually. The destination will come in due time.

## Center Stage for Your Center

Let's type for your center! Are you a Head, a Body, or an Image type? Are you primarily about ideas and mental focus (Head type), down to earth and straightforward (Body type), or image and impression-oriented (Image type)? Image types generally are more concerned with dress, makeup, body build. Head types are learning-oriented and love information. Body types are more basic, going right to straight talk and honest answers. Once you've figured out your center, you're halfway home!

## About Those Subtypes

Self-Preservation, Social, or Sexual—whatever your subtype is, it causes you stress and occasionally grief. Whether it's security, social issues, or intimate relationship issues, once you determine your subtype, you can then see how it fits into the exact description of your type. If the generic and specific description fits, then you're on target. If not, don't stress over it. Usually a person has a primary subtype, and then a secondary. Of course, we visit all the three generic categories, throughout life, so maybe one is dominant right now. Just be aware that people can have very different subtype issues, and don't judge one as better or more important than another. They all are important but obsessive and it's not unusual to have some qualities of all three of your type's subtypes. If you can be sure of your subtype, however, it can help you determine your core type.

## Wings: It's All About Relationships

The wing is secondary to your core type. Sometimes your wing shows up in the thinking aspects of life, as much as in action. Wings can cause some major self-contradictions. You might hide or judge your wing. Accept it! It's part of you. Don't over-identify with anything. Just be honest. We all have contradictory parts. For example, a 9/8 can be assertive, controlling, or angry at times. This vies with the basic intention and self-image of the 9—peace! Your wing can provide you with strengths, as well as difficulties.

# Gender and Type

Theoretically, type isn't gender-specific, but gender still plays a role. For instance, running through the list of descriptors for the types, you might assume that all 8s are assertive, all 9s are accommodating, all 7s focus on fun, etc. But these are generalities. What do we know for sure about the sexes? That's definitely a loaded question.

There is an important difference between sex and gender. Your sex is how you were born—male or female. Your gender and the roles assigned to you because of that gender are culturally and socially determined. Women, on average, are more relationship-oriented than men, but most all 2s, 4s, 6s, and 9s, men and women, are relationship-oriented and other-focused, whereas 5s are less so. It doesn't mean relationship isn't important for 5s. It's just that the priority isn't a demand. Type 2 girls may enjoy playing with dolls, while 5 girls might prefer to use that doll for practicing their first aid skills.

**Lifelines**

Be aware of all the pressures and images of being a gender, personality, or race. Enjoy being yourself, whoever you are. The more *you* accept *you*, the more you can expand.

Typically men are more detached, use less relational language, and tease more without being aware of the effect on others. These are generalizations, stereotypes, even. Yet, within the core type, there is similarity, despite gender differences.

People often try to live up to gender expectations, even if they don't fit their real makeup. Whatever is true about *you*, is true. Gender expectations and reactions from those expectations can detour you from seeing the truth of your type. If you are an assertive woman or a sensitive man, so be it.

# The 7 Deadly Sins Plus 2

Enneagram theory states that each type has an emotional fixation with one of the deadly sins, named as such by Pope Gregory in the sixth century. Two extra ones have been added since then. This information is useful for typing. What sin (limited quality or flaw) drives you and prevents you from feeling balanced? Many people are unaware of their sin and tend to suppress it, even though it is obvious to others. Here are the sins associated with each type, and how to balance those sins:

- **1s' sin is Anger**—anger at what is. This is the judging mind, not accepting what is happening now but thinking there is a right way and a *should* of how things ought to be. Healing this comes with acceptance and serenity of what is *now*.

- **2s' sin is Pride**—pride and arrogance in thinking that you know what is best for people than they do, while hiding your own needs. The balance is humility in being human, acceptance that you don't always know what is best for others, and letting go of control.

- **3s' sin is Deceit**—the focus on image and the willingness to alter the truth to benefit your success. The balance is honesty and letting go of image. Instead of playing a role, be *real*.

- **4s' sin is Envy**—thinking you are missing something, longing for it, and feeling left out—wanting what others have. This longing, hurt, and pain prevent you from joining the human race, feeling good for others who have more than you (as you imagine), and seeing loss as normal. Healing is accepting what you have and enjoying your life.

- **5s' sin is Greed**—wanting to hoard your resources and not share them—whether your mind, your possessions, your time, your needs, or your expertise. You hide away, protecting yourself from engagement. The balance is generosity, sharing what you have and exposing your need to join others and be part of a community.

- **6s' sin is Cowardice**—you focus on fear and danger and problems and security, wanting others to protect you and give you answers. The answers are in you, not in others. Have the courage to be yourself, realizing you are the real authority. Have faith in life itself. Focus on what is good and safe.

- **7s' sin is Gluttony**—wanting to experience everything, not being satisfied with what is, always wanting more stimulation, constant excitement and experience. The balance is to be satisfied with what is and going for depth, as well as variety.

- **8s' sin is Lust**—going after what you want now and taking it. No patience or waiting. It's mine. The balance is to learn to wait, experience others' needs, as well as your own, let go of dominance and territorial control, allow weakness, and seek help.

- **9s' sin is Sloth**—not fully living life, falsely focusing on peace, avoiding conflict. The balance is to include yourself, be more self-centered, and not lazy with your own drive and goals. *Be* your individuality.

## The Least You Need to Know

- Your core type is who you are. Being your type is natural and requires no effort on your part.

- Learning your type helps you understand the truth of who you are.

◆ Friends, family, and intuition can help you discover your core type.

◆ Your subtypes and your wings add depth and complexity to your core type.

◆ Growth comes as a result of understanding the strengths and struggles of your type.

Chapter

# 13

# External Influences on Your Type: Family, Friends, Lovers, Culture, and Your Past

## In This Chapter

- ◆ All in the family
- ◆ Your extended family
- ◆ Power struggles and other issues in the family system
- ◆ Adding the cultural mix

Parents, siblings, grandparents, spouses, and other relatives—everyone who fits under the umbrella of *family* has a significant role to play in your life. Whether you are comfortable with yourself or feel ill at ease may be traced to the way family either accepted you or rejected you. Your personality traits may have been a good fit for the family mix or may not have meshed at all. Regardless of how this has played out in your life, type endures—a testimony to its power. Let's explore your family's role in your type development.

# Close to Home

Parents and guardians have the power to accept or reject you, frustrate you, support you, confuse you, teach you, and guide you. Constant models of personality uniqueness, their power to affect you, and the love and connection you have with them (or lack thereof), creates a tendency to either model yourself after them, try to please them, or rebel against them and their type. Sometimes it's a mix of all of the above.

Parents' type and maturity play a major role in a child's development. Operating from their type perspective, parents clearly can misunderstand you or try to guide you to their ways of seeing. Their conditioning and your responses have significant impact on your type development and self-esteem. Whether you are comfortable in your type or hide your type from them, or even from yourself, begins early in life.

## Mom

Mom almost always plays a key role in your upbringing. If Mom is more reactive in her type issues and not very nurturing, she's unlikely to accept your differences if they conflict with hers. She will try to guide or coerce you to meet her needs or standards or else will demand that you ask for very little. Or you may luck out and you and Mom will have a match of interests. Or you'll adapt. (Some types are more adaptive by nature—2s and 9s in particular.)

For instance, a Type 4 mom might prefer an intense, emotional, creative child—someone like herself. But she's just as likely to find the child a threat, a competitor, and too demanding—someone who overshadows her own needs. A 7 mom, who wants everything positive, will find a 4 child's painful feelings and need for attention frustrating—even though some of those feelings might be the 4 child carrying the 7's hidden pain. The 7 mom will try to cheer up the child or, failing that, will send her to her room. "Get a grip, kid. Be positive or be alone."

If parents can't work out their negative feelings regarding type differences, inner and outer conflicts ensue. When you don't understand your motivations, life is more frustrating and haphazard. Each type reacts in somewhat predictable ways. The more you understand your type, the more likely you'll like your type perspective, child or adult. Of course, some parents *want* a different type child—a 9 to soothe them, a 7 to entertain them and be positive. A Type 5 mom, who tends to be intellectual and detached, rather than emotional, struggles to understand why her Type 6 child is so afraid. It's hard for her to be reassuring, when she doesn't understand such fear.

Whatever the scenario, moms are frequently physically and emotionally exhausted by the demands of child-rearing. Moms either give too much, struggling with setting limits, don't give enough, or don't give what's needed. When we interpret their actions, we do this through the filter of our own type world. These interpretations can be totally off the mark.

If your mom relates to your type world, outside her own tendencies, you are fortunate. In this case, it's easier to be yourself and develop your type's best traits. For instance, if a 6 mom understands her 3 child doesn't want to look at dangers and problems, she won't overload the youngster with all the caveats. Meanwhile, she helps herself, too.

Mothers' types influence their children, so there is something of mother's type in all of us. Called a parental overlay, it's a quality of the type that flavors your personality uniqueness. It's nature! It's natural to imitate or *imprint* the parent—baby ducks follow momma duck. For some, the parental overlay and imprinting is considerable, for others, much less. A 5 mom might encourage a child to be more private and respect knowledge; a 6 will encourage checking the stove, being prepared; and so on.

## def•i•ni•tion

To **imprint** means to create a strong impression; to imitate or take on the qualities of another living entity.

Of course, there are many perfect or nearly perfect fits, in which Mom is delighted by the similarities or differences of her child. She likes what is familiar and also appreciates learning how to relate to what is different. She may realize those differences are exactly what needs developing in herself. Both mother and child experience and experiment with newness, change, and strengthening their bond.

Children are just as likely to react to Mom's type. They may first rebel and, later in life, be both attracted to and repelled by her type. We are drawn to the very things we don't like, in order to resolve conflict or come to terms with it. Love-hate romantic relationships are often a re-creation of some of the dynamics of a parent-child relationship.

 **Lifelines**

What you are repelled by is just as interesting as what you are attracted to. Explore and develop the opposite of your type, and you may be less repelled—perhaps even attracted!

# Dad

Dads and other strong male figures active in the family can have just as much influence in a child's life as moms. We took a general look at moms; let's check out some specifics with dads. How Dad communicates to a child, along with his emotional maturity, are crucial. Let's look in on a few dads and their children:

◆ **I'm right and you're not.** A Type 1 dad is helping his child with homework, but Dad's tone is harsh and critical and he insists there's a *right* way to do the assignments. He's teaching his Type 5 child more than he realizes. The child will decide that struggling alone might be the best way. This experience may also mark future interactions with 1s. Rather than developing a safe and helpful relationship, type is reinforced, along with type limitations.

◆ **You've got some great ideas—let's explore them.** "What have you decided to research for your school project?" asks another Type 1 dad. "I'm interested in your ideas." This dad is patient and supports the child's journey of self-discovery. His more relaxed approach, one which respects diversity, will make a world of difference for his child, who learns to view Type 1s with respect.

◆ **Of course you want to be team captain! I always was!** For this Type 3 dad, good grades are the bottom line and his children's only avenue for success is to capture positions of leadership—soccer team captain or head cheerleader. He might not understand that, to a 7 child, success is *in* the learning or the playing. His child may lead or finish first, at times, but it's not the main goal.

◆ **Never let them see you sweat.** A demanding and blunt Type 8 dad can terrify a 9 child. Dad might assume it's good to *toughen up* his child, but the 9 would be operating way outside his or her comfort zone. As a parent, you have to see what a child needs and what kind of push is appropriate. It has to be for the child, not the parent or parent's projection. Maybe the dad needs to learn to *soften* up.

◆ **Everything's going to be just fine—maybe.** A Type 6 dad can make a child secure on one hand and anxious on the other, exactly what the 6 father tends to feel—secure, insecure, secure, insecure, doubt, certainty, doubt, certainty … Don't overlay your world onto your child more than is necessary. Your type is a gift to the child; it shouldn't be a burden.

The parent may affect the child and type, but the child's type is independent of the parent's. The child will adapt to any situation, from the child's type level. Every type does this differently. 1s will adapt by trying to be good and correct; 2s by pleasing and being positive; 3s by winning; 4s by retreating to their feelings; 5s by detaching; 6s by fearing the unknown, seeking security outside; 7s by having fun; 8s by being in charge; and 9s by retreating to comforts and avoiding conflict.

## Siblings

Siblings sometimes affect a child as much as parents. Depending on whether or not a brother or sister is supportive, there can be more of a peer relationship than with parents, although some siblings bully and compete, while parents usually are supportive. Siblings vie for attention and validation from parents and other adults and peers, and type can play a major role in how that works. The Enneagram is an excellent tool to bring people together for some strengths trading.

If you are a 9 with an 8 wing (9/8) with two siblings who are 1s, that 1 influence may affect your type and be a part of you, though less than your 9 or 8 tendencies. A 1 brother, working hard to make good grades, might not understand a 9 or a 7 brother, who doesn't value hard work as much and just wants to have fun. How will they relate to each other? They could support and teach each other, envy each other, compete with each other, or distance themselves from each other. For example, the 1 could help the other's focus on a goal, and the 7 or 9 could help the 1 relax and play, thus helping with personal development and peer relationships. If you get thanks for what your type does, you generally value your type, yourself, and others to a greater extent; and your relationships with other types work much better.

If two siblings are the same type and their brother or sister is a different type, there could be problems. If the two are 8s and the other one a 6, the 8s could make fun of the 6's fear or simply see it as abnormal. Because 8s don't like fear, they can't stand to see it in others. If the 8s were knowledgeable about their type and had empathy, they could listen and offer reassurance, which the 6 would love. This would also make the 8s feel strong. A perfect fit. The 6 could even teach the 8s a healthy respect for fear, and the benefits of problem-solving.

### Lifelines

The Enneagram is a wonderful peacekeeping tool. Once you understand the types, and realize it's not so easy to change, there's more desire to try to change—less berating, and more and truer interaction and negotiation.

It's sad when kids fight; it's generally not beneficial. Even though competition has its place, every family system could benefit from more cooperation. Some family education in understanding personality differences, handling conflicts, and different ways of looking at life could head off a great deal of strife and confusion. Since people constantly misinterpret motivations, teaching the Enneagram in schools, social clubs, in counseling, in churches—wherever people gather, would help all brothers and sisters get along better!

The Enneagram helps in healing current or past sibling rivalries and differences. When you understand type differences, you can see how your siblings influenced you and why, value what was good, and learn from what was not so good. When siblings get together and talk about type and type influence it makes for better current relating and some good laughs, too.

## Like Parent, Like Child?

It's not unusual for children to be the same types as their parents; in fact, for each parent, the odds are greater than 1 in 9. It's less common to have everyone within the same family be a different type. Genetics plays a role, one that's generally considered greater than conditioning.

Variety is what makes family life interesting, and the way parents relate to their children is fundamentally important. If a parent values one child over another, siblings will notice and act or react to this. Competitive, protective, less than, better than—these peer relationships are greatly influenced by parental interactions with their children.

# Grandparents

Grandparents can also have a role in affecting your type, particularly if they're patriarchs or matriarchs of the family system. Family members can please, avoid, protect, or go against the grandparents. 1 and 8 grandparents, for instance, are probably self-willed, easily conflicting with themselves or others. They'd certainly be opinionated. A 6 grandparent would likely want the family to stay strongly bonded, particularly against perceived external threats, yet fears or a need to control (more likely from a counterphobic 6) could just as easily pull the family apart.

It's also helpful to understand your type from the perspective of how you responded to the type dynamics between your grandparents. One Type 9 had one set of grandparents with the Type 1 grandmother dominant over her 9 husband. Another set consisted of a 6 grandfather and 8/9 grandmother. The 9 child felt more aligned with the 9 grandfather than the 6, though he liked both. The youngster even worked for the 9 grandfather for a short while, picking pecans that his grandfather would sell. Being a 9 child, he adapted to what was expected and got along with everyone. The 6 grandfather felt relaxed around his grandson and liked his innocence.

**Warning!**

Whether families stay together or pull apart is in their make-up. The more tolerance for differences and learning, the more families stay together. The more pressure for conformity, the more they tend to pull apart.

What you've been taught by your grandparents can be significant. If you have a 6 grandparent who reinforced, "Be careful, plan for the future, and watch out for people," that will have a different influence than a 3 grandparent who pushed success, money, and having the best. Everyone in the family may feel a pressure to produce, look good, and have the symbols of success.

Entire families with a 3 background are successful, driven, competitive, and reach the top of their work or profession. The siblings may compete with each other. If your father is a famous 3, you must either succeed even more or drop the 3 success drive. If your grandparent and father were both 3s, then the pressure is often greater. John Sr., John Jr., John the III, etc. President of this, president of that … Your grandparents' cultural values often pressure them to teach you their way, and their values might run deep within you, whatever your type. American values emphasize Type 1 and 3, but depending on where you live, certain types are valued more.

# Aunts, Uncles, and Other Relatives

The extended family includes aunts or uncles, great aunts and uncles, and cousins, all of whom can influence your type development. The more the family agrees on norms, the more you'll either naturally fit those norms or rebel. If your type is not valued and if you are pushed to be different and even punished for being yourself, you can then protect yourself from being, showing, and producing the best your type has to offer, even to the point of wishing you weren't your type.

Certainly life is easier if you fit in or are encouraged to be yourself. Some families reward and value different types—sometimes even more than they do the norm. If you're a 7 in a family that's mostly serious, relatives might appreciate your less serious side. The more welcoming and accepting the family, the better it works.

Maybe a quirky aunt or uncle is exactly the one you want to relate to. A Type 4 might be emotional; a 5 an individualist, bright and mysterious; and a 7, zany with activities and a mind that runs a mile a second. Parents often want their children to be influenced by a variety of relatives—or at least the ones they approve of. The variety within families can be valuable.

Consider cousins, for instance. If you played with them frequently while you were growing up, understanding type differences would help explain why you felt you belonged or didn't:

♦ A 1 could be upset by others' bad behavior and debate whether or not to tell an adult.

♦ A 2 may help her cousins and be alternately satisfied or deflated, depending upon whether her help is wanted.

♦ A 3 is generally the star. Cousins who find themselves being compared to the 3 might come to dislike the 3.

♦ A 4 can be up to mischief and have hurt feelings or elated ones as a result.

♦ A 5, more solitary, studies ants and their building behavior and looks forward to chemistry sets or new computer games.

♦ A 6, trying to build alliances, is concerned about whether the group will include him (or not).

♦ A 7 plays practical jokes and finds fun everywhere.

♦ An 8 convinces the group to do something his way.

♦ A 9 goes along with whatever's being presented, though possibly with mixed feelings.

> **Lifelines**
>
> It's fun to let your relatives play out their types and not try to change or judge them. Just watch what's going on—it's better than TV! Enjoy them, be sensitive, and offer an occasional option, if they need help.

# The Whole Kit and Kaboodle

Family systems are complicated affairs, with much vying for attention, power struggles, and influence peddling. Sort of like international politics! People misread each other, because they are reacting to struggles with their own type issues. Also, self-esteem—or the lack of it—plays a big part in type and family relating. People adapt and control and are in pain or happy and sometimes they're a mix of all these. Your type affects others and others affect you. The more you understand your type, value it, and expand it, the better. The more you understand others, the more tolerance you will develop for their type and the more you can influence in less controlling ways.

Family systems, dominated by 8s with strong opinions and conflicts, have a great deal of energy. Sometimes this is a negative energy. Here's an example of a worst-case scenario: The husband/father/patriarch died. The widow (an 8) and the seven children were present at the funeral. Of the five sisters, three were 8s, one was a 1, and one a 9. There were two brothers, a 9 and a 7. People spoke out, particularly the 8s, while the others mediated or remained detached. The three 8s dominated and fought, even refusing to have a group picture taken. The 9s and even the 1 finally got the picture taken, after pleading for peace, with the 1 also judging the whole scene. The 7 took a back seat and found the scene amusing, though irritating. The family was obviously dominated by Body types (1, 8, and 9), and anger and territorial disputes marred the gathering. What a mess!

Think about some other family systems you're familiar with. How do they function in difficult times?

Here's what to look for in family systems:

♦ 1s probably encompass hard work, judgments, seriousness, commitment, and a desire for order.

♦ 2s compete to please, but there might be many hidden needs and people responding in various ways to giving, receiving, and pressure to be positive and happy.

♦ 3s pressure to perform and achieve and win. Those who haven't achieved, feel less.

♦ 4s have high intensity and want special connections; there can be misunderstandings and much emotion.

♦ 5s may be intellectual, probably not so affectionate, and not into small talk.

♦ 6s drive for security and protection, show loyalty, and have doubts, yet desire certainty.

♦ 7s can be fun and excited but may also avoid dealing directly with problems and pain. Everyone talks at once, subjects fly all over the place.

- ◆ 8s are independent and have power struggles but outspoken expectations. There's less that's hidden.

- ◆ 9s will have indirectness, not much definition, and some confusion, along with sweetness and agreeability.

It's rare to find a family system totally dominated by one type, though it's not unusual to have two types more dominant in a small family unit and several in a larger family network. It all works or it doesn't! The sad news is often that families repeat the same patterns that don't work. Type understanding helps immensely to change this for the better.

# Do a Family Type Tree

Here's a spin on the traditional family tree. It's fun and also highly informative. Sketch a tree with all its branches or use a template, if you happen to have one. Draw the family tree, with grandparents at the top. You can be elaborate, drawing lines or circles that radiate out or squares or triangles or rectangles. Have a blast!

As you write down your relatives' names, write down their types, as well. See how far back you can go. Even if you never knew your grandparents or great-parents, think of stories you may have heard about them and give their types your best guess based on those tales. Do the same for your parents, your aunts and uncles, your siblings and yourself, spouse, and children. When you've finished, examine your work and reflect on what you see.

Who you are today has been affected by your genetic and family history that can go back for hundreds of years. Be aware of that influence, but listen to your own desires, separate from what you've been taught. Then look at what you've been taught and what has been modeled and see if there is a connection or reaction to types in your past.

**Lifelines**

No system is just one type, though usually a few stand out as themes. If you are the different one, are you up for the challenge of being true to your type?

If you can't guess the type, guess the center (Head, Body, or Image) or narrow the core type to two or three. That provides information, also.

You might find a large percentage of your family system is one of the centers or has a disproportionate number of some types over others. One family tree had 21 out of 26 people as Body types (1, 8, and 9), with many issues around anger, boundaries, and territory. Someone else had a family tree that showed mostly Head types (5, 6, and 7) with much knowledge, but not necessarily personal sharing. Out of 35 people, 26 were either Head types or had a strong wing there!

# Cultural Types

Your racial and cultural origins affect your type and its value. Explore genealogy, history, and family stories that reference the deep mix of who you are. Many people in the United States, 3s or not, compare themselves to 3 values. Image, money, success, achievement, and hiding your failures become a focus, even if you aren't a 3. These values are reinforced in your upbringing, and then in advertising, job descriptions, and our reward system. If you aren't striving, accomplishing, or succeeding, then something is wrong. There's pressure to be something you aren't. "What do you do? Whom do you know? What have you accomplished?" If you measure success by learning, developing an interest, or working on some internal spiritual goal—those fields of endeavor that don't measure accomplishment with money, acknowledgement by others, trophies, and outer symbols of success, you may feel excluded from this love fest.

## Types and Countries

By no means are the majority of people of any country or region dominated by one type, but one type or a few types are often more valued as part of a country's history, focus, and tradition. This, of course, can change over time. The country or region you live in often has a type focus that may or may not fit your type, but will influence how people feel about type.

Here's a list of some countries and their corresponding type values. These are stereotypes, of sorts, and are meant to be taken as generalities, not set in stone. It's a bit tongue in cheek, to boot:

- Type 1—England—the King, the Queen, rules and order, traditions, strong beliefs, and propriety, though darker underneath with a history of imperialism and Victorian sexuality. Also, a touch of 5, with pursuit of knowledge.

- Type 2—Italy—the maternal side, eat more, emotional, positive, romantic, seductive. A bit of type 4, too! Drama, intrigue—the Borgias!

- Type 3—United States—show me the money, image, action, symbols of success, be *Number One*, materialism.

- Type 4—France—individuality; art; pursue me, if you want to; nonconformity.

- Type 5—Sweden—learning, travel, rational viewpoint of sexuality, privacy.

- Type 6—Germany—security, order, details, being victim and dominator.

- Type 7— Caribbean in general—festival, fun, pleasure, being outdoors.

- Type 8—Spain—bullfights, colonization.

- Type 9—Canada—socialized medicine, low crime rate, peace-oriented.

## The Least You Need to Know

- Our families play a significant role in how we come to view our core types.

- The influence of parents and relatives extends over the course of our lifetimes.

- Regardless of our upbringings, type remains a strong and dominant force in our lives.

- Exploring your genealogy can give you valuable insights into family types.

# Part 4

# How to Apply the Enneagram

How can you apply the Enneagram to your life? You can use the Enneagram every day to understand how to use your personal strengths to your best advantage. By identifying important growth areas for your type, you'll discover how to meet challenges productively and positively. Whether enhancing creativity, finding ways to enrich your life, or discovering the secrets to successful relationships, you'll find the Enneagram a down-to-earth, practical, and useful tool.

# 14

# Self-Knowledge, Growth, and Enrichment

## In This Chapter

◆ Unique growth paths

◆ Practice new behaviors

◆ Have patience with others

◆ Don't compare yourself to others

◆ Enjoy the gifts of your type

Each Enneagram type has a unique growth path. Growth in your type is a natural, evolutionary process, and most people of the same type will have a similar path. As you will see, what works for one type's self-development and fulfillment works in a very different way for another's.

In this chapter, you'll learn action steps and strategies for using the positive qualities of your core type, along with those of other types, to develop self-awareness and achieve personal growth.

# Personal Growth for 1s

You don't get to experiment and play as much as some other types. Your inner voice restricts anything that goes against your rigid guidelines and built-in punishments. The evolutionary path for 1s leads toward feeling more freedom to just *be*. For 1s to grow, take these steps:

1. **Play more.** Start to see play as part of your growth, rather than as a reward. Integrate play in your life. You might have to set aside time in your calendar! Take breaks, relax, laugh, and open up to following your desires—go for walks; be in nature; or pursue hobbies, sports, or other enjoyable activities. Even if you choose challenging activities—hiking, for example—resist the need to establish the *right* way to hike.

> **Lifelines**
>
> Imagine someone telling you that you are wrong and that there is only one right, correct, or best way. Would you be irritated? Imagine how others feel, when you do your version of that. Do unto others as you want them to do unto you!

2. **Accept that there is more than one right way.** Notice when you control for rightness and pay as much attention to others' viewpoints as to your own. Understand that everyone is on a different growth path, that they have varying maturity levels, and that people will never see everything the way you do, even if your viewpoint is truly enlightened. Notice any anger and irritation that show up for you. Don't act or speak out too strongly. Rather, state your opinion, if you must, but accept that it is *your* viewpoint, not *the* viewpoint.

3. **Be human.** You aren't perfect and aren't meant to be. Stop measuring yourself against unrealistic, overly idealistic standards. Pay more attention to what *you* need and want—not what you imagine or think *should be*. Make a daily list of what you *want*. Include small items, such as going for a walk or eating a particular sandwich or attending an event. Act on your desires, rather than feeling you have to earn them.

4. **Be positive.** Don't trust that your inner critic is on your side. Don't obey it as your guide. Instead of berating yourself for what you did or imagined was wrong, think more about what is positive, what you did right, and what worked out, however imperfectly. Think more about affirmations, rather than complaints. Throughout the day, examine your thoughts, have a positive vision, and focus them on what is working.

5. **Be open to pleasure.** Learn to see pleasure as part of life, not a reward. Open to any anxiety around gratification and relax around the fear. Have a good time, enjoy the five senses, and do activities you like. If you fear you'll go out of control, trust yourself that you can set limits. Sometimes you *need* to go out of control. Add music to your reading of e-mails, do a creative project, go on a pleasure cruise, savor exotic food, or attend a special entertainment. Spend at least 30 minutes a day focused on pleasurable or sensual activities.

6. **Relax.** The focus on doing everything right often makes you tight and rigid. Notice the tightening, when your perfectionist bent is in control. Breathe, release, and lightly scan your body. Relax what is tight! Anger, frustration, and irritation need to be released. Have some down time, chill out, drop those shoulders, and soften the upward lift of your jaw and forehead. Massage your hands and feet and head and ask someone for a back rub. Check in on yourself throughout the day and relax physically, mentally, and emotionally.

7. **Let go of being so serious.** Be silly. Laugh at yourself. Laugh with others. If it's not perfect, laugh, rather than scowl. See the humor in the complexity of life.

8. **Grow less.** Most people need to grow more, but not you. You improve yourself as a way of life, so allow yourself to *be*, rather than trying to change to be better. Change happens best with a relaxed attitude and an acceptance of what is happening now. Improvement means something is wrong, but maybe nothing is!

# Personal Growth for 2s

You focus on the positive. You think you know what others need and tend to be free with advice and gifts. You're quite open to fixing the flaws in others but might not want to see your own. Part of your growth lies in seeing your own limitations as normal and realizing that people often accept you more for your being human. For 2s to grow, take these steps:

1. **Let go of over-giving.** What are your own needs behind the giving? Do you want to be caretaker, instead of allowing others to take care of themselves? Ask permission to help. Let others ask and then give in a limited way. If possible, teach others to do for themselves.

2. **Identify your needs.** Admit you are needy sometimes! We all have needs. Make a list of every need and desire you can think of. Study each one and resolve to

feel good about it. How can you meet that need? Ask for what you want. If you notice you have shame around any needs, allow those feelings to be and relax around them. Don't blame others, if they don't instantly give to you.

3. **Spend time with yourself.** You are a special individual. Get to know yourself. Make sure you spend some time alone each day. Give to yourself. Take yourself to the movies. Sing to yourself. Get to know your preferences. Spend time doing some creative art project. Bring your mind back to you, when it focuses too much on others.

4. **Be more receptive.** You don't have to give to receive. Giving and receiving happen naturally. You have to be receptive, in order for others to give to you! Sometimes you feel embarrassed with too much attention. Relax and feel the joy or good feelings of others' appreciation and gifts.

5. **Let go of territory.** You can be quite territorial. "This is my person to give to and receive from." Be in control of yourself and not others! You don't have exclusive rights in the gifting area, so don't see others as a threat. If you control or cling too much, you might lose the very thing you want to keep. Talk to people, if you feel this is happening. Allow in some uncomfortable feelings.

6. **Watch out for seduction.** It's actually a compliment. You are pleasing and attractive, and you might get what you want but ultimately be displeased by it. Seduction can be emotional, romantic, or sexual. Make sure you want the attention you are seeking. Observe your tendencies to please and see how you get people wanting you. Sometimes you create expectations from others and get in deeper than you want. Don't promise more than you can give, or you'll feel you'll have to deliver.

7. **Say no.** You say *yes* easily but can have a hard time saying *no*. Practice saying it a few times each day. Don't just imply it—do a straight-up *No!* Implications cause confusion. Be direct. Agree to do what you can, as you can, and refuse to do more than that. It won't mean others will stop relating to you.

8. **Know that no one owes you.** You can create unconscious contracts, thinking that others will pay up later. Be careful with these fantasies. Don't give past the point of no return. If you feel others owe you, notice how you set this up and perhaps talk about it. Give in more limited ways, so that if others don't give back, you're okay. Be aware of your conscious or unconscious expectations. Keep a journal about it.

# Personal Growth for 3s

You're geared toward action. Practical growth for 3s is to balance toward being a human *being* rather than a human *doing*. Listen to your inner sense of what's right for you—don't just take on the image of success and stardom. You grow when you reflect, slow down, take in other's perspectives, and do what's right for you. *Inner* stardom. For 3s to grow, take these steps:

1. **Think about what you want before you act.** Even if you can do this project, do you really want to? Do you want to enter this profession? Do you want to be successful in this venue? Think about *you* as much as the success, money, or prestige. Make a list of your values and then take on projects aligned with them.

2. **Don't be afraid to fail.** Failure is a learning process that helps you be more successful the next time you try something new. Are you afraid others will reject you? Your true friends will stand by you, regardless of the outcome. Do you avoid starting projects for fear you may fail at them? Follow what feels right, and you will learn whatever there is to learn from the experience. Make a list of times you failed and how you grew as a result.

3. **Let go of image.** What? Impossible? No, necessary! Your image is not who you are, but it can protect you from seeing who you are. You are more than the image you project. Develop those inner qualities of honesty, patience, and kindness. Make a list of qualities you want to develop.

4. **Don't become a workaholic.** There's nothing wrong with working, but are you so obsessed with work that nothing else is happening? Are you making or supporting others to be workaholics? Examine if this is an addiction of sorts, and see if it's worth it. Look at other ways to be successful. Are you putting time into personal relationships? Personal interests? Be careful that the winning and achieving drive hasn't taken you over!

**Warning!**

A workaholic works or keeps busy compulsively, leaving little or no time to be alone and quiet. Workaholism is a cultural addiction, with so many addicts it's considered normal. In Europe, 6 weeks of vacation time is the norm, and many countries have a 35-hour work week, unheard of in the United States! Food for thought: at the end of life's ride, few have ever wished they could have spent *more* time at the office.

5. **Reframe your thinking so that cooperation fits into your definition of winning.** Do you have to be the star, or can you be a team player as well? Do you think others won't admire you if you aren't winning? Do others compete with you or reject you, because you always have to win? Do you compete unnecessarily? Think about ways you can cooperate and still win. Let others be stars, too.

6. **Examine what you want and make sure it's worth the effort.** Have to have the best? Do you drive a Lexus or BMW for prestige? Wear designer clothes? Have a fancy house? There's nothing inherently wrong with that. It's just that you might drive yourself too much, thinking you have to have the symbols of success. Focus more on enjoying what you have, rather than pursuing symbolic value.

7. **Find your balance.** Stressed to the max? If you enjoy the hard work and drive, great. What do you do to relieve stress? Make sure to exercise, take a few breaks, and have hobbies or activities that allow you to relax and "de-stress." If you thrive on overdrive, you might be driving some folks away.

8. **Make a to-be list.** Besides the goals on your to-do list, include experiencing feelings—sadness, fear, anger, insecurity, joy, comfort, peace. Just tap into them and be with them for a bit. Listen to what is happening inside, as well as outside. Items on your to-be list might include going for a walk, reading a book, smelling the flowers ...

# Personal Growth for 4s

You tend to intensify life, which makes you feel alive, but are you limiting yourself by not having a more balanced approach? Enjoy life and see it from a vantage point of acceptance and worthiness, rather than from rejection and abandonment. Focus on what is good. For 4s to grow, take these steps:

1. **Stay neutral—be objective.** It's terribly hard to be rational and not go to extremes, if you're a 4. When you are hurting, your thinking and surges of feelings are telling you it's the end, that everything is falling apart, and that you'll be abandoned. But hold steady. Things may not be as bad as they seem. Remember, you are not alone. Everyone experiences the fear of loss. Stay calm by focusing on your breathing, get some objective feedback, and take care of yourself. Be in your body and slow down. Don't catastrophize. Just because you think it, doesn't mean it's true.

2. **Focus on the positive.** The good often attracts more good. That may sound superficial, but it's helpful. In your mind and also on paper and in talking with friends, focus on what is working and good. Realize that a good outcome can come from a seemingly bad situation. Don't make it worse by focusing on what isn't working. Work at being objective. See what is true: the good, along with the bad and the ugly.

3. **Don't exaggerate.** From your lens, you're not exaggerating. You are feeling what you feel and it's intense. Highs and lows swing back and forth. Doubt your feelings at times—they may be more intense than what's happening in reality. If you are starting to amplify your feelings or personal story, catch yourself. Don't seek out extra attention by making your feelings much bigger than they are.

4. **Love yourself.** You want to be loved by a special other. At least partially *be* that special other. Love and value your emotions, your love for aesthetics and creativity. Lessen your demand that others love you. Nobody can take care of all the pain or loss now or from your childhood. Don't put that burden on others. Make a list of all your valuable qualities; all that's working and what you can provide to yourself. See yourself as special and unique, without needing others to do that for you. You're the only one on call 24 hours a day to be with you!

5. **Listen to others.** You do listen and are often highly empathic, particularly if someone has an intense decision or dilemma, but you sometimes become bored by those whose lives are mundane. Listen to others as much as you want to be listened to, and you will have the adoration you seek. Be careful to not repeat your story endlessly or demand unequal attention, or your friends may tire. Check in with them, on occasion, to catch this tendency.

6. **Create, create, create.** It's especially important to be creative—draw, paint, sculpt, sing, dance, write poetry or stories, animation, or film. You are meant to create and need avenues for expressing your inner self and desires onto the world. If not, you will implode and become too lost in your inner intensity. Go to art openings, galley shows, avant-garde theaters, and the like!

**Lifelines** _____

Spend time with creative pursuits and you will benefit, along with others, who can gain from your personal spin, pain, and joy.

7. **Get involved in social causes.** It's another way to move outside yourself. Be involved in animal welfare, social politics, global warming issues, vegetarianism, or whatever is real for you. It's wonderful to be with others who have similar concerns. Volunteer for Earth Day, hospice, or a women's shelter.

8. **Be friends with other 4s.** Only 4s can really understand the world of 4. Other 4s will appreciate your intensity and depth. Don't compete for attention, though. You can take turns. You can attend special events together, share your art, cry your eyes out, talk about life and death, show your passion, and go as deep as you want.

# Personal Growth for 5s

You grow by extending yourself beyond the mind. Reveal more of your personal self and live also in your body and heart. Feel your attachments to others and those feelings that well up inside. Express yourself in nonverbal ways. Give hugs, smiles, and your time. For 5s to grow, take these steps:

1. **Be more intense on the outside.** You tend to hold everything in and you speak in a neutral tone. Move away from fear and amplify your voice; show some emotion. You often feel more than you are expressing. Don't always keep your feelings in your head. Tell those special to you how much they mean to you. If you're upset, show it!

2. **Make some small talk.** You hate small talk, but if you want to connect with people, at times it's necessary. You can't always be learning something new and deep. You don't have to tolerate conversations about nails or hairstyles or this week's football scores for eternity; you can change the subject or ask for some more interesting information about nails and hairstyles and football, or just hang in there until the conversation changes to something more substantial. Talk more about what happened at the office, what you are thinking, what you had for lunch, and your next trip. Believe it or not, some people want to hear it!

3. **Feel your emotions as well as analyze them.** Sometimes it's just not possible for understanding to come first. You have to feel the emotions of sadness and fear and pain and anger and joy, before you can understand them. Ride with emotional surges and conflicting desires and allow the understanding to come after. Keep a journal about your feelings. You'll be more compassionate with others who focus on feeling!

4. **Be goofy, wild, silly.** It's not that you aren't funny. You have a marvelous, dry sense of humor but can be overly serious in your heady pursuits. Do stand-up comedy, laugh at silly child stuff, spend time with children. Allow your desires and body to guide you more.

5. **Learn from doing, as much as from reading or thinking.** It's valuable to learn by diving into an experience and knowing you won't be perfect at it. Jump in without knowing what you are doing, and give yourself permission to fall down if this happens. Let yourself be uncomfortable for a while. Don't think before you leap! If you want to learn to canoe, read a book or take a lesson or just rent a canoe and canoe. You're good at learning.

6. **Be in your body.** Sometimes you forget you have a body. Do physical activities or try sports. Typically, you favor individual sports, such as biking, or dual ones, such as tennis, but try a team sport, too—softball, kickball, volleyball. Try out different forms of physical expression—acting improvisation, yoga, or contact improvisation (a type of freestyle dance). Be more animated in your talk. People often misread you, because your hands or facial expressions don't correspond with your words. Watch an Italian film to get the hands and face moving!

7. **Go for love.** You heard right. You tend to spend a great amount of time alone. No need to change that, if it's working, but also allow yourself to enter the fray of relationships—attachment, belonging, risk-taking, pursuit, rejection. It's fun and painful and wonderful and confusing and exhilarating. Cry and laugh. You can only learn by doing. Date, be in a relationship, propose, sing, dance, and do the weird things that people do when they're seeking love or in love!

8. **Go for knowledge outside of knowledge.** Open up to the many ways of learning and wisdom—physical, emotional, spiritual, intuitive. Don't use just your mind to learn. Use music, theater, and mime to express parts of yourself that live outside rational frames.

# Personal Growth for 6s

You grow by not falling prey to your mind. Your mind gives information and intuition but often exaggerates the fear aspects of situations. Trust your instinct more than the fear. Get feedback and focus on the positive. For 6s to grow, take these steps.

**Lifelines**

If your attention is outside, scanning for problems, you forget to come inside yourself and notice that you actually might be feeling secure in yourself. Throughout the day, bring the attention back to yourself and you may feel better.

1. **Trust yourself.** People don't always have answers for you, and that includes authority figures. Listen to your own desires and intuition. Gather the research and believe in your own ability to make decisions. Learn from those who have experience, but don't look to them as having all the answers.

2. **Don't look for trouble where none exists.** You tend to be on the lookout for safety and security concerns, but when all is running smoothly, don't look over your shoulder for problems. Trust that you can enjoy the quiet, comfortable, or fun periods with nothing dangling over your head.

3. **Question if your fear is real.** You can be confused, because adrenaline still kicks in, even when dangers are only imagined. Get feedback from others about what is real to them. Of course, trust your intuition and evidence, but don't assume you always understand others' motivations or intentions. Don't jump to conclusions. Think the best, as well as the worst.

4. **Ask fewer questions and reveal more.** Yes, you heard it right. That's hard to do, as you tend to ask a million questions to gather as much information as possible to be prepared for all eventualities. Sometimes this is hard on others, and they feel barraged by probes or questions that ask too much. Reveal as much about yourself as you want others to reveal about themselves! Put your cards on the table. Answer questions and talk about yourself before you question.

5. **Assume the best.** Let's up the ante. Look for the best in every situation or at least in the part that is good. Don't throw out the whole thing because of a few flaws. Enjoy people for what they can be and don't expect the impossible.

6. **Make decisions.** Sometimes you wait until forever to make decisions, because you feel sure, then unsure, then sure, then unsure. Decide! Some doubt and insecurity are normal. You will seldom be 100 percent sure about anything. Learn as you go and correct along the way. Let go of some of the what-ifs. Catch yourself each time you use that language.

7. **Let go of the past.** You can hang on to past mistrusts of others. If someone apologizes and learns a lesson, let it go. The past is gone. Learn from it, but don't dwell on it. Choose more wisely in the future, if necessary. We all make

mistakes. Everyone, including you, sometimes lies or withholds. Be more forgiving. Look at what does work and have a full memory for everything, not just the bad.

8. **Release anxiety.** You need to let go of some of your anxiety. It's stressful to overly plan, over prepare, and imagine the worst. Do some relaxation techniques, such as breathing, visualization, yoga, meditation, or exercise. Take up some hobbies and get back into your body when your head is working overtime. Do some creative activities or use your head to figure out puzzles or word games.

# Personal Growth for 7s

You enjoy life, probably more than any other type, but you miss some opportunities by avoiding situations that might be painful or difficult. Some difficulties are worth it and some are not. Don't run from challenges that help you grow. For 7s to grow, take these steps:

1. **Go deeper.** Depth is as important as breadth. Many of you are deeper than the 7 stereotype of riding the surface of life. Enjoy all the variety and fun but don't jump too quickly to something new. Stay the course, even during moments of boredom or crisis, delving deeper into problems, and valuing learning and experiencing over a long period of time. Stick with skill development and relationships that are trying, but rewarding.

2. **Have fun but don't avoid pain.** Pain is nothing you have to search for. It will find you and often has some important lesson to teach. Maybe you need to learn something, slow down, choose more wisely, or just experience growth. Not everything can be fun or entertaining, though much is. Don't go to the next stimulating activity just to feel good and avoid when you feel bad. Feel your fear and your sadness. Self-reflect, get some help, and allow in all experience as valuable. Don't worry. You'll find a way to make difficulty a learning or fun experience!

 **Lifelines** _____

Everyone needs to learn and grow. Feedback from others is valuable. Be open to negative feedback about how you affect others. The positive is often held within the negative!

3. **Be patient.** You can be impulsive and it can get you in trouble. Think about consequences before you act. Slow down and see the whole picture. Don't go for the immediate high if, in the long run, it will be a low. Good things sometimes come in slow packages. Learn to wait, meditate, and go with the flow, as well as make the flow happen.

4. **Stay focused on what's at hand.** You tend to get distracted, starting a conversation and easily moving off onto tangents. Stick with the topic until it's run its natural course.

5. **Complete projects.** You often start things—the fun part—and don't necessarily complete them. Ride out the rough times and tough times and finish what feels important. Everything has highs and lows. Not everything can be new and interesting. Repetition and tedium are the norm, and for sure, things will get fun and exciting again. If worse comes to worst, hire someone to do what's more than you can handle.

6. **Accept that there is bad in the world.** Being the eternal optimist that you are has advantages, but there truly is corruption, people out to hurt others, deceit, and greed that you sometimes don't want to see. Face the reality of this, and don't put a positive spin on everything or avoid what's real. There are plenty of good-thinking and positive-sounding people who are crooks, thieves, and vagabonds.

7. **Know that positive thinking isn't enough.** Positive ideas and affirmations don't cure everything. You can affirm yourself from here to eternity, but if someone is starving, that person needs to eat, more than he needs to think positively. Positive thinking sometimes can be an avoidance of doing the nitty-gritty details. It's not the positive thinking that's the problem. It's thinking that thoughts alone are enough. Action, motivated by thoughts, is needed. Generally you do both, but don't give thoughts without offering practical answers.

8. **Listen to difficulties and open your heart to the pain of others.** Sometimes people need empathy more than quick solutions or good ideas. Listening is powerful in and of itself. Have empathy for the complex struggles of others and let your answers come from deep within. Evaluate yourself on listening skills and set goals to increase listening to problems without overly fixing.

# Personal Growth for 8s

You grow by counting to 10 and slowing down your actions and expressions. It's great to speak up but also perfect to hold back at times, quite a challenge for you. Your confidence is wonderful and don't let it hide the parts of yourself that are sensitive and uncertain. You can show it all. For 8s to grow, take these steps:

1. **Be powerful but gentle.** You are powerful and a model for directness and action. Sometimes, though, you come on too strongly and scare people away. Be gentler in your strength. Slow down, lower your voice, and connect to where others are—not just where you want them to be. Have compassion for their process—not what you think they should do. Get feedback from others as to how they experience you. Learn if you are balancing your strong presence with gentleness.

2. **See others as different.** Of course you notice differences, but you tend to think others should think and act as you do. You sometimes think others are an extension of yourself, and they aren't. Everyone is an individual with a very different life process. You don't have all the answers for how others or the world should be. Check with people to see if they feel you are relating to them personally or are being controlling and simplistic in your responses. Let go when you are trying to control.

3. **Don't overdo.** You tend to eat, drink, and be merry; overworking, overplaying, overextending yourself. Find the right balance for you. Notice tendencies to not get enough sleep or have too much pleasure, with consequences that might not be worth it. Keep a log of your activities and set some limits for yourself. It's good to know your limits.

4. **Be sensitive to others.** You love honesty and say or blurt out what you think. Honesty needs to be tempered with sensitivity. Comments need to be measured for consequences. Statements that poke fun at or highlight weaknesses, hurt people. Apologize. People will avoid you if they perceive you as too gruff for their taste.

> **Insights**
>
> I've received lots of feedback to back off and wait before I blurt things out. I've learned to be quieter, pick my battles, and see that others have good opinions. —Sandy, 70, a Type 8

5. **Show your vulnerable side.** You aren't as tough as you seem. The more you show some of your insecurity, fear, doubt, weakness, and vulnerability, the more others will trust you. Others will feel safer with you, when you aren't so overly

confident and cocky. Most people will accept you more and know you've been afraid to expose your softer side. Think of times when you have done this and people accepted you. Vow to do this even more, in the right circumstances.

6. **Be a follower.** You are a natural leader, but don't feel you have to take charge every time. Just let the process unfold. Others may need to lead in their own style and you might take that opportunity away if you take over too quickly. Be part of the gang, without having to lead it. Offer some advice, but don't think you're always right. Be more in the middle and less dominant when necessity isn't calling you to be in charge.

7. **Live and let live.** You generally let go easily. You express what you express and it's gone. But if you feel others have betrayed you, you may go for revenge and make some enemies. Understand that people may be going with their preferences, more than they are betraying you. When this is the case, let it go.

8. **Temper your anger.** You tend to express anger easily. Realize that your anger might be masking other feelings—hurt, fear, pain, sadness. Be in touch with that softer and more vulnerable side. You are as sweet as you are tough, so let that side of you show more. If people remember your quick anger, they may hold back from showing you parts of themselves, to your loss. Don't expect others to be as direct as you can be. It's just not in their nature. Ask others how they feel about your anger. Risk sharing what's behind it.

# Personal Growth for 9s

You grow when you realize it's okay to have a self. You have a right to be the individual you are and that means facing any consequences to that individuality. You want to be liked or at least not disliked by everyone, and that is a difficult task. Accept conflict, misunderstanding, and nonpeaceful experiences as part of the mix. For 9s to grow, take these steps:

> **Insights**
>
> When I go into action, I feel better. I obsess for days or try to avoid an action, than when I do, it's easier than I think.
> —Amanda, 23, a Type 9

1. **Be more assertive.** You let people run roughshod over you and tend to go along to get along way too much. Some people will take as much as they can get if you don't speak up, define your terms, or say no. Take an assertiveness class and practice speaking up. People will often feel more comfortable with you when you can define who you are.

2. **Clarify what you want.** You tend to stay a bit foggy about what you want and what your goals are. Think about that and state what you want clearly and directly. If you are vague, others will relate vaguely to you. Set goals and don't get distracted by secondary motivations. Don't clean up the tool shed to avoid talking to someone. Talk, then organize the tool shed as a reward!

3. **Go into action.** You tend to think about what you want and then dismiss it. Sometimes you don't clarify, because you are afraid to go into action. Things don't get done, unless you do them. Make the call to find out the information. Find out when the check is supposed to arrive. Make no assumptions. Talk to the person in charge. Don't procrastinate. Usually, the task you need to do is easier than your imagination thinks it will be. Make a to-do list right now and do the first task on that list!

4. **Focus on reality rather than imagination.** You tend to be in your imagination, hoping, wishing things were different. Pay attention to what is happening and don't go into some wish fulfillment of what might happen. When you express what you want and work toward having it, you find out what is real. You tend to hope something positive will happen, but it won't, if you don't go into gear. Get to first base to get into the game.

5. **Let go of comfort.** You love comfort, the known, certain traditions. That's nice, but things change, and there are new challenges. Stay abreast of what is current and live in the now, not the distant or recent past. Let it go, as you tend to hold onto it. Enjoy your comforts—food, your favorite TV show, comfortable clothes, your hot toddy, but be open to new comforts. Adjust and make changes to the changing world. Make a list of the changes you need to respond to.

6. **Redefine yourself as nice, but also tough.** It's great to be the sweet, kind, nice person you are, but unfortunately it doesn't always work to your advantage. Understand there is aggression in the world and you must respond in some way. Fight for justice and speak out. Be a protestor and confront situations that are against your values.

7. **Accept your anger and face conflict.** You tend to avoid conflict at all costs, but conflict is natural and can help in personal development. The more you clearly define yourself, the less conflict you may have with others. People get more upset with you when you are unclear, indirect, and angry under the surface. Accept anger as a natural emotion that helps define how you feel, what you want, and what you won't put up with. Be your true self, not your pacifying self, and you'll feel more whole. What do you need to face today?

8. **Be peaceful in a world of war.** It's fine to be peaceful, and you are an ambassador for unity, caring, acceptance, and love. You have to be that, though, in the world as it is. Do your part to make the world peaceful. Be a mediator and help others with tools to deal with differences and conflict. Generally, you accept differences easily but also need to accept that many people are self-centered, rather than other-centered. It is just as valid to be self-oriented, and you need to be more that way. See your own ego and accept it!

# Be All Nine Types

Most people like to stay in their comfort levels and are threatened by too much change, but change is part of life. As you begin to use the growth tips for your type, have compassion for others as they work through their own growth process. You are all nine types, at various times. Genetics and conditioning are strong pulls. What's easy for you is a struggle for another and vice versa. Let go of *should* and never assume you know what is best for someone else.

Attempt to make the best qualities of each type part of your type. Begin by picking one or two qualities to imitate. It will usually feel awkward to do behaviors foreign to your type. Don't feel you are being a sham. You are just trying on new ways of being. Walk with wobbly legs for a little while. You have nothing to lose and everything good to gain!

Affirmations are useful as you begin the process of positive change. In Appendix D, you will find affirmations specifically designed for your type. Locate your type, read each affirmation, and focus on one, until it becomes part of you.

## The Least You Need to Know

◆ Each type's growth path is unique.

◆ To develop yourself, imitate the best qualities of each type.

◆ Have compassion for the growth struggles of each type. As you know, growth is difficult.

◆ Have patience with your own type growth and add a touch of humor to your journey.

◆ Understand that real growth takes constant practice. While you learn, enjoy the best your type has to offer.

# Chapter 15

# Romantic Relationships

## In This Chapter

- ◆ What works for you doesn't work for me
- ◆ Love challenges: how to keep the spark alive
- ◆ Turn-ons and turn-offs
- ◆ How to relate to each type
- ◆ Type and subtype combinations, from mellow to intense

Want to make your current relationship all that it can be? The Enneagram can help you understand the very different perspectives from which the nine types see love and romance. In this chapter, you'll find out what the magic spice is for each type, the reasons why that is, and what you can do to maximize your chances for romantic success. You'll also discover which couple combinations work—and which ones take some work!

## Romance for Thee and Me and He and She

Ah, romance! We think we understand why we're attracted to those who share our values and beliefs and whose backgrounds are similar to ours. It feels good to relate to what's familiar. We are also drawn to the unfamiliar—it's tantalizing and intriguing. The pull of both the familiar and unfamiliar may reflect unhealed wounds from our childhood, reconstituted by our attraction to this new person.

The Enneagram can explain this mystery! None of us is complete, and so we're attracted to those who can offer that which is missing. Together, sometimes, we make a complete person. Whether your desire is to make a current relationship better, increase your chances of success in that new relationship that may be just around the corner, or understand your past *affaires de coeur*, let's see what the Enneagram has to offer.

# Type 1: Perfect Love

In a romantic partner, 1s require honesty, commitment, and shared values (or, at least, values 1s can respect). If you love a 1, remember that improvement, high quality, and integrity are part of the package. Developed 1s can accept differences and imperfection. Undeveloped 1s are rigid and critical. Fall for developed 1—otherwise, prepare for a critical analysis and low grades.

## How Romance Works with 1s

What do you want? Just like everyone else, you want the ideal partner. For you, that means someone with good character—someone who is responsible and can make good choices. You hope to find someone with the courage to stand up for what is right. You like order, neatness, and attention to detail. Of course, you also want romance, gifts, special moments, and sensual delight!

What don't you want? You're turned off by mess and unkempt or slovenly behavior. Watching your partner peel a potato the *wrong* way can cause your tension to build with every scrape of the peeler, until you can't stand it anymore! You give feedback to improve your partner but accepting criticism in return is sometimes difficult. You are already too critical of yourself and too aware of your flaws.

Romantic satisfaction comes as a result of your partner acting with integrity, making some effort, showing appreciation for all that you do, and encouraging a balance between having fun and pleasure and structure and rightness. Pleasure is the logical and acceptable outcome of a good relationship. You've earned it!

> **Insights**
>
> I've worked hard not to nag about what I want my boyfriend to fix around the house. I praise him, try to present my suggestions in a noncritical way, and allow him time to do it his way. Since I've been less critical, he's doing a lot more!
>
> —Sandy, 45, a Type 1

## The Do's and Don'ts of Relating to 1s

◆ "Do what's right!" the 1 says. Right by whose standards? Get that clear up front.

◆ Do speak up for yourself. Get those differences out in the open now, or you'll be trying to live up to the 1's *impossible* standards.

◆ Don't lie to a 1. Ever.

◆ Do be on time. Explain why you're late. Don't make tardiness a habit.

◆ Do follow agreed-upon guidelines. Discuss changes beforehand.

◆ Don't expect special praise. 1s assume that doing what's right is expected. If you want praise, set the example by praising the 1.

◆ Do accept anger, irritation, and differences as normal. Model that you can be irritated and still be in love.

◆ Don't get upset, when your 1 wants to improve you—telling you how you should dress or how to do a task the right way. Affirm what is right for you.

◆ Do encourage 1s to enjoy life without having to earn the pleasure!

# Type 2: The Gift of Love

2s need you to acknowledge their attractiveness. This is an image type that likes to present well, so if you don't notice, you'll be in the doghouse or lose points. Compliment the new haircut or dress. 2s want a positive presentation from you, too. Make your wants known, and you're likely to get what you want. If you want something different, express this *only* with an optimistic perspective. 2s always try to please, but only if you appreciate *them*.

## How Romance Works with 2s

2s like drama, so don't be humdrum. If you like something, say so with zeal. 2s love personal praise. Be enthusiastic and thankful. Romance your 2 with cards, notes, carriage rides, candlelight, and flowers. Be creative and personal with gifts. Small gifts or large gifts—it's truly the thought that counts. 2s receive and bestow affection equally well! Some 2s may be shy, so don't go overboard with attention, but other 2s love it, so don't stop! Find out which one is your 2!

## The Do's and Don'ts of Relating to 2s

◆ Do appreciate the attention 2s give you but set some loving limits, if needed, because 2s can over-give. "Thanks for the attention, but it's too much for me. Can I give you some attention? What do you need?"

◆ Don't take a 2 for granted. Hurt and anger will be the response.

◆ Do actively give to a 2, without being asked. If a 2 withdraws, it's a clear sign of upset. Swallow your pride and ask what you did (or didn't do!).

◆ Do ask a 2 to talk about needs and feelings and be receptive to what you hear. Help your 2 be direct.

> **Insights**
>
> I like personal gifts. You can't give to me if you don't know me, and the gift reflects that. One of the worst gifts I ever received was a clock radio, practical but totally impersonal.
> —Laura, 39, a Type 2

◆ Do ask for what you want. 2s can get over-involved with others' needs. Tell them how much you love how they give, and they'll redirect toward you.

◆ Don't assume a smile means your 2 is okay. Dig deeper, ask how things are going. Go out of your way. Show that you care.

◆ Do affirm what's wonderful more than what's not so great.

# Type 3: The Look of Love

3s love by giving you the results of their achievements and supporting you to be successful, too. They love praise. Remember, 3s are image types, so being the attractive image they want, works. Dress well, work out, be efficient, fit the picture. Achieve on your own and don't compete with their success; support it.

## How Romance Works with 3s

3s might not give you the time and attention you want, because they're working overtime. Often this is to satisfy your material needs and provide both of you with the best. Don't interrupt 3s in the middle of a project, or if you must, at least be clear what it is you want. Tell them the goal first and then talk. Action-oriented, they have limited time! Set up ways for them to win, as they hate to fail. Appreciate them for that, but please or seduce them to focus on personal and relationship needs, as well.

Tell them that's success for you. It might seem manipulative, but 3s love to give in ways that produce a result. The result you want here is happiness for both of you.

## The Do's and Don'ts of Relating to 3s

♦ Do appreciate how you benefit from their success drive.

♦ Do encourage them to have fun and a life beyond work and projects.

♦ Do be like a 3. Be assertive, have goals, and go for what you want.

♦ Do help them to accept feelings that *interfere* with success.

♦ Do demonstrate that it's normal to feel down or sad or have feelings of failure, from time to time.

♦ Do speak the language of action. What projects can you do together?

♦ Do come up with ideas that increase speed and efficiency.

♦ Don't complain, without a definite solution or alternative to make things better.

♦ Don't go on and on. 3s want to move. Get to the point.

# Type 4: The Drama of Love

4s love romance with a capital *R*. They love special attention and special moments, dramatic presents, praise, fun, shared pain, being personal, and even authentic conflict—if it resolves itself. Intensity is okay. What's not allowed? Withdrawal, boredom, too much attention on others. 4s soak up love and appreciation. They can endlessly process their inner life, so set some limits. If you're a really good listener, they might set natural limits.

## How Romance Works with 4s

4s long for the ideal lover who will carry them to new heights. They want to be pursued and chosen and be made love to in unique ways. It's not that others wouldn't choose this, too, but 4s want a steady diet of attention. They love beauty in all forms, so environment is critical. Ambiance and presentation in a restaurant are as important as the food. 4s work at looking exquisite or unique and want a payoff. Their feelings can run the gamut. They want you to be and look special too, though some 4s want your steadiness and consistency.

## The Do's and Don'ts of Relating to 4s

 ◆ Do sing to them, underneath their balcony, late at night.

 ◆ Do whisk them away to a special private beach with a homemade lunch packed in a wicker picnic basket.

 ◆ Do take their clothes off torturously slowly or rip them off quickly!

 ◆ Don't talk in an even tone of voice. Show some passion about your feelings.

 ◆ Do *express* how you feel. Show, don't tell.

 ◆ Do go to exotic places—jazz brunches, special art openings, theater, *Cirque du Soleil*, a ball.

 ◆ Don't get in a rut!

 ◆ Do share your vulnerability.

 ◆ Do be consistent and reliable and follow through on your commitments.

**Lifelines** _____

Typically 4s want the new and different or unusual. The familiar is okay, as long as there's a new twist. Trust your intuition. Let your heart guide you in pleasing a 4. Don't worry about being too dramatic—it's not possible!

# Type 5: Thinking About Love

5s can do the romance dance like everyone else but may be more cautious at the onset. They are concerned about their private space and over-merging, wanting to make sure a healthy dose of individuality and privacy remains intact, over time. Ah, nothing like a stimulating, intellectual discussion or reading to each other or watching a sunset together as hallmarks of foreplay.

## How Romance Works with 5s

5s can be hot in bed, with all that repressed, sublimated physical energy, but may have a difficult time sharing their personal desires and feelings. This can underheat the flames of romance, though many enjoy the mystery it creates. Let 5s know that you appreciate personal information, however mundane, along with secret thoughts and fantasies. Feed the 5s some juicy bits of knowledge, be excited by their intellectual pursuits, and they're yours!

## The Do's and Don'ts of Relating to 5s

♦ Don't be too irrational. Objectivity is a turn on!

♦ Do debate. A bit of the skeptic can light some fires.

♦ Do keep some privacy and independence, as 5s like some of that.

♦ Don't expect words all the time. 5s often like sharing events or music, eating together, canoeing together.

♦ Do start the fire. 5s tend not to initiate, but this doesn't mean they aren't interested.

♦ Do take advantage of 5's willingness to listen, as 5s can listen more than they share of themselves. Start with them listening, and maybe they'll join in.

♦ Do ask for what you want, as 5s are often task or project-oriented. Be specific.

♦ Do expect a 5 to reflect on requests, as thinking and integrating must happen before responding. It'll be worth the wait!

 **Lifelines** _____

You can know a 5 for many years and still be discovering personal information about them. They often under-report and under-express who they are on an emotional and private level. 5s, you are much more interesting than you might appear. Unveil your mystery.

# Type 6: The Practical Lover

6s are practical about romance and the attention is on what might go wrong. Are you the person I can count on? Trustworthy? Honest? Committed? Will you answer my questions? Will you get tired of all my questions? Will you stick around, even if I am doubtful? If the other person can satisfy these requirements, relaxation and romance are likely.

## How Romance Works with 6s

What's the big turn-on for 6s? Reliability. Romance happens best when everything's out in the open and your love interest or partner still sticks around and follows through on promises. 6s can even handle some inconsistency, if you are honest about it and explain! Be real. Of course, go on vacations, make special meals, be entertaining, and show your heart, too.

## The Do's and Don'ts of Relating to 6s

♦ Do realize doubt might remain, for the 6, as part of the mix, no matter how good the relationship. Just let that be. It's not personal.

♦ Do reassure the 6 that worst-case scenarios are improbable. Have the 6 share concerns. You'll be a hero or heroine for listening and reassuring.

♦ Do face challenges together. Live through them to increase bonding.

♦ Don't minimize 6's fears. 6s—Face your fears and also focus on the positive.

♦ Do encourage being in the moment, as much as preparing or planning for the future. See what is real. Look around for what is okay and feel secure for *now*.

♦ Don't over-plan. Be more spontaneous and accept what happens. Open to the excitement of the new.

♦ Do let go of bad memories. Remember the good. Enjoy what is.

♦ Do show self-confidence, as 6s want to feel secure.

> **Warning!**
>
> A 6 on her honeymoon expressed her worries about details: money, getting to breakfast on time, concerns about the hotel. The 3 husband reached his limit and said, "Can you just shut up for a minute?" It's difficult to hear 6's over-concerns. Trust that things will work out, even if you are late for breakfast. After all, you're on your honeymoon!

# Type 7: Love Is Fun

7s have the energy for fun and interesting activities. This is a great fire-starter for romance. Enjoy yourself and let the enjoyment show on your face. Look at the bright side and put new spins on the familiar. 7s don't like overly focusing on the negative, so that will put the fire out. Freedom is important, so express yourself, with options in mind.

## How Romance Works with 7s

7s want to have a good time. Pleasure is in and pain is to be avoided, if possible, though developed 7s can face the music. 7s can easily come up with mental or practical solutions. Things can change quickly. If this experience isn't turning out, let's try another. 7s can bolt, if they feel trapped over a period of time. Feeling free creates the opportunity for more commitment.

## The Do's and Don'ts of Relating to 7s

- ◆ Do brainstorm alternatives.

- ◆ Do be spontaneous. Last minute changes are fine.

- ◆ Do choose excitement over low-key options. Be playful and humorous.

- ◆ Don't overly process. Use a positive focus to solve problems.

- ◆ Don't set too many limits. There is no limiting for 7. Always have options.

- ◆ Don't pressure for commitment or owning mistakes. Rather, present your version and let the 7 think about it.

- ◆ Do trust for a positive outcome, no matter what's happened.

> ### Insights
>
> No dog collars on me. On the other hand, I desperately need grounding. Speed and intensity spark me. I prefer being with 1s, 3s, 7s, or 8s who have a strong energy. So hard for me to be with the slower energy of others.
> —Joy, 42, a Type 7

# Type 8: I'm on Top

8s want to be in charge. Typically they are strong pursuers in a relationship and generally up front with their desire and attraction. They will lavish much attention on you. 8s tend to want you to adapt to their lifestyle or desires and won't overly alter themselves or their lifestyle to accommodate yours. They are outspoken, passionate, and physically present.

## How Romance Works with 8s

8s are direct and will go out of their way to bring you onto the map of their life. If you are looking for subtleties, this is not your type. Sex? Let's speak frankly! Expectations and expression of wants are easy to talk about. What do you want and can you meet it? Fun, laughter, and good times, with energy to burn. Intensity, both physical and emotional, adds to the relationship. Let's fight! Making up is just as intense.

## The Do's and Don'ts of Relating to 8s

- Do be honest and direct about what you want and confront your partner, when necessary.

- Do accept and relish in the pleasure of satisfying your desires. Express direct appreciation when your 8 fulfills them.

- Do tell jokes, enjoy yourself fully, be your full-out self, and be open to receiving energy from the 8.

- Don't try to control your 8. Say what you want, but easy on blame, demands, or telling an 8 what to do.

- Don't overexpose your 8's vulnerability. Encourage your 8 to express that softer side.

- Don't do whatever you want, without letting an 8 know what you are up to. 8s want to be independent but worry if *you* are, in ways that leave them out. They prefer to know everything.

- Do create some wild times, the more unusual the better.

# Type 9: Easy Rider

9s prefer a softer approach to romance. It's not that they're not attracted to more intense types, like 4s and 8s; they often are. But after a while, they need some peace and quiet or they get overloaded. Many other types are drawn to 9s' gentler, accepting approach. 9s are initially easy to be with, but perhaps not as attractive later on, if not enough self-will comes forth. Too much peace is a sedative, not a stimulant.

## How Romance Works with 9s

Generally, 9s don't like overbearing or pushy people. 9s like comfort and can't sustain too much anxiety or pressure. At the same time, 9s learning to be more assertive often attract assertive types. Also, assertive or anxious types are drawn to the calming, laid-back attitude of the 9s. Unless the opposites can see and value the need for each other, over time, conflict and withdrawal are inevitable. Owning your opposite or hidden side ensures more acceptance of the other. Easily satisfied, 9s love when others support 9s' individuality. 9s will adore anyone who receives their attempts at assertiveness.

## The Do's and Don'ts of Relating to 9s

♦ Do communicate to a 9 in a gentle, nonabrasive tone. Tone is much more important than content.

♦ Do support the 9 to be assertive and more direct, knowing that it's difficult for 9s to even know what they want.

♦ Do be positive, though 9s are great supporters of people in pain and struggle. 9s are nurturers.

♦ Don't push or confront a 9 too much, or you'll meet with withdrawal, stubbornness, or a blown gasket. The pressure builds!

♦ Don't assume a 9 has an agenda or goal. Help 9s clarify what they want.

♦ Don't expect the 9 to be dramatic. 9s typically make a molehill out of a mountain. 9s underplay their issues. Encourage a 9 to talk about what's uncomfortable.

♦ Do praise, nurture, or give to a 9. You will be rewarded, as 9s are receptive and deeply appreciate any positive attention.

> **Insights**
>
> I am so concerned about conflict that I don't express myself strongly, fearing another's upset or rejection of my need. Feels like I have to yell or be dramatic to get my point across.
> —Jean, 29, a Type 9

# Type Combinations: Creating the Right Mix

If you are in the beginning stages of a relationship, some conversation and observation will help you learn just where your romantic interest is on that all-important journey of personal growth. Has this person developed qualities outside his or her core type or worked to change some of its limiting or dysfunctional aspects? Undeveloped people of each type present challenges. They will, without question, do what you would expect of their type:

- ◆ 1s will criticize you, because they're self-critical.

- ◆ 2s will over-help you and expect something in return.

- ◆ 3s will be successful but have little time to devote to the nuts and bolts of relating.

- ◆ 4s will be emotionally flailing, projecting abandonment.

- ◆ 5s will be withdrawn and unavailable.

- ◆ 6s will be paranoid and see the worst.

- ◆ 7s will be high on excitement and tuned out from reality.

- ◆ 8s will dominate; you will be an extension of their wants.

- ◆ 9s will be so undefined you can't find them.

With development comes all manner of wonderful things:

- ◆ 1s show understanding and accept differences.

- ◆ 2s both give and receive with little or no expectations.

- ◆ 3s are successful, loving, and available to share more and prioritize relationships.

- ◆ 4s find balance and equanimity.

- ◆ 5s become emotional and personal, as well as competent.

- ◆ 6s are courageous and secure.

- ◆ 7s are focused, deep, and unafraid of difficulties.

- ◆ 8s are firm, yet open to revealing their inner feelings.

- ◆ 9s become direct and spacious in their perspective.

# Some of the Easier Couples Combinations

Some relationship combinations tend to be easier than others. Development plays an important role here, as well. Undeveloped versions of any type are difficult to relate to. They tend to not take personal responsibility, are demanding, and not open to change. This puts great demands on others and makes it difficult to be your natural self. As a consequence of this, you will withdraw, limit yourself, attack, or go else-where.

Any combination can work well, particularly if a couple works to understand and enjoy each other's differences. Generally couples that have an easier time relating may have a more rewarding relationship, but it's just as true that couples that struggle more may grow more, particularly if they value and respect each other. Many couples love strong differences. There's no right way to do *coupleness*.

The easier combinations tend to be the ones with some strong similarities, as well as differences. A Type 2 and 3 couple is a good example of this. The 2 and 3 are both image-oriented, savor success, have a positive focus, and like validation—the 2 from pleasing others and the 3 by pleasing both self and others in ways that produce suc-cess. 2s can easily support 3s to be successful. This benefits the 2, who reaps the rewards of 3's success; it also benefits the 3, who feels the 2's support in giving, mak-ing network connections, looking good, and praising the 3. They are different, yet similar enough, particularly if the 3 has a 2 wing and the 2 a 3 wing: very similar with a touch of difference. Their worlds make sense to each other.

Any adjacent numbers with an exchange of wings can work fairly well. For instance, a 4 and 5 couple can expect challenges, but a 4 with a 5 wing and a 5 with a 4 wing can work more easily.

5s and 8s often do well together. 5s are objective and withdraw, to think before they act, quite different from 8s' tendency to be impulsive with decisions. 5s admire 8s' directness. This is refreshing for 5s, who spend too much time thinking before act-ing. 8s learn from 5s' thoughtfulness, research, and patience.

Other combos that might work more easily than others include 1-5, 1-6, 2-2, 2-7, 3-7, 5-5, 5-7, 5-9, 6-9, 7-8, 7-9, and 9-9. With so many factors involved, including sub-types, family background, and, of course, development, predicting couples success cannot be an exact science.

## Middle-Range Relating

Most couples find themselves in the middle range. The same combination may be fine for one couple and not so great with another. It just depends how your chemistry works together. It often has to do with past type associations, your developmental process, past experiences, subtypes, wings, and other differences the Enneagram doesn't touch. For instance, let's look at a 1-7 couple. The 1 longs to have permission to play and let things be, like the 7; and the 7 balances by being more serious and focused, like the 1. They might support each other *in* their differences, or could torture each other *with* their differences. The 1 could criticize the 7's lighter side and the 7 not want 1's more serious and evaluative nature. On average, this combination works well over time. Middle range relationships might include the 1-2, 1-3, 1-7, 1-9, 2-4, 2-8, 2-9, 3-3, 3-5, 3-8, 3-9, 4-3, 4-5, 4-6, 4-8, 5-6, and 6-8.

## Same-Same Couples

There is a real advantage in being with your own type. You will probably understand each other and speak somewhat the same language; however, your own issues are mirrored in your partner, so you could experience double vision. Some same-same couples compete with each other:

- 1s might be scolding and have different values, but it's more likely their values will be the same.

- 2s could help each other and be appreciative.

- 3s can either compete with each other or work together for the same goals.

- 4s often blow each other out of the water with too much intensity or competition for attention, though, when developed, they can support and understand each other.

- 5s often do well together with knowledge-sharing. They feel safe together, respecting each other's space.

- 6s could outdo each other with fears or protect each other and be empathic with concerns and mutual goals.

- 7s can have a blast together but could have difficultly staying grounded.

- 8s can vie for power.

- 9s generally work well but need to support each other to be assertive and individually oriented.

# Some of the Harder Couples Combinations

All combinations can work, when more developed people are involved. Some of the most challenging combinations can be quite enriching, but combos with too much difference can create inherent conflict for most people. Some of the most challenging combinations include …

♦ 3-6 couple—3's foot is on the gas, careening toward action, and the 6 is cautious. 3 is image-oriented, and 6 is matter of fact, often disdaining image. It takes some real understanding and appreciation of difference to make this combo work.

♦ 2-5 couple—This one is common, but a challenge. 2 wants to please and expects repayment of appreciation and emotion, yet 5 is typically private and skeptical of someone who gives too much, which can feel invasive to them. 5s may be appreciative, yet not verbalize it. 5s prefer others being up front, without hidden agendas; 2s are typically indirect, with hidden needs. This coupling is fraught with misinterpretations and disappointments. Patience and practice and insight are required here. Over time, 2-5 can learn so much from each other and be more like the other, with great integration of their differences.

♦ 1-8 couple—Both have strong opinions, wanting to take charge and be in control. 1s have rules; 8s break them. It's typically a marriage made in hell, unless the types are developed. Even then, it can be challenging. Power struggles are inherent. Typically a 1 calls on God to get advice on what's right or to get a reference for some spiritual guidelines. The 8 doesn't need to call God, as he or she is already sitting on the throne and doesn't need outside authority!

♦ 4-9 couple—Common; they're almost inevitable magnets for each other. The initial, wonderful attraction of opposites later leads to challenges. 4s become bored with the humdrum, while easygoing 9s scream to get out of 4s' emotionally intense force field. 4s are looking for passion, not calm. The 9s are avoiding their passion, and the 4s', in the need for more evenness. If both develop the opposites and integrate the full range of who they are, then this combo could be in heaven together or at least pass *Go*.

Other typically challenging relationships are 1-4, 2-6, 4-7, 8-8, and 8-9. Even these combos can work well, if the partners develop all parts of themselves and accept differences and challenges. Admiration and respect work wonders, and if you've had good friendships with these combos, that helps, too.

**Lifelines**

There are couples workshops for a number of the type combinations. Imagine a room full of same-combination couples—with amazingly similar issues. It makes you feel less alone.

# Subtype Combinations

Maturity, type differences, family, and cultural history all play significant roles in how couples, or any twosome, interrelate. Subtype differences also play a major role. How you perceive your bottom-line survival issues are crucial, along with how you negotiate for personal survival and enjoyment. The combination of type and subtype differences can produce infinite possibilities of misinterpretation and threat or satisfaction and learning.

## Sexual/Sexual Couples

This combination is hot. Mutual Sexual subtype couples prioritize sex and romance over social or survival issues. Often these couples have a great sex life or certainly desire that, but at the same time may feel overly threatened when problems intrude. Sexual subtypes are intense. Expectations to have an ideal lover are high and much can get projected in the romantic atmosphere. This is the romantic couple *par excellence*, with each feeling the other's desire for heat, intimacy, and wanting to fulfill the other's fantasies. Longing, romance, some fighting and jealousy—this is the stuff of soap operas.

## Sexual/Social Couples

The Sexual subtype wants to spark, and the Social subtype wants to be in the spotlight of groups and social concerns. The Sexual subtype wants private time with the partner, and the Social subtype wants social time often away, possibly with the mate included. Take the time to negotiate. Don't judge the differences; instead, talk about them and see if you can have both. Maybe you can go to the convention and still have some private time, too. The Sexual subtype could come along or visit with a close friend, and the Social subtype could hobnob and network. Don't see the differences as problems so much as opportunities to learn the concerns of the other. Everyone has need of all three subtype areas, so intensify your interests that are similar to your partner's.

## Sexual/Self-Preservation Couples

The Sexual subtype feels rejected if the spark isn't the same as it used to be. The Self-Preservation subtype understands that time changes the level of intensity that characterizes the beginnings of romance. Self-Preservation subtypes want a stay at home weekend to go over the budget, clean the home, and plan renovations; and the Sexual subtype wants quality moments with the mate and romantic getaway weekends. Conflict and misinterpretation can result, unless each makes time to engage the needs of the other or the couple decides to alternate weekend activities between their subtype differences.

## Social/Social Couples

Maybe you're the jet-set couple, attending social engagements with other couples, hosting dinner parties for your friends, and juggling invitations to join prestigious groups. Having the same interests can help here. If one of you favors political groups, while the other prefers religious groups, there can be some tugging around these differences. Still, there's a shared respect for the social arena of life. Making those personal or group associations is all-important. At parties, you might want to connect with everyone important to you. Feeling in or out socially is important and the role you play in these individual or group relationships is vital.

## Social/Self-Preservation Couples

One of you prefers to stay at home, and the other is out and about socializing. This can work well, as Self-Preservation subtypes often are introverts and want to spend some time alone. Maybe the Social subtype can encourage the partner to attend some parties and go out in public, and the Self-Preservation subtype can help the Social subtype spend some quality time alone. Do some socializing at home, if that works. Because neither of you is the Sexual subtype, there's less demand for your partner to please your core needs.

## Self-Preservation/Self-Preservation Couples

Both of you tend to be homebodies and prioritize money in the bank, security, health, hearth, and home. Your priorities and values are similar, and you aren't into high risk adventures. You enjoy doing what you always tend to do. You have regular habits, are predictable, and don't like to shake things up. Change is difficult. Have that special meal together and plan for the future! *Bon appétit!* Travel together and don't get too tied to the house. Take some risks and have some adventures, either together or apart.

## The Least You Need to Know

♦ For each type, love and romance vary as much as the stars in the heavens.

♦ True and enduring love? You have to work at it.

♦ It's important to relate to the type world of your romantic interest.

♦ Understand your type combination and *your* combo will be easier and more fun!

♦ Subtypes play a major role in your romantic mix.

# Chapter

# 16

# Relationships with Friends, Acquaintances, and Other Folks

## In This Chapter

- ◆ The past lives on in the present
- ◆ The value of true friends—priceless
- ◆ Working through the rough spots
- ◆ Relating to acquaintances
- ◆ The benefits of people watching

It's a fun exercise to type people from both your past and your present. It also helps you understand the circumstances surrounding what happened then and what is happening now. Even if you aren't totally accurate about type, narrowing it down or at least knowing the center can greatly help you understand. This chapter gives you the details on understanding type differences and improving your relationships with others.

# Going Back to School

Significant authority figures affect how you feel about your type. Teachers, professionals, religious leaders, Scout leaders, and others can all have a major effect on you, both positive and negative. Once you learn the Enneagram, you will see that the ways you once viewed people from your past may be different from how you see them now.

If you have a negative or painful history with someone, there is some likelihood this person is an immature version of their type. Look to heal any bad memories and also look for current, healthier examples of the types. Reflect on the important people in your life and learn what types they are.

> **Lifelines**
>
> Type your school teachers, professors, doctors, dentists, and influential people in your life. In what ways did type affect your relationships with these people? Knowing how this has worked in the past can help you relate to similar types in the present.

If a teacher's type is the same as yours, or if your type is a natural fit for what the teacher wants, you are likely to be validated. If a teacher liked that you were helpful (like a 2) or peaceful and agreeable (like a 9), your type was validated. If, however, you enjoyed playing pranks (more likely a 7, 8, or counter-phobic 6), which the teacher didn't appreciate, then you might have rebelled even more, reinforcing your type. If the teacher liked humor or pranks and valued a more fun approach, then you might have become more open to your type.

A Type 1 teacher may follow the rules to the letter, but a 1 teacher who is growing knows she needs fewer rules and more humor. A 5 teacher could be boring—focusing too much on dry knowledge—but another 5 teacher may have brought everything to life. One 5 American intellectual-history professor brought in props of the period he was teaching to enliven understanding and generate ideas. The students were captivated.

Development plays as big a role as type. Children can be immature, but they are supposed to be! Many people have painful memories of immature teachers demanding unrealistic behavior or over-punishing minor errors.

Part of the Enneagram's purpose is to help you value your type and learn the best strengths of the other types. Maturity comes with knowledge, acceptance, and developing new aspects of yourself. Humility, curiosity, objectivity, and a willingness to be vulnerable help you grow and expand beyond your type. Hopefully, your relationships have supported the value of your core type and you have learned to be parts of all the types you've been with. People are unique mixes of the nine types and, by the time you are forever young, you will have integrated everything!

# Friends and Type

Certainly friendships can affect your type—in some cases, even more than lovers or relatives. Ongoing or deep friendships model valued type bonding. If you are esteemed for your strengths, you expand who you are and add dimensions beyond your type. Life is richer and deeper. Conflicted friendships (not unusual to have some conflict on occasion), possibly indicate needed growth for making better choices. Your type, type development, and maturity have a profound impact on your relationships.

Friendships often are safer than love affairs for learning about differences and trying new perspectives, though emotional intensity in friendships can be just as strong as any other relationships.

It's wise to have friendships with different types in order to develop parts of yourself you otherwise wouldn't. Going through different kinds of conflicts and misunderstandings can be useful in understanding how different types perceive life and its circumstances. Friendships can help heal same-type issues with relatives and lovers, and you can enjoy new vistas. Your type will be rounded and edged, moved and shaped.

**Lifelines**

A true friend doesn't try to change you as much as enjoy you, learn from you, and value the way you are. A good friend, though, does offer caring, non-controlling ideas or advice, particularly if requested.

Many people have closer ties with friends than they do with family or romantic partners. Friendships often pass the test of time, enduring long beyond romantic connections and the ins and outs of family politics or loyalties. And while there may be fewer preordained obligations in a friendship, relating to friends can be just as intense as relating to family or a lover. Friends accept us for who we are, faults and all. We choose our friends, the saying goes, but we can't choose our relatives.

We are usually more realistic about our expectations with a friend. Over time we grow to understand what to expect, how to enjoy each other, and what topics or situations to avoid. Some friends want the contrast of our differences reflected in type, and others want the support of similarities. Friends often do well with their own type, and this is recommended for at least some of your friends. Similar type friends will understand each other in ways other types can't.

What about friends who are different types? That's also great! It's easier to practice growth with friends than it is with family or lovers. For example, 4 and 9 friends can

**Warning!**

Don't project past painful feelings, often related to love relationships and family, onto your friends. Your friends often provide more support than anyone else.

trade off intensity and relaxation in ways beneficial to both. 3s and 5s often work well together, as both like competence. 3s could coach how to make a project happen, with 5s providing the information or technical expertise. 8 and 9 friends benefit from the comfort and acceptance the 9 offers and *oomph* that the 8 provides in going after a goal. In the 2 and 4 combo, both like some emotional intensity. 2s can listen well to a 4, who supports 2's individuality.

# Healing with Friends

Everyone makes mistakes. What we did yesterday, we might not do today. The Enneagram can inform why you did what you did and offer alternatives for today. You fought with your friends who were trying to control you. Now you see other options. Listen to others' views, as valid for them as yours are for you, acknowledge them, but do what you feel is best for you, without fighting or losing yourself in any destructive way. Learn to diminish the need for approval and still be respectful. As you understand more why people do what they do, you'll have more options to enjoy more and defend less. You'll understand why you get defensive. Why defend anything?

## What Brought You Together

With choosing friends, mutual interests or mutual friends may have been the connection. In the beginning of a friendship, the shared interest may be the major relational focus. As time goes on, the friendship deepens, as you learn more about each other. With a wider perspective, you can see that everyone's contribution is necessary and working out the differences, in and of itself, is beneficial. For example, a 9 needs the practice of being assertive with an 8, who even appreciates it. A 7 needs to understand the world of a 6 and, rather than make fun or avoid, see the value of looking problems squarely in the face. You need the input of other perspectives, however difficult it may be.

## What Pulled You Apart

Differences can pull you apart; a 7 gets exasperated by the 6's worst-case scenarios or a 4's abandonment fears and decides not to hang around. 7 will acknowledge pain and problems but doesn't want to dwell or obsess about them. 1s can see 7s as too loose or not serious about what the 1 thinks about, such as consistency. 8s can't stand the indecisiveness of 9s or phobic 6s. Other types react to the image-making of the image types. Specific events snowball into fights, misinterpretations, and separation. Emotional scenes linger in our memories. It's sad if the past made us feel hopeless and gave us few options but to fight or withdraw.

## What You Learned from Differences

Differences can lead to useful learning. Even if a situation is difficult or painful, it could be the very thing that takes you to a new level of *integration*. Learning from challenges or even from enemies is sometimes the best learning. Possibly another's qualities that drive you insane relate to the very parts of yourself that you avoid. When we balance out what our type needs to learn, conflicts with others diminish somewhat. Type conflicts reflect what we need to balance in ourselves. For example …

**def•i•ni•tion**

**Integration** is the organization of the psychological or social traits and tendencies of a personality into a harmonious whole.

- ◆ A 2 feels the pain of a 5 not telling her, "I appreciate you." She learns that the 5 shows appreciation in different ways. She learns the importance of appreciating herself.

- ◆ A 9 learns to relax more, when a 1 passes judgments, rather than reacting in anger or withdrawing. Conflict isn't seen as bad, but something to work out. Respectful assertion becomes an option.

- ◆ A 7, who likes high energy, finds ways to maintain that perspective, while dealing with his friend's demands that he follow her directions on when to do a specific task, or how to do a certain procedure.

Opportunities are always there to learn what we need—9s to be more assertive, 1s to relax their structures, 2s to accept others' versions of love, 3s to see more varied versions of success. See life's problems as opportunities for growth.

## Forgiving a Type

Why did you stay on when the situation was grim? You stayed because you weren't ready to leave. You took on certain challenges to learn, even beyond your practical concerns of security and survival. The culprit might be ignorance, addiction, or not knowing optional ways of making better choices. People do what they do, in a large way, because of type tendencies. Other people of the type tend to do the same. Knowing the type helps you to let go and have better options for the future. Your choices reflect your learning and self-esteem.

If you feel you've wasted time in certain relationships or jobs, as the result of choices you've made or in going along with others' choices—let it go, if you can. There's so much to learn in life and many roads to take. Start fresh each day.

Forgiving is as much about *you* as it is forgiving others. You are learning, and you can't learn without making mistakes. Appreciation for mistakes increases future integration. Guilt tends to limit it. Give yourself a break and forgive yourself, even for the big mistakes and certainly for the little ones. Of course, learn your lesson, so as not to repeat the error. Even then, be easier on yourself. Forgiving others and your past is all to your advantage.

> **Insights**
>
> A friend is, as it were, a second self.
> —Aristotle

## How to Maintain a Good Relationship Today

Good relationships are maintained by understanding differences, having compassion for the difficulties of each type, developing other type qualities, and admitting your mistakes. There's no point in defending yourself, if someone points out what is true. Be affirmative, more than complaining. See how you grow, even with the challenges. Good things can come in difficult packages!

Don't project onto others. Own what is true in yourself. Remember you need to develop some of the good qualities of every type to be well rounded. Keep healing your past, while living in the moment. Live in your heart, as well as in your head, and you'll be fine. Ultimately, you are typeless! Meanwhile, enjoy the types and have fun with every one of them. Keep practicing what you need to learn and be easy on yourself. Growth is the goal, not perfection.

# Relating to Acquaintances and Type Differences

Acquaintances are the folks you may see every day or only occasionally. Whether it's the barista who delivers your morning latte, your favorite checkout worker at the supermarket, the postal worker who delivers your mail, or the mechanic you've patronized for 20 years—acquaintances are not quite friends, but they're definitely closer than strangers. Sometimes, being able to understand their types can help in transacting business, smoothing over a misunderstanding, or simply expanding your knowledge of human nature.

Casual acquaintances can add much value to your life. You expect less from them than you do from friends and you can also see their type more clearly. For example, a nitpicky acquaintance 1 is less difficult to deal with than a friend or lover 1 with the same trait.

When a 6 acquaintance questions you, there's no need to take it personally. You can recognize this as a type habit. It may be easier to see that this person operates the same way with most everyone. Question back! Find a way to enjoy the type interchange. If you notice someone unique or intriguing, ask yourself what type this person could be. Consider imitating traits of that type for your own enhancement, if that seems valuable. For example, if you are feeling down and meet a 7, spend some extra time with that 7 and see the bright side of life.

If it's appropriate, initiate a conversation about type with an acquaintance. Learn how that person perceives life. Discover the strengths and quirks of that person's type. Even though certain traits may be missing from a person, each type seeks its traits. For instance, a 9 isn't always peaceful inside but likes peaceful feelings. A 6 wants your loyalty but isn't always loyal. A 3 isn't always successful but strives to be around success. An added benefit is that just spending some personal time with an acquaintance may be all that it takes to form a new friendship.

# Relating to the Public and Type Differences

People watching is great fun and provides a practical exercise in Enneagram typing! We're talking about strangers or public figures—those people you don't know on any personal level. Observe the bank teller, waitress, politician running for public office, TV anchor person, or cab driver and watch them play out their types. The cab driver who drives too fast may reflect an 8 who likes power or a 3 getting you to your goal as quickly as possible. A 2 waitress is ready to serve you and anxious to please. If you feel mellow, you're probably in the company of a 9. If you feel overloaded with rules, you might be dealing with a 1 or a 6.

You can easily say just the right words to a 6, "Here are some safety tips; here's what not to do; please ask any questions; these are the probabilities." If you're being waited on by an overwhelmed 9, keep your voice calm and reassuring, "Take your time, there's no hurry." And about that cab driver? "Slow down, please," if speed isn't what you fancy.

**Lifelines**

Stop by a café with an Enneagram friend for coffee or tea and some people watching. Try some typing. How do people walk? Do their gestures reflect type? What are they talking about? Are they helpful, sticking with technical ideas or subjects, a bit manic? Strong and loud? Quiet? What's their body language telling you?

## The Least You Need to Know

♦ Authority figures from your youth played a role in how you see and value your type today.

♦ An appreciation of differences leads to deeper and more satisfying friendships.

♦ We may have closer ties with friends than with family, and in times of need friends may offer us more support than family.

♦ Type conflicts reflect what we need to balance in ourselves.

♦ Forgiving others, as well as yourself, helps you grow and develop beyond your type limitations.

# Chapter 17

# Work, Career, and Type

## In This Chapter

- Types in the workplace
- Career growth and personal development
- Do's and don'ts for each type at work
- How each type defines job satisfaction
- Facing your worst fears: challenges worth taking on

Work is an integral part of life and your work identity is extremely important in most cultures. It determines how you see yourself and how others see you. It transfers to your personal life, as well. Aligning your work choices and career paths with your type can give you personal satisfaction. Working against your type can be difficult, unless you are consciously trying to challenge yourself. Enjoyment, personal growth, and feeling in charge of your work and professional development have important implications for your personal life. Development, strong wings, subtypes, family history, and how one likes to challenge one's self are important factors in work and career decisions. (Refer also to the "Work and Career" sections of each of the nine types in Part 2.)

This chapter will look at tendencies and preferences, professional development and disaster paths, what settings tend to work well with each type, and a tongue-in-cheek look at work settings unlikely to bring happiness. Included are lists of important workplace characteristics for each type.

Each type tends to gravitate toward certain career and work choices, but understand that any type could potentially do well in any work or career setting. Which work choices will make you happier than others? How can your type strengths be used to your advantage? Know thyself! Meet as many of your requirements as possible. Interview others to make sure a job is right for you. The Enneagram can help.

# Career Paths and Professional Development for 1s

1s usually do well in work and careers that require attention to detail, have clear guidelines, offer an ethical purpose or right cause, or produce high quality products or services. Typical jobs that work well for 1 include town manager, police officer, independent house cleaner or carpet cleaner, office organizer, fashion consultant, financial planner, or real estate agent. Whatever 1s do, they do well and thoroughly. 1s develop professionally when they find professions that support their type strengths, learn to relax, interrelate well to others with different standards and values, and can handle a few mistakes without committing *seppuku*.

## Disaster Paths

Disaster jobs would be high profile, with shady ethics or jobs that support sloppy work. Characteristics of the jobs from hell would include nonspecific job descriptions, inaccurate accounting practices, overlapping shift schedules, production geared toward inferior products or services, and quantity stressed over quality. Additional levels of torture would include the allowance for innumerable mistakes, constant redefinition of job descriptions, inconsistent or nonexistent standards, support for pleasing the boss valued over doing what's right, and no targets for outcomes. Worst professions would include being an odds maker at the racetrack, teaching in a Montessori preschool, or traffic officer in Beijing.

## Checklist for a Good Working Environment

- Cleanliness
- Efficiency

- Order
- High quality standards, services, or products
- Proper dress codes or other reasonable standards
- High ethics

- Consistency and reliability
- Fairness
- Adherence to schedules
- Acknowledgement for good work
- Clear job description

# Career Paths and Professional Development for 2s

2s do well in professions that require a positive image and include service, people contact, helping others, and giving personal attention. 2 would be perfect as *maître d'hôtel* or waiter, service manager, educational consultant, childcare provider, physical therapist, or yoga and workshop center instructor or owner. Professional development includes acknowledging personal limits, working on areas of improvement, saying no, and finding the right boundaries for giving to others.

## Disaster Paths

Jobs to avoid include those with no people contact, appreciation, or reward systems. To make this worse, include physical settings that are spare, with no pictures, windows, or décor, and add complaining people who never smile, never share anything personal, and punishment for engaging with people during work or breaks. Worst professions here might include working on a factory assembly line, professional chicken plucker, shelf stocker on the night shift at a grocery store, heavy machine operator, or sewage pond maintenance personnel.

**Lifelines**

Doing work you love is essential to your health. Your stress level lowers with work that satisfies, even if it challenges you. Make sure your work utilizes your type strengths.

## Checklist for a Good Working Environment

- Beautifully appointed environments—pictures, plants, brightness, and sunlight
- People contact—the personal connection
- Appreciation and acknowledgment

- Fun, cheery atmosphere
- Positive focus
- Service orientation

# Career Paths and Professional Development for 3s

3s do well in jobs that offer possibilities for advancement, leadership potential, competition, and good reward systems. Professions such as real estate investment, business consulting, sales, prestigious teaching positions, entrepreneurial ventures, modeling, and project management are good fits. Professional development includes having tolerance for project slowdowns and complexities and doing work less concerned with image and acknowledgment. 3s need relationship development beyond their work connections. Well-rounded 3s have interests that add dimensions to their lives, and that are outside work.

## Disaster Paths

Worst-case scenario jobs for 3s include those where everyone is treated equally, with no perks for productivity and where there are no clear goals, leadership potential, ability to advance, or job titles. No extra pay, no trophies, no benefits—just one of the boys or girls. We'll inflict filing as an office job for our hapless 3s—also teaching socialism, maintaining the electronic scoreboard for the Chicago Cubs, or being a researcher for a cloning project.

## Checklist for a Good Working Environment

- Clear goals
- Reward systems
- No limits to advancement, quick advancement
- Can-do, winning atmosphere
- Efficiency and speed focus
- Leadership potential
- Special recognition and star potential

# Career Paths and Professional Development for 4s

4s do well with work and careers that stress individuality and meaningful, personal values, along with aesthetic pursuits. Unusual jobs with a dramatic flair and potential for variety and change are well suited to 4s. Interior decorator, a psychology professor who teaches about trauma and abuse, artist, dancer, flautist in a symphony orchestra, or writer of erotic novels could be perfect. Professional development includes integrating the mundane at work in unique ways and developing skill sets and conforming to standards, while still standing out.

## Disaster Paths

Disaster 4ness would include not having disasters, living an ordinary work life with no drama, no special recognition, no beauty in the environment, and pleasing the boss as the top priority. Jobs that elicit no feelings would be hell. The inability to express yourself personally would be the worst tragedy. Jobs that would fit this description could include manufacturing paint-by-numbers kits, method acting, mathematics, and surgical scrub nurse.

## Checklist for a Good Working Environment

- Aesthetic and creative possibilities
- Acceptance and support for passion, mood, and drama
- Ability to express one's feelings and inner state
- Openness to the new and different
- Appreciation for artistic quality
- *Positive stress*, essential for 4s

## def•i•ni•tion

**Positive stress** is the type of stress that enhances life and keeps it exciting. The thrill of a roller-coaster ride, a fun challenge, a promotion, getting married ... all are examples of positive stress.

# Career Paths and Professional Development for 5s

5s do well in knowledge-based careers such as engineering, systems analysis, psychiatry, physics, mathematics, or higher education. Anything that relates to analysis, developing advanced knowledge, creating more integrated knowledge with other systems, new theories of learning—all are part of the 5 experience. 5s like to constantly learn and don't want to stay in jobs with no ability to deepen or create more knowledge. Professional development includes support for 5s' need for learning, knowing that personal relationship education is part of that learning, and that knowledge isn't the same as outcome. 5s need to be careful not to isolate at work. Share your knowledge and process, so others can benefit too. Personal engagement can add to more knowledge!

## Disaster Paths

Worst-case 5 work would be dull jobs that don't challenge the mind. Structures that limit you from learning or developing new strategies and ideas would be awful. Authoritarian structures that limit pursuits of research or the ability to challenge authority, particularly if that inhibits your individual process, would not be the job for you. You often like to *be* the authority when it comes to the latest ideas and theories about subjects that interest you or in which you want to be expert. Disaster jobs would be charismatic televangelism, swimsuit model, or professional wrestler.

## Checklist for a Good Working Environment

- Time alone and privacy at work
- Intelligent people to engage with
- Learning opportunities
- Information and knowledge valued
- Appreciation for introversion
- Clear guidelines along with an openness to innovation
- Appreciation for objectivity
- Discussion groups that challenge the mind

# Career Paths and Professional Development for 6s

6s do well with work that supports their strengths of research, analysis, awareness and incorporates support for safety systems, combating danger, and ways to support relationship security. Engineering, the legal system, safety standards, the insurance industry, and the home security system industry are 6s' areas of work. 6s need some structure at work, with guidelines for grievances and a clear hierarchy. Professional development includes managing your anxiety; making alliances with most people instead of *us against them*, therefore eliminating the need for enemies; acting without having to overly plan or predict in advance; and seeing the best-case intentions of people who challenge your assumptions.

## Disaster Paths

Areas to avoid would be working at jobs that over-promise security and those would include dangerous jobs with no safety standards (though some of you counter phobic 6s aren't always safe, as you challenge the boundaries). Specific horrible situations for 6s include regulator at an enriched plutonium plant, astronaut for a third world nation's fledgling space program, or circus trapeze artist working without a net.

## Checklist for a Good Working Environment

♦ Clear lines of leadership and authority

♦ Guidelines for challenging authority

♦ Strictly enforced safety standards

♦ Orderly environment

♦ Allowance for questioning

♦ Supportive groups

♦ Appreciation for problem-solving skills

♦ Critical analysis and feedback opportunities

**Warning!**

6s like order and control from outside, yet are also concerned about too much order and control. 6s can't solve this dilemma around control until they focus on themselves for security and feel control from inside.

# Career Paths and Professional Development for 7s

7s need freedom and variety at work to be their best. They do well with a system for brainstorming before decisions, a support system to help with carrying out tedious details, and fun and extroverted environments. They thrive in jobs that have plenty of new, nonrepetitive dimensions. They can write exciting computer games, motivate others as public speakers, and shine as masters of ceremonies. They develop professionally by accepting limits as part of the process, following through on action and commitments, and realizing that authority, not total egalitarianism, is sometimes necessary. They need to realize and allow that others aren't as positive as they are, possibly due to others facing bottom-line realities.

## Disaster Paths

7s think that everything is possible, so real disasters can be a challenge for 7s, who can focus on favorable possibilities and forget that real dangers do exist. Disaster paths for a 7 would include work and career journeys that focus too much on real or imagined danger and rules and limitations. Worst-case jobs would be telephone solicitor working in a cubicle, prison guard, coroner, or compiler of actuarial tables for an insurance company.

## Checklist for a Good Working Environment

- Freedom to move physically in the environment, independence
- Options to do your job the way you feel is best
- Dynamic, exciting, engaging environment
- Plenty of change
- Openness to new ideas
- Appreciation for what is good, positive focus
- Fun, entertainment, and pranks as part of the mix

# Career Paths and Professional Development for 8s

8s want their independence and a strong sense of autonomy. Telling an 8 what to do doesn't land well. 8s prefer to be in charge, or at least feel in charge of their choices. They need environments in which they don't feel dominated or restricted. 8s speak up, so work settings need to tolerate that, to some degree. They are the head nurse; they're in charge of the high school physical education department; or they own a lumber company, run their own business, or manage the department in which they work. To develop, they need to practice patience, allow for differences, appreciate their own insecurities (without needing to fight to cover them up), and think before they leap. Other people are also learning about power and control, and there needs to be some give and take in the process, between the 8 and others.

## Disaster Paths

They would hate to have a million bosses over them, competing with each other. Having confusing leadership above is torture. People trying to be nice, with undercurrents of power swirling about, is like having spider webs in the face. 8s feel trapped and little. Feeling and reality can be different. Worst-case jobs would be Army recruit being ordered around by a bully sergeant and working front counter of a complaint compartment.

## Checklist for a Good Working Environment

- Room for independence, self-determination
- Comfort in people being direct with each other
- Leadership position potential
- Strong and clear leadership from others
- Group goals, defined and consistent
- Room for joviality and good times
- Environments that have a sense of boldness, action, conviction, and passion

# Career Paths and Professional Development for 9s

9s like work that's not overly stressful, in a pleasant environment, with a tolerance for differences and minimal competition, fighting, and mixed messages. 9s prefer to please and create harmony, if possible, so if that is difficult, it's a challenge to be motivated. Unappreciative environments or organizations, rife with conflicts, are challenges. 9s do well as mediator, human services director, spiritually-oriented therapist, x-ray technician, repairperson, or almost any job that does a service that ideally benefits others or improves the environment. 9s need the challenge to be more self-oriented and speak up with their desires and intuitions.

## Disaster Paths

Worst-case scenarios include 9s being in or witnessing constant conflicts in a highly stressed work setting with major power struggles. Constant pressure to produce wouldn't work with a 9, unless it fits the 9's individual purpose and the approach is somewhat comforting. 9s are flexible but hate to be pushed or taken for granted. Worst-case jobs would be bullfighter, fashion model, stockbroker, hockey player, or Donald Trump's assistant. It's not to say a 9 couldn't do these jobs, as 9s adapt to anything and everything, but typically they struggle both inwardly and outwardly in stressful environments, with competition or infighting. 9s pick up stress easily, so everyone's inner conflicts are felt by the 9.

## Checklist for a Good Working Environment

- Opportunity to take breaks as needed
- Congenial atmosphere
- No back-biting
- Cooperation, rather than competition
- Appreciation for differences
- Higher purpose
- Inclusive environment

# Facing Your Worst Fear

At times, all the types will face their worst fears at work and need to confront the challenge. Until you master all the strengths of the nine types, you haven't fully played the game and faced your own type fear. Face that and life is more abundant and less fearful. Have compassion for the fear of each type:

- 1s—Face your anger, imperfection, and hidden desires and you can relax, have pleasure, and still strive for excellence.
- 2s—Face your needs, your self-drives, your limits on giving, and your need to receive love with openness, and you will have the love you want.

- 3s—Face your fear of failure and you'll no longer experience it, because you'll know it's an illusion. You can relax and not try so hard to win every time. You can have love without winning.

- 4s—Face your fear of abandonment and you can't be abandoned. Accept yourself as you are now, and let go of longing for a future that is better. Be here now. That's the meaning.

- 5s—Face your fear that your learning will never be enough. It won't be. Nothing in and of itself will be fully satisfying. Allow emotions, the unknown, lack of control. It's all part of the dance. Wisdom is beyond knowledge and accepts all of what is.

- 6s—Face your fear of insecurity and allow it in. When you allow your fears, rather than try to fix them in some desperate way, you can accept fear as a teacher. Security lies within.

- 7s—Face the fact that unlimited freedom actually traps you. Certain commitments and limits give freedom. See the illusion and you'll still be free.

- 8s—Face your inadequacies and fears and share them. Don't worry, you can protect yourself, but don't overprotect yourself. There is strength in admitting weakness.

- 9s—Be your assertiveness. Have an ego. Say what you think and want and go after it. Most people will accept you, but you need to see and accept your own strength. *Be yourself* rather than blend.

## The Least You Need to Know

- Career choices need to be made with your type in mind.

- There are professional development challenges unique to type in your work and career.

- Each type has a list of important qualities to look for in work.

- Use work to grow beyond some of the limited qualities of your type.

# Chapter 18

# Relating to Colleagues and Managers: Team Building and Type

- ◆ Teams that work and teams that don't

- ◆ How the Enneagram helps with team cohesion

- ◆ How an ideal team works together

- ◆ Creating your best team at work

- ◆ How to relate to your boss

Most organizations and teams have a mixture of types. Just as with chemicals, explosions can occur with the wrong mix. How do you minimize the explosions and maximize the chemicals that work well together? How can the types interrelate on a team for the most fun and efficiency? How do you relate to someone who has power over you?

Understanding the type strengths and limitations of your boss and managers will help in knowing how to optimally communicate your preferences and differences. Knowing what communication and leadership skills you need to develop will position you for efficiency, confidence, and more camaraderie. The more you know about yourself and differences with others, the more you can work on a team, using your individual strengths, yet having the ability to interrelate who you are with others' skill sets and strengths.

# How Teams Work and What Works Best

A team is a group of individuals who work as a unit to produce a specific outcome. If the team dynamics are productive, there is minimal conflict and each member works to achieve the goal, rather than being the Lone Ranger, vying for attention or acclaim. When each type contributes his or her best, individual differences are optimized, bringing forth fresh ideas or new perspectives. Clarity and understanding are keys to team cohesion. What is easy for one type may be difficult for another. The Enneagram is a useful tool to understand type differences and make sense of each person's perspective and concerns.

# What Doesn't Work

When a team clashes internally, the worst culprit is likely to be type prejudice. When this occurs, certain types and type characteristics are consistently valued over others. Misunderstanding about type perspective can kill a team. Whoever has the most power can either enhance others' creativity or dominate and shut it down. Safety, clear goals, and structures are important. If something isn't working, whatever is causing the problem needs to be fixed. If team members start protecting their image or ego, or over compete, rather than relaxing and supporting everyone's best aspects, stress ensues. Some real-life examples of an Enneagram trainer working with various teams are presented in the following sections. Each team was greatly enhanced by the Enneagram information and strategies.

## Questioners Want Their Questions Answered

The background: a team made up of 10 individuals worked in a research-development company, creating software for voice-recognition devices. Four of the members were 6s, two were 5s, and the rest were a mix of other types.

The concern: team members were worried about how long their contract would last, as the company shareholders didn't want to extend funding for the project. The unknown was creating anxiety and affecting work. The 6s were especially concerned.

The solution: taking into account the 6s, who would rather have bad news than no news, the Enneagram trainer coached the top management, a 4 and an 8, to share more about the possible longevity of the company and project with the employees.

The result: the bosses, with the trainer's support, immediately shared what they knew, which was still probability rather than fact. Even though the news wasn't concrete, there was some relief and better productivity during the remainder of the project's run. The team training included ways the Head types—the majority—could work more effectively with the Image and Body types.

> **Insights**
>
> Certain types have an affinity to certain projects or work environments—5s and 6s are more drawn to research projects whereas models, for instance, are more likely to be Image types.

## Boss and Mediator Clash

The background: A small training company had four employees. There was the boss (8/9), an administrator/trainer (9/1 with a Stress type of 6), and the other two trainers (9/8 and 1). The administrator and the boss were in conflict.

The concern: The Type 8 boss wanted paperwork and proposals to move more quickly, which would move training projects along and generate revenue. He preferred to speak without having to think about his words before he spoke. He was direct and tried a, to him, peaceful approach with the Type 9 administrator, but found it difficult. The 9/1 administrator didn't like the perceived rough and quick tone of the 8. This caused the 8 boss to hold back too much and eventually explode from the repression. The 9/1 wanted to do things right and orderly, and her Stress type of 6 contributed to the hesitancy and slower pace. The 8 didn't care about that, "Just get it done and send it off." The other two employees were being affected by the 8 and 9 conflict and felt pressured to choose sides. The 9/8 already got along fine with the boss.

The solution: With coaching, the team recognized there were some big differences in their communication—both delivery and reception. Several role-plays built confidence in talking and interpreting what was happening. The boss was coached to be direct, not hold back, but talk in a more sensitive, connecting tone. The 9 was coached to listen and accept that the 8 was speaking in his normal tone, which was somewhat loud and direct, but not demeaning.

The result: With everything out in the open and some tools to work with, the operation worked much better for a while, until it needed some reinforcement the following year.

## Church Headquarters—Peace and Prejudice

The background: Over a period of years, an Enneagram trainer worked at the head-quarters of a Unitarian Church with four teams, each consisting of approximately 15 people. All nine types were represented on the teams. Type 9s were the majority on each team, with one exception, which had 1s dominant. 2s or 6s equally ranked third in representation.

The concern: The major conflict was between 1s and 9s. The 1s tended to want things done in specific ways, with more detail and conviction. 9s, wanting to avoid conflict, were less outspoken. 1s complained that the 9s wouldn't or couldn't take a clear stance on what they believed or wanted. As is often the case, the silence of the peacemakers was creating conflict. Because Type 9 was predominant, they were having a powerful influence, not only on each team but on the whole organization. Others wondered about, and sometimes misread, the 9s' seeming reticence to express themselves.

The solution: The Enneagram trainer encouraged the 9s to see how powerful they actually were, both in positive qualities and acceptance abilities, as well as in their passivity and avoidance, and coached them to speak up more for what they believed. The 1s discovered that sometimes they were too strong in their beliefs and more crit-ical than they realized. Their criticism related to adherence to certain principles or guidelines. The 6s were good at strategic planning and noticing problems or poten-tial problems. The 2s, small in number, kept the group focused positively and helped individuals to connect to each other and take action. A few 3s and 8s led the charge.

The result: Overall, the teams worked well together, both internally and across teams, as purpose and mission were very much in alignment. There were just some differences with carrying out the mission, some normal power struggles, and some misinterpreta-tions. The types were encouraged to have more dialogue and share their viewpoints and differences. The 9s in particular were encouraged to speak up more. Most under-represented were the Image types; therefore, the teams lacked a marketing focus. There was discussion about ways to compensate for that. The Image types volunteered to concentrate more on those areas and bring forth their power.

# How the Enneagram Helps

Using the Enneagram system, the Enneagram trainer clarifies what is happening, relative to personalities, and puts the problems on an objective plane. There's less blame, more accurate information, ways to utilize the best the types have to offer, and tips on personal development and communication skills related to each type.

During the training, participants learn to understand each type's motivations and then role play, practicing specific new communication strategies. They see immediate verification of the training's benefits.

Once we learn to communicate in ways that are appropriate to people's types, everyone is happier. Confidence grows and there's more fun and less stress, once we know what's really true (accurate), instead of *wondering* what's true (inaccurate). Not every problem is type-related, but much positive change can come from understanding the type differences and relating directly to them.

# The Dream Teams

An ideal team works together fairly easily. Maybe there is some conflict, but it's generally not destructive. There's fun and appreciation for team members' differences. People aren't pushing each other to be other than who they are. There is little or no type prejudice but instead an intuitive understanding of differences. Here, the Enneagram enhances what is already working.

There might be a few power issues but no major power struggles. On average, the members are open and honest and are aware of different members, who have their own version of power and control. While this is the ideal, it unfortunately doesn't describe most work situations. Because work settings and relationships are reflections of families and the culture at large, all the problems, conflicts, and issues associated with them play out within the organizational context.

# Sales Staffs and Teams

In business and sales, many teams and team managers are 2s, 3s, and 7s, though all the types are represented. 8s are frequently supervisors or bosses. Salespeople are competitive and, in the best teams, are also jovial and encouraging of each other.

Most systems assign territory or have other structures in place to diminish jealousies and power struggles. More so than human-services personnel, salespeople are expected to be self-oriented. An Enneagram trainer worked with several real estate companies to coach Realtors on selling to different types and also discovering the effects their own types might have on sales.

**Lifelines**

Good strategies for sales personnel involve practice or role play, influencing potential clients, or closing sales to each type.

People in sales can benefit from coaching on how to sell to different personality types. 5s tend to give product information over personal connection, while 2s create a personal connection first. A 5 or 6 customer certainly wants information as part of the presentation, whereas a 2 customer wants personal connection, and 7s want a fast and entertaining approach. 3s might want to be sold on the image the product or service will provide, and 8s want to get to the point. A 9 wants a connection, but not an approach that's high pressure.

# How You Can Create Your Best Team at Work

Strengths are naturally enhanced when no obstacles block them. You create the best team when you utilize the strengths of all team members. Enneagram awareness speeds up the process by which each team member can push beyond type limits and develop positive traits outside the type.

An understanding of conflict resolution skills, knowing when certain types take precedence over others, and seeing how that limits creativity and production are essential skills for managers.

Teams work together when their type mix works together. Whether all nine types or just a cluster of a few types are present doesn't matter as much as how well people can utilize their skills in their individual work and communicate and intermesh with others' skill sets. The Enneagram is a useful predictor of what to expect from someone. People can obsess and misinterpret others' behaviors and motivations, and that also wastes time and energy, therefore affecting output. Seeing what's objectively true cuts obsession time.

It helps to allow or support everyone to be his or her most natural self. Not everyone has a cheerful demeanor or is animated or extroverted. 1s tend to be precise and can be critical and teacherly; 2s cheerful and helpful; 3s goal-driven and time-bound; 4s emotional, personal, and different; 5s often quiet, introverted, and intelligent; 6s planning and analytical; 7s upbeat, humorous, and quick; 8s direct, in charge, and action oriented; and 9s laid back, gentle, and agreeable. The Enneagram describes the type, but people develop beyond these descriptions. It's important not to stereotype but rather to accept and appreciate people's tendencies.

Egalitarian power structures do exist in business, but they're infrequent and, even when attempted, certain individuals tend to take charge, anyway. Teams often work better when the team leader is not so dominant or judging and when the leader's type doesn't become the prototype of how others should be. Though on a practical level, it's a good idea to understand the *boss* type, the type more in charge, and relate to his/her world. Time to explore the boss world!

# Type 1 Boss and Management

Type 1s are leaders with strong convictions and can speak up, particularly if something needs fixing. You like to model good behavior, though at the low end, you can be a critical boss with the one-right-way approach. If that's the way you manage, your employees will typically try to avoid you!

## How to Deal with Your Boss

Honesty is the best policy in relating to a Type 1 boss. Realize you might be criticized for wrong or inefficient actions or what you neglected to do. You may feel you're being watched by the eagle eye. 1s are evaluative. Expect some critical feedback as normal. We all need feedback, and you can evaluate its usefulness. Appreciate the 1's comments, even if the delivery is unpalatable. 1 bosses typically don't comment on what is good or what's working. You could risk saying you need positive comments that motivate and reinforce good behavior. You could also risk saying that while you appreciate feedback, you have a different approach that you think will accomplish the same goal—that getting a particular job done is more important than how you accomplish the task.

> **Warning!**
>
> It's painful to watch a Type 1 manager yell at her employees in public on how to do procedures right. They were having a good time beforehand, probably providing better service for the fast-food clients, before the barrage. If you could see yourself in a mirror doing your worst type stuff, you'd think twice!

## How to Develop Your Own Leadership Style

As a 1, realizing there are many ways to accomplish the goal enhances leadership development. Practically speaking, you will anger many people by being too demanding of a *right* way. Many 1s require training in anger management in order to realize their anger is spewing out in critical, scolding, or snide remarks or a preaching tone. Be aware of this. Accept your anger without putting a negative judgment on it. Give yourself and others more allowance for learning or forgetful mistakes. Focus on people acceptance as much as task completion and you might get both. Allow for differences.

# Type 2 Boss and Management

2s manage by persuasion. You want to influence others in ways that don't appear controlling. Look at what might be controlling, even if your delivery doesn't seem that way to you. You can be positive, yet still be demanding. Your personal touch often works well. Sometimes you may need to focus on task completion, as much as on the personal connection.

## How to Deal with Your Boss

2s want to be seen well, so don't embarrass your Type 2 boss. Appearance is important, so think about how you present yourself. The task certainly is important, but so is the personal connection. If your 2 is sharing a personal story, listen with interest. Maybe you could offer a helpful comment. 2s love it when you go the extra step to support them or another team member in ways that make the boss or group look good and positively affect the bottom line. Be upbeat and noncomplaining. Look at a positive direction and a way of heading there through action. Gratitude and praise are welcome.

## How to Develop Your Own Leadership Style

As a 2, your leadership development is enhanced by being as task oriented as you are people oriented. Be careful of over-involvement with employee's problems, though it's great that you care and often that enhances production. Don't demand that people be overly positive, as their efforts to please you may detract from their natural talents. Don't expect praise. Don't punish or withdraw from those you feel don't appreciate you. It's your job to get the job done and not overly enter into personal dynamics. By all means, keep your positive focus and encourage employees to engage personally with each other. Have parties and acknowledge birthdays, performance, anniversaries, and the like as a way of connecting people.

# Type 3 Boss and Management

3s are naturals at management. You like to achieve, win, and be on top. You don't mind going the extra mile to get the job done and, as you see it, the faster the better. You appreciate competitive employees who excel, if they don't compete with you to your detriment. At the same time, you create a cooperative environment that may make productivity happen even more. Be careful not to take too much credit, if it's undeserved. You might get anger directed toward you, as a result. Put recognition where praise or reward is due.

**Lifelines** _____

3s who praise others or share the praise with the team get more praise in the long run.

## How to Deal with Your Boss

If you're working for a Type 3, be efficient. 3s typically don't care so much how you get there, as long as you do. Of course, everyone has ideas on what's faster or more efficient, and your 3 boss will share his or her ideas, if you ask. On average, 3s care less than 1s about having a job be perfect, so err on the side of speed over excessive detail. Slowing down is the wrong direction. 3s also are upbeat and don't want a down energy, as they tend to see that as impeding the goal. 3s can be critical and angry if you are slow, talk too much, and aren't committed to completion. 3s often expect overtime (completion and winning being an important focus), so you might have to negotiate on that issue if that isn't something you're willing to do.

## How to Develop Your Own Leadership Style

As a 3, you need to see that others don't always have a bottom line of winning. Many people feel a 40-hour workweek is plenty and don't want their lives dominated by work. Don't load your work beliefs on others who are balancing work, relationships, family, and personal goals. Prioritize people as much as tasks, and you'll accomplish what you need. If you overwork, your stress level might be too high to get the job done as efficiently as you like. Support what can get you what you want with less stress—such as breaks, variety, feedback, and having balance in your life.

# Type 4 Boss and Management

Type 4 bosses will support aligning work and personal goals. 4s are individualists and don't expect others to conform to a unified way of doing things. 4 bosses are open to the personal level that includes feeling, creativity, new or unique approaches, and fitting work with life purpose. Of course, an undeveloped 4 boss could be overreactive and lost in personal feelings, making it hard to be objective. Often, in the world of work, a 4/3 will lead with her 3 wing and seem like a 3.

## How to Deal with Your Boss

It's okay, on average, to be personal with a Type 4. 4s can be empathic with your personal needs and desires and want to please you, if you are personally developing yourself as well as accomplishing a task. You can show your emotions more than with other types, but don't be competitive with your boss. Type 4 bosses are open to new ideas and some risk-taking and like new spins or twists. 4s can be moody, so don't expect a consistent demeanor. Listen to what's going on for them. Don't take it personally, if they change quickly. They can embellish for effect, so don't be surprised if facts become analogies, rather than exact details.

## How to Develop Your Own Leadership Style

As a 4, attempt to stay objective and goal-oriented and not let your feelings or desire for aesthetics overshadow goals and how others see you. You can't lose it at work. Avoid personal reactions and others perceiving you as unstable when you're upset. You can be a leader to support others in their personal process and even in using their unique growth process and goals to coincide with work goals. As a leader, learn to balance your individual pursuits with containment of personal expression.

# Type 5 Boss and Management

As a Type 5 boss, you tend to keep on an objective and analytical level. Let's get the facts and understanding first and action will follow. As a boss, you often must act *before* all the facts are in. You need to engage with your employees or audience. Information alone is not enough to lead your group. Other people need strength, inspiration, encouragement, and personal engagement, even small talk. There are many ways to get people aligned with group outcomes and purpose.

## How to Deal with Your Boss

5s like to know that you understand what's important and can critically analyze a situation. Knowledge and rational thinking engage a 5 immediately. 5s can be private, so don't overly push for personal information. 5s sometimes post their hours to talk, so don't assume a Type 5 boss will be chatty or want to engage at any time or during lunch. Know the boundaries and protocol. Ask for time to engage and how much time is available. 5s generally like some preparation and planning, so do your homework first. 5's don't always respond off the cuff. 5s will reflect before making commitments and generally wait to respond until you end your sentence—so end it, and don't repeat yourself!

> **Insights**
>
> If you ask me a question, I listen to it and often need to get back to you after I think about it. I don't like to give quick responses to important questions.
> —John, 37, a Type 5

## How to Develop Your Own Leadership Style

5s develop by seeing that leadership extends beyond knowledge to personal engagement, emotional awareness, and risk-taking. Delegating power to others, with different styles of leadership, helps with that integration. Hiring people as coaches for self-development certainly can be valuable for all types, and especially beneficial for 5s, who can isolate and lead from an ivory tower. 5s do well to get feedback from constituents in their information gathering. 5s are wise when they can lead from a detached, intuitive, and compassionate level. Give people information to process, as you research issues. Don't just give them your conclusions.

# Type 6 Boss and Management

6s tend to lead through building alliances and support. At the same time, 6s can be afraid of negative outcomes and can overplan and overprepare, isolate too much, and not build those alliances. Balance among research, planning, and action. 6 bosses want to make sure what they are doing is right and need feedback from those who can be objective, courageous, and clear about the deeper purpose. Type 6 bosses question, but it's important not to overly test as a way to check loyalty. Be directly honest.

## How to Deal with Your Boss

6s want any concerns allayed, so do your research and present your case on what is safe, what is problematic, and how to manage the discrepancy. An overly positive focus won't work, if it isn't backed up with forethought and practical solutions. Vision alone isn't enough, though you can help your boss with having a positive vision and remembering what is already good. A 6 boss wants as much information and insight as possible, so don't hold back. Be as rational as you can and present data, though share your hunches, too.

## How to Develop Your Own Leadership Style

6s develop when you can keep a positive vision, and, at the same time, have clear guidelines for dealing with real or potential problems. It's important to have faith in your ability to handle situations and not create major problems from minor issues. Focus on what's at hand, instead of possible or imaginary problems. If 6s can use humor and be less crisis-oriented, more relaxed and self-secure, problems remain problems and not disasters. 6s can utilize the strengths of others, who trust in the good and aren't anxious about what might occur. Lead with a focus on what's constructive and create the reality you want from the inside out, with hopeful vision, as well as with outside action steps. Check out all information to relieve anxious concerns that may be untrue.

# Type 7 Boss and Management

7s lead with a positive vision and trust in a can-do spirit. 7s might not acknowledge all the important details in depth or deal with immediate painful problems head-on. 7s expect others to remain positive and can be critical of those who don't. The right attitude cures all, from the 7 view. 7s create an affirmative environment of excitement and possibility and are optimistic and energetic in maintaining it. Commitment can wane if others don't stay optimistic or problems seem too difficult. Follow through can be a challenge.

## How to Deal with Your Boss

Type 7 bosses love positive, upbeat people so be that, yet offer all the practical information that a 7 needs. Talk about the problems, yet be encouraging. Anything can be fixed! Be oriented to the present and move toward the future, not the past. 7s love brainstorming options. Talk about the positives in your *let's get it done* attitude. Mention ways the situation is getting better and what a good outcome looks like. Type 7 bosses want to feel free with options, so don't use the language of crisis, unless you're actually in one!

**Lifelines** _____

7s can't stand slowness and hesitation, so make your point quickly and succinctly. Move it or lose it!

## How to Develop Your Own Leadership Style

For 7s to develop, leadership style needs to be a balance of the positive with an awareness of dealing directly with the negative. Sometimes 7s transfer ideas onto future solutions, rather than handling a current issue. Deal directly with others' concerns, before affirmations are mentioned. Stay connected to your ability to hold a positive vision, but be open to the inclusion of other ideas and attitudes. Don't see others as obstacles. It's your job to include their vision and put a positive spin on it for them.

# Type 8 Boss and Management

A Type 8 boss is *The Boss*. This is a strong match, as 8s feel comfortable being the boss and uncomfortable not. 8s take charge, and that's the issue: you can be too much in charge and not inclusive enough of other's opinions. Learn to hear those opinions, even if you disagree. Inclusion creates more buy-in and less resistance. *Your way or the highway* attitude causes others to take secondary roads to avoid you and that delays the mission. Some detouring is okay. You can't force a unified approach. Allow some unresolved conflict and trust it will be resolved later.

## How to Deal with Your Boss

Be direct. State your opinion and back it up with evidence. 8s will often consider what you say, if it makes sense. 8s like strong character with backbone. Disagreements are fine, if you aren't challenging an 8 on power itself. Then it's like two bucks vying for territory. There are plenty of female 8s who do the same. Don't talk behind an 8's back, or you'll be perceived as either a wimp or an enemy. Ask questions of the 8, if you need clarification, but get to the point. 8s are impatient if you are unsure.

## How to Develop Your Own Leadership Style

8s need to back down when you're wrong and admit mistakes. You'll still be seen as strong, even more so, if you can be human, too. Humans make mistakes! You are not the only authority, and people aren't betraying you if they have a different opinion or create an alliance with someone else. People have a right to their individuality—what you so preciously protect in yourself. Fight a bully, but not those who are just expressing who they are. Don't threaten people, as that will create the very enemies you are trying to avoid.

# Type 9 Boss and Management

9s don't like to boss. It's against your nature to be in charge or be focused on power and control. But that's exactly why you often can be a great boss! You aren't in it for the ego or power. You are in it to include others, create harmony, and please your employees and customers. You can see all sides and you validate and include others. Step up to the plate, as you are often the best boss possible, but only if you can be commanding, state your beliefs, hold your opinions, and not let anyone run roughshod over you or others. You can redirect the egomaniacs and not let them be in charge.

## How to Deal with Your Boss

Type 9 bosses want harmony, so don't go in with your guns blazing. A peaceful approach that is inclusive is best. If you are in it for your own ego and gratification, it won't work. A weak 9 boss may be influenced and give in just to stop feelings of conflict or to please; in the long run, however, you will lose. 9s always think of the whole. Support your 9 boss to be strong and more self-centered. Listen to his or her struggles. 9s can be indecisive, so maybe brainstorm with them or listen to their process, in order to support clear decisions.

## How to Develop Your Own Leadership Style

9s need to be assertive. You have so many good qualities already, but you need to trust yourself more and state your ideas with assertion, passion, and conviction. Back up what you say, and go into action from your intuition. Listen to others, but trust yourself with a clear conscience, as your purpose is to include all. You have good solutions. Don't doubt. You can edit your decisions, but typically what you say and do from your heart is the truth. Commit to truth, rather than to pleasing. You already are compassionate, so you don't have to worry so much about displeasing or conflict. That will occur on occasion, and it's normal.

Of course, use any of these leadership development tips, no matter what your type. We are or have the potential to be all nine types and the ultimate purpose is to have a richer, more meaningful life. Don't limit yourself to your one type!

## The Least You Need to Know

- All perspectives need to be included and validated on any team.

- Each type has unique leadership skills and challenges.

- Bosses vary, so it's important to vary your approach accordingly.

- It's best to know all the typical type strengths and weaknesses and be prepared in advance.

# Appendix A

# Glossary

**affirmations**   Positive statements or judgments; something declared to be true. Affirmations offer us a method to affirm the future, in order to create that future.

**archetype**   A prototype, the original model or pattern from which all other things of the same type are made. *See also* mother archetype.

**Body types**   Sometimes called Gut types, these are Types 1, 8, and 9. These tend to be more basic, with no frills—things are what they are. Body types perceive life from body instinct, preferring a direct form of expression and honesty in love.

**centering**   A way to connect to yourself, to go inside, to feel grounded, clear, and unscattered. People often center with practices such as breathing techniques, visualization, and meditation. Simply closing the eyes and connecting more to your individual, higher, or universal self, removed from day-to-day problems.

**centers**   A grouping of three different concentrations, each containing three types. Each center perceives reality, first and foremost, through a similar focus of attention, different from the other 2. These centers are Body or Gut types 1, 8, and 9; Image or Heart types 2, 3, and 4; and Head types 5, 6, and 7.

**counterphobic**   Subcategory of Type 6. The tendency to challenge real or imagined fears. Attacking the fear creates a surge of feeling more secure.

**defense mechanisms**   In psychoanalytic theory, an often unconscious mental process (such as repression, projection, denial) making possible compromise solutions to personal problems or conflicts. The compromise generally involves concealing, from oneself, internal drives or feelings that threaten to lower self-esteem or provoke anxiety.

**developmental levels**   The three levels of maturity within each type. These are a developed version, average or "most of the type" version, and an undeveloped version. Type descriptions change, depending on a person's level of development. These levels can shift, due to stress or growth.

**Enneagram**   A theory of personality types, the Enneagram describes nine core types, each of which has a filter or lens that deeply flavors one perspective over the others. The lens is both an amazing strength and an amazing limitation.

**Growth type**   A specific type, based on your core type, whose best traits you take on, when you are growing beyond the limitations of your core type.

**Gut types**   *See* Body types.

**Head types**   Types 5, 6, and 7, perceive life from the mind (mental representation) and like to plan, think, and understand before they act. *Cogito ergo sum.* I think; therefore, I am.

**Heart types**   *See* Image types.

**Image types**   Sometimes called Heart types, these are Types 2, 3, and 4. Image types perceive the world from an image they create and project. They want to be seen from that perspective and be rewarded for what they can produce from that projected image.

**imprint**   To create a strong impression; to imitate or take on the qualities of another living entity.

**Instinctual subtype**   A subcategory of three different types within each Enneagram type, each of which correlates to one of three basic survival instincts. Each subtype, with its own unique name and description, is generally more prevalent and a lifetime concern and stress area in a person's life. There are 27 separate Enneagram subtype descriptions in the Enneagram, three for each type.

**integration**   The organization of the psychological or social traits and tendencies of a personality into a harmonious whole.

**mother archetype**   An archetype that encompasses all the virtues and vices of motherhood.

**passive-aggressive**   Refers to behaviors that are anger-based and that come out in passive, resistant, or indirect ways such as avoidance, withdrawal, delay, or forgetfulness, and expressions such as negative comments, criticism, or negative comparisons.

**phobic**   Subcategory of Type 6. The tendency to suffer from irrational fears.

**positive stress**   Stress that enhances life and keeps life exciting. The thrill of a roller-coaster ride, a fun challenge, a promotion, or getting married—all are examples of positive stress.

**projection**   A defense mechanism by which your own traits and emotions are attributed to someone else.

**Self-Preservation subtypes**   These focus more on issues and concerns regarding basic, personal survival. These issues are related to security, protection, food, the home, comfort, money, planning for the future, and health.

**Sexual subtypes**   These focus on issues relating to the mating instinct and are obsessed and often stressed about sex, romance, relationships, love, rejection, jealousy, and commitment.

**shamanism**   A belief and practice in the existence of spirits and the mediation between the visible and spirit worlds. Can also include the spirits of living objects—trees, plants and animals, as well as inanimate objects, such as rocks. It is also the belief that the vital principle of organic development is immaterial spirit.

**Social subtypes**   These relate to the herd instinct and focus more on issues of social rank, position, prestige, social recognition, causes, group or community inclusion or exclusion, and group or social acknowledgment or appreciation.

**Stress type**   A specific type, other than your core type, whose worst traits you take on when you are undergoing sustained stress.

**Sufism**   A system of mysticism within Islam.

**type**   One of the nine categories of Enneagram personalities.

**typing**   The process of determining the core type of a person.

**wing**   Refers to the two type numbers on either side of your core type. For instance, a Type 2's wings would be 1 and 3. Wings flavor the way you exist in your core type. Most people have a *strong wing*. Though less important than your core type, the strong wing has type characteristics that mix as a second strong feature of your core type. A 2 with a 1 wing has a different day-to-day type focus than a 2 with a 3 wing.

# General Type Questionnaire

This questionnaire will help you narrow down what your core type might be. As you answer each question, reflect on your personal qualities and attributes.

1. What three or four or adjectives best describe you? What do your friends consistently say about you? Think of a story or life experience that describes who you are.

   _____

   _____

   _____

   _____

   _____

2. What are major themes/obstacles in your life? For example, not assertive enough, too direct, success-driven, too critical, don't share enough, too emotional, I don't know what I want, run away from commitment, always worried.

   _____

   _____

   _____

_____

_____

_____

_____

3. What are your most important beliefs, values, and guidelines?

_____

_____

_____

_____

4. What do you think about during the day? What bothers you the most? What do you mentally obsess about?

_____

_____

_____

_____

5. Describe your ideal partner. How are you similar or different?

_____

_____

_____

_____

6. What's impossible for you? Think of qualities you'd like to possess but can't seem to develop.

_____

_____

_____

_____

7. Whom do you admire? What about them do you admire? How are you similar or different?

_____

_____

_____

_____

8. Think about your relationships. Why have you left others? Why have others left you?

_____

_____

_____

_____

9. What two or three types are you most like? Why? (See Chapter 12 for tips on narrowing down your type.)

_____

_____

_____

_____

_____

10. What types are you definitely *not* like? Why?

_____

_____

_____

_____

_____

_____

11. What type is your ideal? In what ways are you not like this?

_____

_____

_____

_____

_____

12. What types do you have the most trouble interacting with or understanding?
    Why?

_____

_____

_____

_____

_____

# Questions That Reflect Type

Here you will zero in on your own core type. You've narrowed down your possible core type to two or three possibilities, so as you work your way through the questions for each type, one type should ring true. You should have a strong response of identification to practically every question in the core type that you are. Other types may describe parts of you, but your core type will be the closest match. Ask your close friends to take the test for you as an additional backup verification.

## Type 1

- ◆ Are you critical? Do you evaluate everything against a "should" or right way of doing something?

- ◆ Do you tend to think in black/white, right/wrong, good/bad ways?

- ◆ Are you clear about your moral values and often upset if others don't seem to have a strong or similar sense of values?

- ◆ Do you work hard to do the best job possible? Are you concerned about mistakes, ruminating how you could have avoided them?

- ◆ Do you like order? Are you irritated when things are not in order?

- ◆ Do you feel guilty if you don't measure up to your expectations? Do you have guilty pleasures?

- Do you have a hard time relaxing? Do you find yourself worrying about what's wrong, judging yourself, evaluating yourself harshly?

- Is it hard to trust the natural unfolding of things? Do you tend to try, to make an effort, to make it happen, often making things worse from too much effort?

- Do some people avoid you because they don't want your judgments and critical advice?

- Do you cross every *t* and dot every *i*? Can't turn things in or complete things unless they are perfect?

# Type 2

- Do you notice what people need and have a hard time not providing it for them?

- Do you offer advice and expect that people should be grateful to you for offering it?

- Are you upbeat and positive and don't think others would accept you if you weren't? Have to look good and please?

- Do you hide your own needs, even from yourself?

- Do you long for someone to take care of you, give to you without your having to ask?

- Do you love being appreciated? Acknowledged? Loved?

- Are you generous but become angry when you aren't given back to or at least acknowledged?

- Do you make people dependent on you?

- Are you romantic, focused on relationships?

- Is it hard to focus on yourself? Make yourself as important as others?

# Type 3

- Do you focus on success and love to compete and win?

- Would you be devastated if you failed? Do you imagine others would reject you if you failed?

- Are you always about doing, accomplishing, rather than just being?

◆ Are you positive, with a can-do attitude all the time?

◆ Are you action oriented and can't stand people who talk on and on, slow you down or who don't act?

◆ Do you have a constant to-do list?

◆ Do you dress for success? Are you concerned about your image? Is your image who you are?

◆ Do you long for praise and recognition for your work?

◆ Can you relax, play, learn with no goals in mind?

◆ Are speed and efficiency very important? Does it excite you to save time? Do you do several things at once?

# Type 4

◆ Do you have to be unique? Refuse to conform?

◆ Do you have intense emotions that tend to change often, from elation to despair?

◆ Do you think about ideal love and feel you never get what you need?

◆ Do you feel misunderstood? Not listened to deeply enough? Abandoned?

◆ Do you thrive on depth, personal relating, authentic communication? Are you easily bored by day-to-day reality?

◆ Do you have a large emotional vocabulary?

◆ Are individuality and creativity extremely important to you?

◆ Do you love passionate expression and tend to exaggerate?

◆ Do you love life but feel that at times life is too painful to manage?

◆ Do you get feedback that you are very intense?

# Type 5

◆ Do you pride yourself on being objective? Can't stand people who always put a personal spin on things?

◆ Are you private and only share personal things with people you know well?

◆ Are you smart but feel otherwise because there is so much more to learn?

- Are you irritated by slow people, small talk, people who repeat or have nothing real to say?

- Would you rather stay home than attend a social gathering where you feel you won't have any depth or learning potential?

- Do you enjoy going to interesting lectures, topic-discussion groups, and learning events?

- Do you read a great deal, love the Internet, and prefer to spend time alone, preferably learning?

- Do you repress your feelings or have a hard time sharing them?

- Do you like to think things through before you make decisions? Not share your process with people until you reach your conclusions?

- Are you in your brain all day long thinking about what you are learning and paying less attention to daily basics such as what to eat, what to wear, what to share?

# Type 6

- Do you find yourself frequently worrying what might go wrong? Worry about worst-case scenarios?

- Are you safety and security oriented?

- Do you read below the surface, paying as much, if not more attention, to what's not said as what is?

- Do you tend to be alert, noticing most everything that is happening?

- Do you like to plan in advance and are you thrown off by last-minute changes?

- Is loyalty a major issue for you?

- Do you test people to see if they are reliable? Consistent?

- Do you ask questions—outwardly or in your head?

- Do you like information? Is there never enough?

- Do you have major issues with authority? Concerned about how they use power? Tendency to challenge authority? Other times too trusting?

# Type 7

- Is fun a major motivator for you?

- Do you adapt to change more easily than the next person? Excited by change?

- Do you do all sorts of activities? Are you concerned you might miss out on something?

- Are you optimistic? Your mind mostly filled with positive thoughts?

- Does your mind run a mile a minute - thinking, planning for future fun possibilities?

- Do you dislike being around negative, worried people?

- Do you get distracted easily? Change subjects easily?

- Do you tend to avoid pain, always coming with solutions to avoid pain and find pleasure instead?

- Do you enjoy life, no matter what is happening?

- Is freedom important to you? You can commit but only if you have plenty of options?

# Type 8

- Do you like to be in control?

- Do you avoid feeling or sharing your vulnerabilities, fear, doubt, and insecurities?

- Are you impulsive?

- Are you strong, doing anything to avoid being weak?

- Are you a leader and not a follower?

- Do you tend to overdo everything you do? Is it hard for you to have limits?

- Are you irritated by indecisive, insecure, dependent, needy people?

- Are you independent and tend not to ask for help?

- Are you direct, honest, and sometimes blunt?

- Do you like to empower people?

# Type 9

- Are you peace and harmony-oriented? Avoid conflict a lot?

- Is comfort important to you?

- Do you avoid risk? Prefer what is easy, known, and comfortable?

- Are you indecisive? See all sides of an issue which often all seem equally important?

- Do you go along with others fairly easily? Do you have a hard time saying no?

- Are you stubborn to change, once you come to a decision on your own?

- Are you passive? Or passive-aggressive? Instead of showing your anger or saying "no", do you avoid, resist, imply yes, but don't act?

- Do you tend to get along with most people and feel perplexed if someone isn't accepting?

- Are you more cooperative than competitive?

- Are you more okay with comfortable feelings but struggle with envy, anger, jealousy, and self-centered, competitive emotions?

# Affirmations

## Affirmations for Type 1: The Perfectionist/Improver

1. Thank God, I don't have to be perfect. What a relief.

2. I let go of trying to be good. I just am myself, with my flaws and desires and needs.

3. I have a good time, no matter what.

4. Mistakes are fine. They're certainly nothing to stress about.

5. I accept people as they are, including me.

6. Some feedback from my inner critic is okay, but I let go of using the critic for constant evaluation. You're fired!

7. Life is fun, and I do lots of fun things.

8. I don't have to earn good things. It's okay to enjoy the bounty.

9. Pleasure is good and I am good.

10. Life is easy. I don't have to try so hard.

## Affirmations for Type 2: The Giver/Cheerleader

1. I make my needs important to me. No one has to guess them.

2. I express myself directly. No more hinting for me.

3. I'm positive, but I accept my self-centered and upset sides.

4. I love to give and I love to have limits, too.

5. I give to myself as much as I give to others.

6. I love appreciation and love to be given to but don't demand it.

7. I give freely. No one owes me.

8. I sing and dance and fly kites to please me as much as others.

9. I ask for hugs as much as give them.

10. I love to receive. I am one of the most receptive and appreciative people I know.

## Affirmations for Type 3: The Success Striver/Winner

1. I love to win but also love for everyone else to win.

2. Competition and cooperation are equally fun for me.

3. Whether I succeed or fail makes no difference. I learn and grow either way.

4. I love to do hobbies and interests as much as winning at a big project.

5. I love my work but also spend time developing my relationships.

6. I love my feelings and inner life. They support my success.

7. Whether I get the results I want or not, I enjoy life to the hilt.

8. I am more than my image or role. I am natural and what you see is what you get.

9. I don't have to be the star, though it's natural to shine and let others shine.

10. I relax when I need to and don't overly push my edge.

## Affirmations for Type 4: The Romantic/Depth Seeker

1. I feel deeply and sensitively and accept myself.

2. I like feeling centered, being at peace, yet still being the passionate person that I am.

3. I love life and focus on the positive, as well as the difficulties.

4. I love relationships, and feel safe in them. As long as I love me, no one can abandon me.

5. I listen to others and they listen to me. I love the back and forth of supporting each other.

6. I love my creativity. I am always creating something of beauty.

7. I love drama, playfulness, and excitement, as well as loss and pain. All experience is valuable, and I am special that I can go so deep.

8. I am learning to be more objective and observe my feelings and thoughts without losing myself.

9. I let go of longing and focus more on having and accepting how much I have right now.

10. I'm happy with what is. Nothing is missing. I focus on what I want, which increases the odds of creating it.

# Affirmations for Type 5: The Observer/Knowledge Seeker

1. I love my mind and also my body and heart and spirit.

2. I open to and let go of my fear of people. People are fun to be with and learn from.

3. I share more about me, and people like that.

4. I show my emotions more and realize I don't have to understand everything.

5. I passionately express what I like and want.

6. I observe life and also jump in to learn from experience.

7. I don't know everything and that's fine. There is much to learn and I stay excited about that.

8. I express from my intuition and body sense of things, as much as expressing from my ideas.

9. I am rational but appreciate the irrational. I learn from many ways of expression.

10. I live life joyfully and love to engage with others.

## Affirmations for Type 6: The Guardian/Questioner

1. Live and let live. I don't have to know everything.

2. I trust that unseen forces support me and I don't have to control things to be safe.

3. I allow things to unfold at their own pace and I am open to feeling peaceful.

4. I feel more and more comfortable with my body and mind.

5. I don't have to get reassurance from you to feel safe and it's fine to get reassurance, too.

6. I am my own guardian and protector and I like that.

7. I trust that I can handle future situations. I don't have to plan and prepare so much in advance.

8. I know much of my fear is about the past or in anticipation of the future. I trust that I can feel safer in the present.

9. I have many gifts of solving problems, protecting others and creating important bonds.

10. In taking care of myself, I take care of others.

## Affirmations for Type 7: The Optimist/Fun Lover

1. I face pain and discomfort with excitement and opportunity.

2. I love the new, and I accept and enjoy what is known and reliable.

3. I love to experience the quick version and I like to go deep with things, too.

4. I am a jack-of-all-trades and a master of everything.

5. I stay centered and clear, as my mind races from one thing to the next.

6. I listen deeply to people, as well as offer solutions to problems when asked.

7. I enjoy all the ventures in life, including the detours and difficulties.

8. I cheer people up but also listen to and relate to people's pain.

9. I have empathy for all feelings, including my own.

10. I am a bright shining star and also weather storms well.

# Affirmations for Type 8: The Director/Powerhouse

1. I am powerful yet also sensitive and patient.

2. I realize others are not as direct as I am and I accept that.

3. I understand peoples' fear and insecurity. I support them to have courage and confidence.

4. I'm a leader, yet equal to others and open to their feedback.

5. I don't have to have it my way. I want to hear your opinion.

6. I love to live life fully and find the moderation I need.

7. I inspire others in my leadership and support others' leadership.

8. I am committed to serving the best that humanity can be.

9. I am giving and generous and back off if I become too controlling.

10. I am in charge only to the degree that is necessary.

# Affirmations for Type 9: The Harmony Seeker/Accommodator

1. I am assertive and direct when necessary.

2. I face conflict, as I know that I will grow from that.

3. I accept myself as much as I accept others.

4. I clarify and focus on what I want.

5. I act on important self-goals and don't get distracted.

6. I passionately express what is important to me.

7. I am important and realize the powerful effect I have on others.

8. I realize that it is okay to be an individual and have an ego.

9. I notice when I go along with others too much and need to focus on me instead.

10. I am tolerant of others but can say no and challenge someone when he or she goes against what I believe in.

# Resources

If you're intrigued by what you've read so far and would like to learn more about the Enneagram, here are some suggested books and websites.

## Books

### General Enneagram Books

Baron, Renee, and Elizabeth Wagele. *The Enneagram Made Easy: Discover the 9 Types of People.* New York: HarperCollins, 1994.

————. *Are You My Type, Am I Yours?* San Francisco: HarperSanFrancisco, 1995.

Beesing, Maria, Robert Nogosek, and Patrick O'Leary. *The Enneagram: A Journey of Self Discovery.* Denville, New Jersey: Dimension Books, Inc., 1984.

Daniels, David, and Virginia Price. *The Essential Enneagram.* San Francisco: HarperSanFrancisco, 2000.

Hurley, Kathleen, and Theodore Dobson. *What's My Type? Use the Enneagram System of Nine Personality Types to Discover Your Best Self.* San Francisco: HarperCollins, 1992.

———. *Discover Your Soul Potential: Using the Enneagram to Awaken Spiritual Vitality*. Lakewood, CO: WindWalker Press, 2000.

Ichazo, Oscar. *Interviews with Oscar Ichazo*. New York: Arica Institute Press, 1982.

———. *Letters to the School*. New York: Arica Institute Press, 1988.

Keyes, Margaret Frings. *Enneagram Personalities At-A-Glance*. Muir Beach, CA: Molysdatur Publications, 1992.

O'Hanrahan, Peter, and Susan Forster. *Transformational Leadership, A Guide to Developing Your Leadership Skills Using the Enneagram System of Personality*. Go to www.enneagramwork.com to order.

Palmer, Helen. *The Enneagram in Love and Work: Understanding Your Intimate and Business Relationships*. San Francisco: HarperSanFrancisco, 1995.

———. *The Enneagram: Understanding Yourself and the Others in Your Life*. New York: HarperCollins, 1988.

———. *The Pocket Enneagram: Understanding the 9 Types of People*. San Francisco: HarperSanFrancisco, 1995.

Riso, Don Richard. *Discovering Your Personality Type*. New York: Houghton Mifflin Co., 1995.

———. *Enneagram Transformations: Releases and Affirmations for Healing Your Personality Type*. New York: Houghton Mifflin Co., 1993.

Riso, Don Richard, and Russ Hudson. *The Wisdom of the Enneagram: The Complete Guide to Psychological and Spiritual Growth for the Nine Personality Types*. New York: Bantam, 1999.

———. *Understanding the Enneagram: The Practical Guide to Personality Types*. Boston: Houghton Mifflin Company, 2000.

Riso, Don Richard with Russ Hudson. *Personality Types: Using the Enneagram for Self-Discovery.* Boston: Houghton Mifflin Co., 1996.

Rohr, Richard, Andreas Ebert, Marion Kustenmacher, and Peter Heinegg. *Experiencing the Enneagram.* New York: Crossroad Publishing Co., 1992.

Wagner, Jerome. *The Enneagram Spectrum of Personality Styles: An Introductory Guide.* Portland, OR: Radius Press, 1996.

Wright, Dick. *The Enneagram Triads: A Key to Personal and Professional Growth.* Muir Beach, CA: Molysdatur Publications, 1997.

## Enneagram in Business

Bast, Mary, and Clarence Thomson. *Out of the Box: Coaching with the Enneagram.* Portland, OR: Stellar Attractions, Inc., 2003.

David, Oscar. *The Enneagram for Managers: Nine Different Perspectives on Managing People.* Lincoln, NE: Writers Club Press, 2001.

Goldberg, Michael J. *The Nine Ways of Working.* New York: Marlowe & Co., 1996.

Lapid-Bogda, Ginger. *Bringing Out the Best in Yourself at Work: How to Use the Enneagram System for Success.* New York: McGraw-Hill, 2004.

Palmer, Helen, and Paul B. Brown. *The Enneagram Advantage: Putting the 9 Personality Types to Work in the Office.* New York: Three Rivers Press, 1998.

Tallon, Robert, and Mario Sikora. *From Awareness to Action: Emotional Intelligence, the Enneagram, and Change: A Guide to Improving Performance.* Scranton, PA: University of Scranton Press, 2004.

## Enneagram in Education

Callahan, William J. *The Enneagram for Youth: Student Editor and Counselor's Manual.* Chicago: Loyola University Press, 1992.

Levine, Janet. *Enneagram Intelligences: Understanding Personality: What Every Educator and Every Student Needs to Know.* Westport, CT: Bergin & Garvey, 1999.

## Enneagram in Film, Literature, and the Arts

Condon, Tom. *The Enneagram Movie and Video Guide.* Portland, OR: Metamorphous Press, 1999.

Searle, Judith. *The Literary Enneagram: Characters From the inside Out.* Portland, OR: Metamorphous Press, 2001.

## Enneagram and Parenting

Levine, Janet. *Know Your Parenting Personality.* Hoboken, NJ: John Wiley & Sons, Inc., 2003.

Wagele, Elizabeth. *The Enneagram of Parenting: The Nine Types of Children and How to Raise Them Successfully.* San Francisco: Harper, 1997.

## Enneagram and Psychology

Bartlett, Carolyn. *The Enneagram Field Guide: Notes on Using the Enneagram in Counseling, Therapy and Personal Growth.* Portland, OR: Metamorphous Press, 2003.

Keyes, Margaret Frings. *Emotions and the Enneagram: Working Through Your Shadow Life Script.* (Revised ed.) Muir Beach, CA: Molysdatur Publications, 1992.

Linden, Anne. *The Enneagram and NLP: A Journey of Evolution.* Portland, OR: Metamorphous Press, 1994.

Naranjo, Claudio. *The Enneagram of Society: Healing the Soul to Heal the World.* Nevada City, CA: Gateways Books and Tapes, 2004.

———. *EnneaType Structures: Self-Analysis for the Seeker.* Nevada City, CA: Gateway Publications, 1990.

———. *Transformation Through Insight: Enneatypes in Life, Literature and Clinical Practice.* Prescott, AZ: Hohm Press, 1997.

## Enneagram and Relationships

Keyes, Margaret Frings. *The Enneagram Relationship Workbook: A Self and Partnership Assessment Guide.* Muir Beach, CA: Molysdatur Publications, 1992.

Olson, Robert W. *Stepping Out Within: The Enneagram as a Guide to Relationships and Transformation.* San Juan Capistrano, CA: Awakened Press, 1993.

## Specialty Enneagram Books

Keyes, Margaret Frings. *The Enneagram Cats of Muir Beach.* Muir Beach, CA: Molysdatur Publications, 1990.

Thomson, Clarence, and Thomas Condon. *Enneagram Applications: Personality Styles in Business, Therapy, Medicine, Spirituality and Daily Life.* Portland, OR: Metamorphous Press, 2001.

## Enneagram and Spirituality

Addison, Howard. *The Enneagram and Kaballah: Reading Your Soul.* Woodstock, VT: Jewish Lights Publishing, 1998.

Almaas, A. H. *Facets of Unity: The Enneagram of Holy Ideas.* Berkeley, CA: Diamond Books, 1998.

Bakhtiar, Laleh. *God's Will Be Done: Volume 1: The Sufi Enneagram.* Chicago: Kazi Publications 1993.

Empereur, James. *The Enneagram and Spiritual Direction: Nine Paths to Spiritual Guidance.* New York: Continuum Publishing, 1997.

Jaxon-Bear, Eli. *Healing the Heart of Suffering: Using the Enneagram for Spiritual Growth*. Kula, HI: Pacific Center for Sacred Studies, 1987.

———. *The Enneagram of Liberation—from Fixation to Freedom*. Boulder, CO: Leela Foundation Press, 2001.

Maitri, Sandra. *The Spiritual Dimension of the Enneagram: Nine Faces of the Soul*. New York: Tarcher/Putnam, 2000.

Mortz, Mary. *Overcoming Our Compulsions: Using the Twelve Steps and the Enneagram As Spiritual Tools for Life*. Chicago: Triumph Books, 1994.

Nogosek, Robert. *The Enneagram Journey to New Life: Who Am I? What Do I Stand For?* Denville, NJ: Dimension Books, Inc., 1995.

Rohr, Richard. *Enneagram II: Advancing Spiritual Discernment*. New York: Crossroads Publishing, 1995.

———. *The Enneagram: A Christian Perspective*. New York: Crossroads General Interest, 2001.

Rohr, Richard, and Andreas Ebert. *Discovering the Enneagram, An Ancient Tool for a New Spiritual Journey*. New York: Crossroads Publishing, 1990.

Thomson, Clarence. *Parables and the Enneagram*. Portland, OR: Metamorphosis Press, 2002.

Zuercher, Suzanne. *Enneagram Companions: Growing in Relationships and Spiritual Direction*. Notre Dame, IN: Ave Maria Press, 1993.

———. *Enneagram Spirituality: From Compulsion to Contemplation*. Notre Dame, IN: Ave Maria Press, 1993.

# Enneagram Websites

**www.breakoutofthebox.com**   Leadership and types. Mary Bast Consulting.

**www.ennea.com/ennbooks.htm**   List of books and tapes about the Enneagram by 30 authors.

**www.ennea.com/links/ennlinks.htm**   Complete list of Enneagram videos, books and tapes, resources.

**www.enneagram.com**   Website for Helen Palmer. Enneagram courses, products, training, newsletter, and more.

**www.ennea.org**   *Enneagram Monthly*. Monthly magazine of Enneagram articles.

**www.enneagraminstitute.com**   Website for Don Richard Riso and Russ Hudson. Free articles such as type compatibility, misidentifying types, famous people examples, books, tapes, workshops, typing assessment, discussion group, teacher certification training, lists of other Enneagram books and website links.

**www.EnneagramWorldwide.com**   Website for Helen Palmer and David Daniels. Free video clips, books, tapes, videos, DVDs, workshops, typing assessment, teacher certification training.

**Enneagramwork.com**   Website for Peter O'Hanrahan. Enneagram consulting, coauthor of *Transformational Leadership*.

**www.herbpearce.com**   Website for Herb Pearce. Enneagram workshops, psychotherapy, coaching, training, teambuilding, typing.

**www.internationalenneagram.org**   Website for International Enneagram Association. Enneagram Resources organized by topic, a very comprehensive list of Enneagram books. List of organizations and universities that use or teach the Enneagram. An international membership association open to anyone. Many other resources.

**theenlightenedsociety.com**   Famous examples of types. Ken Jenkins Enneagram consulting.

# Index